TARGET RAN

SOCC
FIEL

THE ARMORY

MW01613147

INGRAM BARRACKS

THE NATATORIUM

RICE ACADEMIC
BUILDING

GYMNASIUM

Castle Heights
Military Academy
Lebanon, Tennessee

UNKEN GARDENS

ATHLETIC FIELD

TENNIS CO

Readers Guide:

• Periodically through the book, the following feature appears:

Breaking Ranks

This is material added during 2013-14 preparation of the book to expand on key individuals, items and events about which JB Leftwich wrote.

• Author's legal name was JB Leftwich, without periods. Because multiple editors through the years added that punctuation after his initials, correction became too time consuming, so "J. B. Leftwich" became a pen name of sorts. This book will refer to him throughout as JB.

• Though efforts were made to make photographs as sharp as possible, many are from old catalogues, yearbooks, newspapers and other historic publications -- or are very old pictures -- and thus reproduction was difficult.

• When possible, research was done to update information on cadets, faculty and others written about by JB during his almost 40 years as a newspaper columnist. These data appear, usually at the end of a column, in a tint block.

Cover Photo:
Late '50s spring Sunday dress parade by JB Leftwich.

Overleaf Photo:
Taken by JB Leftwich in mid-1950s. Used in multiple Academy catalogs for many years, though for two of them - including this version - Armstrong Hall was mislabeled "Smith" and Smith Chapel as "Rice Academy Building."

VIEW FROM THE HILL

★ MEMORIES OF CASTLE HEIGHTS MILITARY ACADEMY ★

JB LEFTWICH

RECOGNIZING
Glyn Ed Newton
(1942-2014)
Primary proponent of publishing
the work of JB Leftwich

COMPILATION, RESEARCH
James L. Leftwich '63
"Jim"

EDITOR
Philip S. Huguenin '59
"Stan"

Printed in the United States
First Edition

ISBN 978-1-938315-36-7

For information about the book, contact:
Castle Heights National Alumni Association
611 Hill Street
Lebanon, Tenn. 37087
•
HNAA President Rob Hosier
1045 Woodmont Drive
Gallatin TN 37066
•
Email: shosier@msn.com / HNAA site: www.castleheights.com

Graphics/Printing:
Gina Scinto, Renaissance Printing
Gainesville, Fla.

Introduction

JB Leftwich was a man of many interests and passions. He never considered himself an intellectual, but he was always in intellectual pursuit. He never considered himself a politician, but he was almost fanatical about politics. He would never have called himself religious, but he certainly lived by moral and Christian principles. He would not have called himself an historian, but he could name every president, vice-president, opposing presidential candidates, and all the first ladies. (As a point of interest, he used these recitations as a cure for insomnia.)

He was passionate about the written word, correctly written. He once wrote of his friend and fellow-teacher, Paul Wooten, that Paul was "an observer with the unique ability to interpret meaning in what he observed in nature, politics, or just people watching." He noted that Wooten's compositions showed a diversity of moods, sometimes "twisting wry humor from the commonplace." JB Leftwich could have been describing himself, although he would never have done so.

Early in his life he resolved to be a writer. Speaking of his formative years growing up in the hills of Tennessee during the Depression, he wrote, "It was in this environment of isolation from modern transportation and communication that I determined to write for a newspaper or magazine or anybody that would publish my project."

And write he did, publishing a weekly column in the *Lebanon Democrat* and periodically in the *Nashville Tennessean* for more than 45 years [1965 until 2010]. Even though he wrote in columns the equivalent of some 20 novels and mentored others who wrote much more, he never quite got around to committing to paper the novel that rattled around in his head for most of his life; perhaps more our loss than his.

He was fervent about teaching and about Castle Heights Military Academy, where he joined the faculty in 1941 and would spend the next 40 years teaching mathematics and journalism, overseeing the school's newspaper and yearbook -- *The Cavalier* and *Adjutant*, respectively. He also loved photography, and photographed students, facilities, faculty and all other aspects of life on "The Hill." He never quite got over Heights' closing in 1986, even though he spoke and wrote of its obsolescence and financial travails, and of periodic efforts of individuals and/or companies to save some of the Academy buildings for modern-day usage. It saddened him watching the subdividing of campus and razing of its old buildings.

He never considered himself athletic -- once describing his golf group as one golfer, two has-beens and a never-was -- but he loved sports and remembered Heights football and basketball games in great detail. He took enormous pride in the accomplishments of all former cadets, but especially those who wrote on the school's publications under his sponsorship.

There was an amazing range of subject matter in his approximately 2,500 columns. He brought to life mundane daily events, made local/state/national politics humorous, roasted politicians, critiqued books and movies, brought to light obscure historical people and events, spoofed and lampooned fiction and autobiographies. Some columns were serious, some emotionally touching, some amusing and some downright funny. He frequently took positions on very delicate issues, but never in a mean-spirited or condescending way, often writing stories or parables to soften or add humor to sensitive questions.

Sometimes JB was called on to write objective news reports for newspapers, but his gift for writing showed in his columns -- where his best always had an undercurrent of passion and emotion. His career at Castle Heights, and his "View from The Hill," provided inspiration for many of his most memorable.

James L. Leftwich

James L. Leftwich '63

TABLE of CONTENTS

FROM THE AUTHOR....
Written in 2007

Born: November 26, 1919, near Buffalo Valley, Tenn., in a house that still stands, but is not listed in the National Register of Historic Places.

Education: Attended one-teacher schools during first four grades before Dad moved me to a three-teacher school where I was woefully behind other pupils. To my credit, I progressed and graduated third from the top in my eighth grade class. I was also third from the bottom. There were only five of us.

Attended high school at Baxter Seminary [1933-37], a private four-year school operated by the Methodist Church. My most notable achievement was president of the Senior Class, a position I won by default since no other boy wanted the job. I found out on Arbor Day why others rejected the honor when I, as president, had to make a speech about trees. From that time forward, I always asked – Chamber of Commerce, civic clubs, professional organizations -- if their president had to make a speech on Arbor Day.

Attended [1937-41] and graduated from Cumberland University. During my last two years, I was editor of the *Cumberland Collegian,* which was named an All-America paper my last year. I thought that was pretty good. I majored in mathematics and minored in journalism. I wanted to be a novelist, but I lacked talent. I had a knack for mathematics but lacked the depth to become a mathematician. But I found out I was pretty good at teaching math. So, I did – for 34 years.

During my last two years of college, I worked part-time for *The Lebanon Democrat.* I wrote minor news stories during the first three days of the week, and was a "printer's devil" during the last three. There were only three on the news staff – the editor, society editor and me. Hence, I was associate editor, the highest title I ever had in newspapering. I made $7.50 per week, and I was overpaid. I loved the *Democrat* and have remained connected. I still write a weekly column for this paper, now a daily.

Career: In 1941, I became a mathematics teacher—also eventually director of public relations and director of student publications—at Castle Heights Military Academy. I remained 38 years as a faculty member. It was a great school and I dream about it all of the time. All instructors wore US Army uniforms, so I became an instant captain, wearing bars briefly but soon switching to three discs. One time, a couple of Army privates and I met on a Lebanon street. They saluted, and I returned the salute. Then I heard one of them say: "What in the hell was that?" and the other say, "Damned if I know."

Publication Advisor Leftwich screens photos for '40s newspapers, yearbooks.

At Castle Heights, I was assigned to sponsor *The Cavalier*, the cadet bi-weekly newspaper and a very good publication. We made it into a pacemaker. Annually, it was an All-America and a Medalist newspaper in contests sponsored by national associations. Twice, it was selected as one of the six best in the country. I also served for many years as advisor to the CHMA yearbook, *The Adjutant*.

About 1945, I guess, *The Tennessean* lost its Wilson County correspondent. Veteran editor Elmer Hinton persuaded me to take the job temporarily, which I held about 45 years [correspondent and photographer] on a temporary basis. I endured through a number of state editors, and I thought the best of the lot was Jimmy Carnahan who became a close friend.

Initially, I was paid 10 cents per column inch. At the end each month, I pasted all of my stories into a string and mailed them to the state desk. I thought the pay was pretty good, and I enjoyed knowing the staffers.

I was never a Bob Woodward or an Ernie Pyle, but I was a pretty good reporter, covering politics, sports and breaking news.

One favorite editor at *The Tennessean* was Frank Ritter, who for many years edited the op-ed page. Frank liked my columns, especially the humorous ones, so I became somewhat of a regular guest columnist.

Biggest story I covered: Actually, I can't remember many. There were the usual murder trials, train wrecks, floods, political intrigue, et al. I covered no Columbine or Virginia Tech, but I came close. And at Castle Heights, a half-century ago. A cadet smuggled a rifle into a barracks, and shot three fellow cadets, all from South or Central American nations [*page 15*]. I may be wrong, but I think this was one of the first of the epidemic of school shootings.

Another big story: our state representative shot and killed his brother-in-law, a prominent lawyer. I broke the story in *The Tennessean*, but after that staff reporters took over, and I returned to my classroom.

Personal: Met Jo Doris Prichard at Cumberland in 1938, and we married July 12, 1939. We have four children -- Lynda, Barbara, Jim and Jack -- and nine grandchildren, 11 great-grandchildren. We've belonged to the First United Methodist Church for more than 50 years, and have been active in the community as well. I served as president of such organizations as the Lions Club, Lebanon Jaycees, Lebanon/Wilson County Chamber of Commerce and as a longtime Lebanon Library Board member. Jo Doris was early member and officer of Lebanon Young Women's Club, which became La Coterie, and was an excellent school teacher. We also shared duties as longtime Sunday School teachers.

Best story I ever wrote: It was a column about one of our granddaughter's infant daughter who had heart surgery at age two months, survived against the odds and today is 8 but totally disabled. It was good because it was personal but detached [*page 257*]. Maybe the funniest story I ever wrote was about my battles with a squirrel that totally out-witted me too many times [*page 251*].

Major accomplishments: Starting cadets in newspapering who became major players on the big stage. They're retired now, but some were: David Hall, former editor [in-chief] of *The Bergen [NJ] Record*, the *Denver Post* and the *Cleveland Plain-Dealer*; Jim Fall, editor of a slew of Missouri and Arkansas papers and most recently executive director of the Montana Press Association; Frank Sutherland, editor of *The Tennessean*; Sam Hatcher, former editor of *The Democrat*; and Albert Smith, former owner of a string of newspapers in Kentucky. Many of my editors entered other fields, but continued to write. Three are Charles Ward, Tulsa, Okla., architect; Jack Robinson, senior partner, Nashville law firm; and Gordon Baskett, former owner of a major printing operation.

What I would do over if I could: All of the above. I loved scholastic journalism at Castle Heights, I enjoyed working for *The Democrat* and *The Tennessean*. I even enjoyed being a landlord during the last 20 years of my working career.

OBITUARY

The passing of a beloved institution....

• JB Leftwich, Fall 1986

Taps for Castle Heights Military Academy came on an August afternoon in the summer of 1986, just as the proud old institution prepared for its 85th school year. And she died with her head high as if she expected reveille to sound as usual the next day.

But reveille did not sound the next day despite efforts of Lebanon business and professional people to pump life into her once again. Castle Heights was a tough old institution which had weathered other crises and fought back to full strength. Indeed, only 12 years before, in 1974, the Castle Heights Foundation was formed to buy the school and more than 100 acres from the floundering Bernarr Macfadden Foundation.

In the final analysis, Castle Heights died because there was no longer a body of cadets large enough to sustain her. Year after year following the Vietnam War, which changed so many attitudes and altered so many institutions, school officials hoped and prayed for a halt in declining enrollment. But aside from an occasional flurry, increases in enrollment did not come. And so, Castle Heights ran its course and the time came for the final Taps. There had been many casualties among the ranks of military schools prior to the demise of Heights; there will be many more. Education in this country is on a different track, and the future of military schools at the secondary level is, at best, hazy. Factors responsible for a weak response in the market place include escalating tuition and proliferation of private day schools. Another factor, perhaps as important, focuses on home discipline in which children make the decisions -- particularly with regard to leaving home and friends to attend a school.

Add to these the tremendous overhead of operating a boarding school -- salaries, utilities, maintenance of ancient buildings, transportation, food and administration become more costly each year.

And so, the heyday of boarding schools in general and military schools in particular is long over, and this is sad. These schools have meant so much to so many. The stronger, richly endowed boarding schools will survive, but even for them maintaining enrollment will become increasing difficult.

It is not easy to write the obituary for one you love. On a personal note, I have been a part of Castle Heights Military Academy as teacher, administrator or trustee for 45 years... and I loved her. But the time had come for her to go, because she could only be a shadow of what she once was. I am not precluding the possibility of another school operating on her campus...I am saying the Castle Heights I knew and loved and supported is gone. ⛊

Chapter One
Looking Back

"The working efficiency of a well-equipped, wisely managed military academy is such to disarm all hostile criticism. Its advantages so far outweigh any possible limitations inherent in the military system that ... it is the very best type of school for the training of our American boys. Tangible advantages of military training include loyalty, respect for authority, self-confidence, self-control, courtesy, dependability, neatness of appearance, and the inculcation of promptness and obedience."

-CHMA President Laban Lacy Rice / 1917

THE DRILL:
During his more than 45 years of writing columns for the *Lebanon Democrat* and *Nashville Tennessean*, JB Leftwich expressed his love and devotion for Castle Heights Military Academy while at the same time describing historical, entertaining, noteworthy and intriguing individuals, events and facilities that populated The Hilltop.

Overleaf Photo:
Cadets chatting at the gates, columns originally framing portions of the 1940s CHMA campus.

Photo Credit: 1950s Heights Catalogue

Castle Heights about 'men from boys'

• November, 1994

Near Lebanon, Tennessee's peak of The Hilltop, storied and celebrated when Castle Heights Military Academy existed, is a newly paved
parking lot on which Armstrong Hall, known to thousands of cadets as
"Halls," once stood.

This was my building -- the building that housed my office, my
classroom, the student publications office, the school photo lab. In more
than 45 years association with Castle Heights as teacher, administrator
and finally as a member of the Board of Trustees, I spent more time in
Armstrong Hall than in any other area of a campus that sprawled over
more than 100 acres.

I recently visited the
new parking lot and tried
to figure out exactly where
Armstrong had been lo-
cated. Even the huge ma-
ple tree that stood out-
side my office window is
gone. Nothing remains of
the building that during
much of the life of Castle
Heights housed two floors
of rooms populated by ca-
dets as well as classrooms

JB Leftwich assists early '40s cadets with math.

and eventually offices.

To the west of the Armstrong site stood Bullard Hall, built in the late
'30s, and razed before my tenure with the Academy ended. Across the
street and southeast of Armstrong was Benarr Macfadden Gymnasium
-- which yielded earlier this year to a wrecker's ball and now is the site
of a rising office complex.

Marked to come down in the near future is Rice Tower [cornerstone
laid 1905], a spike of a building that was home to hundreds of cadets
throughout the decades. No practical use can be made of Tower because
of prohibitive costs of renovation and because of its impractical design.

Proposed extension of Castle Heights Avenue through the original
campus site is scheduled to take out Ingram Hall, once better known as
"Gym;" Smith Chapel, then referred to simply as "Chapel," which also
was a memorial to the Academy's war causalities; maybe even the old
Armory Building, which housed staffs of the Reserved Officers Training

Corps [ROTC].

Mitchell Hall, once headquarters of the Junior School, stands in ruins -- though some efforts are being made to restore it. Macfadden Auditorium, under construction when I came to Castle Heights as a freshman teacher in 1941, is a hazard to those who would illicitly enter it.

Main Building, to many the heart of the Heights complex, broods silently as it dreams of former splendor on The Hilltop and dies a slow, painful death.

Even newer Academy buildings, constructed during the '60s, are deteriorating as buildings do when vacant. Of the original older buildings, only Rutherford Parks Library, an oddly shaped structure, has new life -- restored and occupied by American Family Life Assurance Corporation. This and two of the more recently constructed barracks buildings, restored by a dentist and a physician, are promised continuation in the next century.

Fortunately, there is "new life" on campus. On either side of the original Academy entrance -- on West Main Street -- is a commercial bank in a new building, and a medical facility for recovering patients. As time goes on, other new buildings are expected and different uses will be made of the property.

Nevertheless, the greatest function of this expanse began in 1902 and ended in 1986, a span of years when Castle Heights Military Academy made men from boys.

o o o

What follows is by no means the history of Castle Heights Military Academy -- I am not sure all dates are accurate. These are personal observations. A history should be the task of an historian -- someone gifted in research who could put into print the records of great athletic teams and the players who made them great, and the student writers, the singers, the debaters, the military leaders, the academic leaders.

Specifically, light should shine on the Heights graduates. However success is measured, they would rank with the best anywhere.

No matter how nostalgic we become over the physical plant of Castle Heights Military Academy, buildings and grounds were not what the school was about. Castle Heights was about men and boys -- some great, some average, but the overwhelming majority better for having had the Castle Heights experience.

Some time after the turn of the century, an idea incubated in the mind of **I. W. P. Buchanan**. He looked at the open space outside the western city limits and envisioned a school for boys in Lebanon. But the city had problems -- at least in the mind of Buchanan, it did. Thriving in town were a number of saloons, which he viewed as obstacles to his

4

| I.W.P. Buchanan | David E. Mitchell | Laban Lacy Rice | O.N. Smith |

dream. So he went to the city council with a proposition.

"Close the saloons and I will build a school which will become one of the finest," Buchanan reportedly told the council. In essence, they did and he did.

In partnership with **Dr. David Mitchell**, already famed as an educator at Cumberland University, Buchanan opened Castle Heights School in the fall of 1902 -- not Castle Heights School for Boys as he was said to have envisioned, but a school for boys and girls. Females continued as pupils until 1917, when Heights became a military academy for boys only. And thus it remained until 1973, when girls were again accepted.

Two other giants in the school's early history joined the Academy in 1903. Professor **O. N. Smith** [his daughter, Helen, was a 1908 graduate], who came to Lebanon from Princeton University and named the athletics teams "Tigers" in honor of his university's teams, and **Dr. Laban L. Rice**, who in 1913 became sole owner of the school. Dr. Rice, later chancellor and president of Cumberland, sold the school to a group of faculty members in 1921, when it was on the decline

Again on the verge of collapse, the school was placed on the auction block in 1928, when **Bernarr Macfadden**, publisher of confession magazines and of *Liberty* and *Physical Culture*, rescued it and made it a part of the Bernarr Macfadden Foundation. And there it remained until 1974, when poor leadership and poor planning forced the Macfadden Foundation to offer it for sale.

At this point, in March, 1974, with prospective buyers inspecting the facilities, Lebanon banker and businessman **J. Roy Wauford Jr.**, a 1948 alumnus, stepped in. With **Carl Wallace**, then editor of *The Democrat*, and to a lesser degree with me as a member of the lead trio, the Castle Heights Foundation was formed to purchase and operate the Academy. Wauford, who headed the Board of Trustees for two years while the school made adjustments, must also be considered one of the giants in the history of Heights. Without his financial wizardry, the life of Castle Heights would have ended suddenly following the 1974 commencement

J. Roy
Wauford   *Thomas*
                 Phelan, Jr.   *Batey*
                                      Gresham, Jr.

exercises. Despite oppressively difficult times, other leaders -- **Thomas Phelan Jr.** '51, **Batey Gresham Jr.** '52, **Dan W. Evins** '53 -- emerged to head the board and to keep the school moving until the hard decision to close came in the summer of 1986.

In retrospect, the Macfadden Foundation -- which saved the school in 1927 -- was the primary cause of its failure in 1974. Macfadden himself drained the school's assets in his latter years when he made an expensive race for governor of Florida, and when he married his last wife who proved costly to him in his old age. After Macfadden died, the Macfadden Foundation's New York-based board allowed **Col. Harry L. Armstrong** autonomy in operating the school until Macfadden's son-in-law, **Joseph Wiegers**, wrested control from board members to become chairman in 1961.

The Academy continued to thrive during an era when military schools were in high favor, but Wiegers dissipated assets when he formed a secondary school naval academy in Florida. The net result was no reserve for Heights' hard times that were to come in the following decade. Because the Macfadden Foundation always cloaked its financial operations in strict secrecy, repeated fund drives failed. Alumni and other potential donors balked when financial disclosure was refused. Thus, when the Castle Heights Foundation assumed control in 1974, alumni had to be cultivated and simultaneously solicited for funds. Despite earnest and

• The Sanford Naval Academy was established in 1963 by Joseph Wiegers and the Bernarr Macfadden Foundation in a Sanford, Fla., complex purchased from the New York Giants when that team moved to California. The facility originally was a resort hotel on Lake Monroe called the Mayfair Inn. The first senior class of 25 graduated in 1967, women were admitted starting in 1973, and the school closed in 1976. First SNA Superintendent was US Army Lt. Col. Henry J. Furman, who came to CHMA in 1956 and taught math and military science in the Junior School. He came to the Senior School in 1961, serving as Alumni Secretary before leaving for Sanford. His twin sons, James and Richard, are 1964 Heights grads.

often inspired efforts, financial campaigns were never as successful as in other private schools because Heights at a critical time had no developed base for private giving.

The constant drain on Academy funds during the latter years of the Macfadden Foundation kept CMHA in a syndrome of emergency maintenance. When the Castle Heights Foundation assumed control, the buildings were in sad need of repairs. But the funds were not there for renovation as the administration faced declining enrollment in the midst and aftermath of the Vietnam War, and as private day schools -- sprouting like mushrooms in the wake of forced busing and as a consequence of new religion-based educational institutions -- siphoned potential pupils.

To complete the equation leading to disaster, new regulations imposed by government agencies, higher salaries to compete for quality teachers, and a comfort-and-entertainment oriented youth unwilling to surrender their automobiles and march in a battalion of uniformly clothed cadets were key factors.

All of these ingredients and others coalesced to force the closure of many of the nation's military secondary schools. Only the strongest and best financed survived. Castle Heights was not one of them.

o o o

Maj. Dan Kendall joined CHMA in 1929, having served as public schools teacher, coach, principal, superintendent.

And now, remembering some of those who for me made Castle Heights great:

• **Harry L. Armstrong**, superintendent from 1928 until he was ousted by Joseph Wiegers in 1962. Colonel Armstrong, remote and unemotional but a truly outstanding educator, presided during some of the greatest years of Castle Heights. For decades, he and Macfadden made a fine team.

• **Dan Kendall**, headmaster at Heights when I arrived in 1941, and in that office until his death in the early 1950s, was another of the geniuses the school was able to attract and hold. His forte was in molding young teachers and in understanding teenage boys.

• **Dan T. Ingram**, Mr. Chips of Castle Heights, was commandant and in charge of discipline from the early 1920s until 1963. Even the largest All-Mid-South tackle quaked when he answered a report to Colonel Ingram. Unequivocal but infinitely fair in meting out justice, he won the respect and even the affection of most cadets. He was the first teacher that alumni visited when they returned

Archie Potter joined the CHMA Junior School faculty in 1955, and was named Headmaster in 1962. He earned his AB from Peabody, MA from Middle Tennessee State. He retired as a Lieutenant Colonel. His wife, Mildred, lives in Nashville.

to The Hilltop. Colonel Ingram served as superintendent 1963-65, but was never comfortable in this position. He was a man born to be commandant.

• **Jonas Coverdale** was the first headmaster, and indeed an excellent one, of the Junior School, located on the Mitchell property acquired in 1936. **Archie Potter**, a later headmaster of that department, was a dedicated educator.

• **Ralph Lucas**, in my opinion without peer as a basketball coach, was superintendent from 1965 until 1977. His was a record of merit. He faced and solved problems created by a board chairman who never understood the school's mission.

• **Stroud Gwynn**, for 25 years head football coach and winner of more games and championships than I can remember without research. In his last years at Castle Heights, he was a fund raiser. His integrity and pragmatic approach to monumental tasks were instrumental in prolonging the life of the school.

• **Leonard Bradley**, for many years headmaster of the Senior School, was a developer and defender of a fine academic program that guaranteed Heights graduates an initial advantage when they entered college.

• **Robert Hosier**, for decades the highly successful coach of the school's swimming teams, may have taught at Castle Heights longer than anyone. He still fights for and defends what is left of the Academy.

These were men whom I knew best during my tenure at the school. There were many more great teachers and administrators. This is not an attempt to name all of them. They, along with many others, made Heights a superior educational institution.

o o o

A graduate of Dartmouth University, Daniel Webster, once said of his alma mater: "It is a small school, but there are those who love her."

This could be said of Castle Heights. There are those who love her. I among them.

Death of a beloved landmark
• *April, 1994*

Opened in 1937, Macfadden Gymnasium was scene of memorable athletic and social events.

As I watched the Castle Heights gymnasium being torn down, I remembered what was and mulled over what will never be again.

Just as every other member of the Heights family, I experienced a mixture of emotions as the gymnasium -- more specifically, the Bernarr Macfadden Foundation Gymnasium -- fell to the wreckers' ball and hammer.

Among the memories, mostly good:

• • • *No time showing in the semifinal game of the Mid-South tournament that February day in 1956.* **Billy Smith**, *the Tigers' leading scorer, launched a shot three-quarters of the floor from the goal just milliseconds before the half-time buzzer. The ball sailed through, touching only net.*

• • • **Ralph Lucas.** *For many years a fixture in the Heights gymnasium. Coach extraordinaire. The ultimate strategist. Always cool during the pressure of athletic competition. Never emotional. No chewing out of a player. Relaxed. Thinking. Legs crossed. Viewing the game as if completely detached. As if he were a mere spectator. Never challenging a referee. Appearing to be 20 points ahead instead of five points behind. Winner of a record number of championships.*

• • • **Billy Smith.** *The tournament's most valuable player. Unusual selection because Heights lost. In overtime. The MVP usually is on the champion team. The Tigers were not to repeat as champions. Even in a tournament played in their own gym.*

Ralph A. Lucas' contributions to CHMA were extraordinary, and his basketball coaching skills legendary.

9

The Castle Heights gym was new when I became an instructor in 1941. It then was one of the best high school gyms in the state. But time passed it by. Lighting and seating [most of it in the balcony] became obsolete. In the Academy's latter years, most gyms were better.

Macfadden Gym was scene of hundreds of commencement formals, Christmas dances, sock hops and generational music shifts.

•••*The boxing team.* **Pete Rademacher** *and brother,* **Johnny**. *Mid-South champions in 1948. Pete later won the Olympic heavyweight championship. Heights won the '48 team championship. Coached by* **Stroud Gwynn** *who leaned heavily on the Rademacher brothers' knowledge... And wrestling. The 1963 team featuring* **Buzzy Fryer, Bobby Langford, Johnny Ogles** *and our son,* **Jim Leftwich**.

Buildings run their course. Nevertheless, the Heights gymnasium was built to endure. Solid construction. The demolition people encountered unusual resistance when they tried to knock down the walls.

•••*Formal dances in the gym. The cadets in dress uniforms. Whites in the spring. Their dates in formal gowns. In the earlier days, Francis Craig and his orchestra. Later, the ear-splitting, skull-shaking rock bands. Sock hops. Commencement and Christmas formals.*

I was saddened to see it go. The community rues its demolition. Many alumni shed tears. I started teaching in its basement. 1941. Room No. 5. Four classes of geometry and one class of algebra in a six-period day. After teaching four classes of geometry, I felt the whole world knew how to prove triangles congruent and how to circumscribe polygons.

Some would like to kill the messenger. That is unfair. The new owners wanted to renovate, but decided the idea was impractical. We hoped for a renovation. Such as AFLAC did to the Heights library. It is easy to find fault when we are hurt and when fate takes a turn not in our plans. Some blame the City. Some blame the community. Maybe the community was to blame -- not just for the gym, but for failing to commit itself when Heights became locally owned in 1974. Then and during the 12 years that followed marked the time to "rally 'round the flag."

Too few did.

Rice Tower and the mysterious 'cologne'
• *April, 1995*

There it lay. The Tower. A pile of rubble, a heap of bricks that once cloaked a noble building. In little time, the wrecker's ball had razed Rice Tower, formerly the target of cadet jokes and formerly militantly defended by its cadet residents.

Rice Tower was the oddest building on Castle Heights' campus -- named for Col. L.L. Rice, who owned the Academy during some of its early glory days -- and part of a circle of buildings which included Rutherford Parks Library, Main, Ingram, Smith Chapel and Armstrong.

I never learned why Tower was built four stories high with three rooms on each floor. It made no architectural sense. Maybe there was this little plot of ground too small for a conventional building.

It was never "Rice" Barracks. It was always The Tower. To the cadets who were assigned rooms in Tower, the building was fiercely defended. There were stories told by the cadets on the top floor about how the building swayed during wind storms. The "Fourth Floor boys" loved to brag about the building's swings. They graduated heroic in surviving the rigors of the fabled floor.

I always suspected cadets living on the upper floors loved their quarters because it was impossible to surprise them with an "after Taps inspection." The old building creaked and groaned with every step on its uncarpeted stairs. Everything always was in order by the time an inspecting officer reached the top.

There was only one "bathroom," on the second floor—with a concrete floor sloped to a center drain. There were tales -- unconfirmed, of course -- that in the wee small hours, some cadets on Fourth simply raised a window. Most of us thought those, like so many others coming out of Tower, were greatly exaggerated.

It is fact that during the late '50s, a desk chair "mysteriously" flew from a third floor window, barely missing a faculty officer on patrol. Shaving cream in the night watchman's security key box was common. As was ice on the inside of the latrine windows during winter. And around 3 a.m. one spring day, three cadets arranged for a brief Tower-only power outage -- after which all lights and radios in every dorm room came on.

Here is another one of those tales: **John Granville** came to Heights from Texas, where he was an amateur boxer of some fame. John was hardly ready for military discipline, and before he settled in, there were a few confrontations. One occurred with me in algebra class. Both of us emerged with greater respect for the other and became friends. I am using his real name because he became a fine cadet.

John lived on Tower's third floor. Usually, when I was Officer in Charge for a day and making barracks inspection during evening CQ [Call-to-Quarters, supposedly used for night study], I would stop and chat with John.

One night, I noticed on his cabinet shelf a cologne bottle with a brand I had not seen before. I picked it up, and started a discussion.

"Never heard of this brand," I said. "Where did you get it?"

John stalled a moment.

"A Christmas present from my girlfriend at home," he replied.

I discarded the idea of taking a sniff of the new cologne, terminated the conversation, and left the room.

Characteristically distinct cadets assigned to Tower through its 80-year history matched the dorm's unique architecture.

Years later, now teacher and alumnus, we picked up our conversation.

"You remember the time you stopped in my room and picked up my bottle of 'cologne'?" he asked.

It took some memory searching, but I finally recalled the incident.

John Granville
as '54 senior.

"Did you know what was in the bottle?"

"Cologne?"

"No," he said. "Not cologne. Gin."

I registered my surprise.

"I always wondered if you knew what was in the bottle and used a ruse to let me know you knew. Or if you just idly picked it up and were ignorant of its contents," John said.

"I was totally ignorant," I said.

"I took no chances," John said. "Before you were out of the building, the gin was down the drain. I never touched another drop as long as I was in Heights."

In those days, possession of booze would have resulted in dismissal.

Listing Bernarr Macfadden [center] and Heights President Col. Harry Armstrong [right], editors of a Wilson County history book unfortunately failed to identify a key World War One general and CHMA benefactor [left] in this JB Leftwich photo.

The 'Third Man' in the Heights picture?
• *March, 1966*

Remembering Wilson County, published by Wilson Bank and Trust, contains several pictures I took during my long tenure at Castle Heights -- among them a photograph of three men, one elderly.

Two are correctly identified as Col. Harry L. Armstrong, president of the Academy for many years, and Bernarr Macfadden, rescuer of the school when times were bleak in the late '20s.

Macfadden was internationally known as a magazine publisher, some daringly risqué then but no eyebrow raisers in this bare-it-all era.

So, who is the third man in the picture? Obviously, compilers of the book did not know. Indeed, few people living today would have the slightest clue as to his identity. I had the pleasure of knowing him personally, albeit on a limited scale.

During the World War II years, he frequently visited the campus. He

September, 1939, and 440 cadets -- 40 over capacity -- were enrolled. Bullard Hall, named to honor Gen. Robert Lee Bullard, was completed, adding 72 rooms and faculty living quarters in the center of each of three floors.

was a member of the Bernarr Macfadden Foundation Board of Trust -- which ran Castle Heights -- and in this capacity enjoyed seeing the cadets at drill. He was immensely popular with students, roaming the campus with an entourage surrounding him.

He was especially proud that one of the Academy buildings was named for him.

He was born Jan. 15, 1861, in Youngsboro, Ala., graduated from West Point in 1885, and served in the Spanish-American War and in the Philippines. Early in World War I, he was promoted to brigadier general in command of the 1st Division in France. Soon he was in command of the 3rd Corps, which defended the vital Château Thierry against the Germans in the Second Battle of the Marne. Later, he led the 2nd Army in the Argonne Forest offensive which culminated in the armistice ending the war.

He was Lt. Gen. Robert Lee Bullard, second in rank only to Gen. John Pershing.

JBL Note: Although he wore only four stars, General Pershing was the highest ranking general in the history of the United States Army, outranking Eisenhower, Bradley and Arnold of World War II fame. Pershing was General of the *Armies*.

* Leave it to a colonel to set us straight on "generals." "It may be confusing," notes USAF Col. Thomas Bradley [Heights '69], but "journalists often refer to all generals in the Army, Air Force and Marines as 'General' -- from Napoleon and Julius Caesar to today's lowest brigadier. Common form of address for all is 'General,' but in fact the four grades in American usage are brigadier general (one star), major general (two), lieutenant general (three) and general (four). On occasion in wartime, Americans have been promoted to five-star rank, as were several during WWII. John J. Pershing eventually was promoted to six stars in World War I -- and called General of the Armies -- but I do not think he ever wore all of them. George Dewey was promoted to the six-star rank of Admiral (USN equivalent of General) of the Navy by Congress after the Spanish-American War, but I do not think he ever wore all of them either."

Campus shootings plagued even Heights
• *April, 2007*

Col. Gene Hale, a great Castle Heights teacher, assisted me in the research of this column.

The tragedy at Virginia Tech [Virginia Polytechnic Institute & State University, Blacksburg, Va.] this week revived a bank of memories of a frightening and traumatic incident at Castle Heights Military Academy 50 years ago. But in this instance, the "goddess of trauma" smiled on the Academy which emerged, compared to Virginia Tech, relatively unscathed and without loss of life.

As far as I know, the Heights' event was at least one of the first school-shooting incidents in this country, but my research was limited.

On a beautiful Saturday in April, 1957, Castle Heights was the scene of a new experience – one destined to be repeated in other U.S. schools with more tragic results.

For readers unfamiliar with the nature of Castle Heights, hundreds of boarding cadets passed through its portals, many from foreign coun-

Completed 1904 as the first stand alone CHMA gymnasium, the building -- scene of a 1957 shooting -- was converted to Ingram Hall in 1937.

tries. Most alien cadets came to the Academy from Mexico, Central America and the northern tier of countries in South America.

Highlight of each Academy military year was federal inspection when a team of Army officers came to review the cadet corps and the school facilities. A frenzy of activity played out before the inspection began. Cadets and faculty worked together to assure school facilities were spotless. Extra military rehearsals were conducted on the drill field.

On this April Saturday afternoon, all of the cadets, except the foreign pupils, were on the drill field honing skills for inspection scheduled Monday and Tuesday. Cadets from foreign countries who were not citizens of the USA were excused from this exercise. This offered a wonderful opportunity for them to loll around in their rooms, play 45 rpm records or, in rare instances, even study for upcoming exams.

Three Latin-American cadets were goofing off in Ingram Hall when a Cuban cadet burst into their room and started shooting. One cadet was critically wounded, another had serious wounds, and a third suffered only superficial injuries.

Here, my memory lapses. I don't remember how Academy officials came on the scene or how long after the shooting occurred before Lebanon police were informed.

I do remember it was learned the shooter smuggled into the barrack piece by piece a .22 rifle, then reassembled it. And I remember the shooter was a troubled boy, a loner and a target for torment from the other Latin Americans. He was sullen and unresponsive in class, and he appeared consumed by anger. If we had had a psychological profile, it may have resembled the profile of the man who massacred 32 pupils and teachers at Virginia Tech.

The victims were taken to the old Martha Gaston Hospital in Lebanon where Dr. John Hill Tilley brought them through the crisis.

The Academy was fortunate in the quality and judgment of the parents of the three victims. They did not assign blame or neglect to the Academy. They were grateful for a skilled surgeon and the medical care they received. All of the victims returned to their classrooms, finished the school year, and in due course graduated from Heights.

Even the legal issue was solved satisfactorily. The shooter's father flew to Lebanon where a meeting of him, school officials and the district attorney followed. The district attorney agreed to release the shooter to his father, who agreed to take the boy home to Cuba.

o o o

JBL Note: I do not remember who served as district attorney, but I think it was Baxter Key Sr., whose common sense decision made it possible for the school to move on without the burden of criminal litigation. No complaints of neglect were heard from the victims' parents. Obviously, they could have sued. Instead, they returned their sons to school, their confidence in the Academy unshaken.

I still cringe at the thought of the mayhem that could have resulted under our system in those years. Barracks buildings were never locked. One unarmed guard patrolled at night.

I was the Academy's public relations officer. I also worked part-time for *The Tennessean*. I hoped to use my influence on the editors to go easy on playing the story. The next day, the story appeared on the front page under an eight-column banner head.

My vague memory recalls three victims. *Hail, Castle Heights!*, a history of the school, tells of only two.

Macfadden's razing recalls
Macfadden's raising
• *March 2010*

The proposed razing of Macfadden Auditorium calls to mind the raising of Macfadden Auditorium at Castle Heights in 1941, my first year.

The new building was much more than a school auditorium. It became a community center where many plays and other entertainment functions were staged.

I remember the Gilbert and Sullivan operettas produced jointly by Castle Heights music department and Ward Belmont School for Girls in Nashville. Mrs. J. H. Kremer, known affectionately by

A most valuable Heights building, Macfadden Auditorium opened in 1941 to be used for multiple activities. Classrooms were in the basement.

cadets as "Ma" Kremer, directed the cadet glee club and co-directed the operettas. They were professionally produced and staged.

The auditorium was completed early in December, 1941, and was opened the beginning of the second semester. I was one of the first half-dozen instructors to teach in a spacious classroom in the basement.

Two days each week—Monday and Wednesday—we held chapel exercises mid-morning. [And on Fridays during appropriate seasons,

The corps convened twice weekly in Macfadden Auditorium for chapel services, and faculty/administration announcements and reports.

pep rallies were staged]. Annually, the graduation crowds often over-heated the auditorium, and we wished for air conditioning -- which the building never had.

Bernarr Macfadden in the early years often was present at graduation exercises and delighted in handing graduates their diplomas. The colorful publisher and physical fitness guru took pleasure in doing or saying things that often affronted Col. Harry L.

Armstrong, long-time Castle Heights president.

Once Macfadden, well advanced in years, excited graduates and embarrassed the colonel by finishing his duties on stage and making a running leap as he exited the building.

Civic clubs made use of the building. I remember appearing in drag in a Lion's Club skit. Mattie Donnell graciously allowed me to use one of her dresses, which I managed to squeeze into. (My sons have a picture of me in the dress, and enjoy showing it.)

Musical performances featuring cadets and Lebanon groups theater productions were held in the Macfadden Auditorium.

The Kiwanis Club held its minstrels in the auditorium, a part of their history they now would like to erase. Community religious services also often were conducted there.

One interesting note: During the early 60's, two rooms under the main steps were used by several cadets—who had to shower in the gym across the street.

After the school was forced to close in 1986, Cracker Barrel Restaurants Co. eventually bought the building, and Dan Evins, the company's CEO and a Heights alumnus, hoped to restore it as a community center. But times were changing and interests were shifting. Restoration plans never developed, and the building suffered a fate common to most vacant buildings.

In recent months, a group of alumni, including engineering firm official Tom Clemmons '75, made valiant efforts to purchase and restore the building. But its goal was never reached.

Just as alumni and other teachers, I rue its demise. But it can meet its doom with dignity and pride, and as a symbol of the times.

Remembering Christmas at Heights

• December, 1991

In a recent letter-to-the-editor, a Mt. Juliet, Tenn., reader commented that Christmas comes from memories, not tinsel and toys.

"Our children will not remember the expensive toys, large or small, but the anticipation of the season, the participation in a church or school pageant, choir or caroling, the family traditions of decorating, baking, wrapping gifts, reading together the Christmas story, visits from relatives and friends and the happy greetings of 'Merry Christmas!'"

Christmas dances in Macfadden Gymnasium were among highlights of campus seasonal events.

Anticipation of Christmas reached its purest form at Castle Heights Military Academy during the years when its barracks were filled with boarding students, many of whom had not been home since the previous September. In them there was true anticipation and excitement. In each room, there was at least one calendar with each day in December crossed off, usually the first thing in the morning, to mark the approach of Christmas vacation.

And there always was the Christmas Dance. The gym was decorated in appropriate colors, a cedar tree with a full complement of lights seemed to grow from the roof of the porch on Main Building, and each division [floor] of each barracks was festive in its decorations.

My memory travels to Christmas 1941, 50 years ago, when, according to author Ferrol Sams in his new novel, *All the World Was Young*. I am not sure which Nashville orchestra, probably Francis Craig, played for The Dance, but it was a date of great cheer.

I, too, was young, one month into my 22nd year, and my wife was 20 and pretty and no older than many of the cadets. So a constant stream of them "cut in" and danced with her. Since we did not live on campus, many cadets had not seen her before the Christmas Dance. So, they pretended they thought she was my sister.

Even though the country was two weeks into World War II, the occasion was festive and the anticipation near its peak -- just as author Sams described this period in history.

The Division Christmas parties -- usually one or two nights before classes were dismissed for vacation -- were events to behold. [*Guest*

Columns, pages 169 and 181.] The cadets pooled their resources and bought more food than they could have eaten in a month of Sundays. They gorged themselves. Some threw up. But the fun and happiness.

Deeply embedded in the memories of hundreds of former cadets -- now parents and grandparents and even great grandparents -- are the memories of Christmas at Heights. Or, more nearly accurate, Christmas anticipation.

Christmas 1941. The Christmases that followed during those war years were not as festive. Many of the boys living through the excitement of Christmas 1941 were even farther from home during subsequent holidays, celebrating the event on foreign fields and wondering if ever again there would be another like Christmas '41.

For some, Christmas 1941 was their last. They fought and died on foreign battlefields, carrying with them the memories of happy days at Castle Heights as the days dwindled to late December.

How wonderful to imagine the stories the survivors of the War years may have told their children and grandchildren about those Christmases, "when all the world was young."

A pre-1917 advertisement for Castle Heights School. Subsequent Heights Military Academy ads for some reason neglected to mention "discipline firm but sympathetic," "delightful home life," and "wholesome social advantages." And note cost of $43/month, assuming nine-month school term.

Gen. Dwight D. Eisenhower, in June, 1944, challenges paratroopers preparing to participate in first assault in D-Day invasion. Sixty-nine Castle Heights grads died in World War II, with hundreds more serving.

'The Longest Day'
• *June, 1994*

I marvel at our fascination with numbers, especially the ones that end with a zero or a five. Such as 50.

And such as our observation of the 50th anniversary this June 6 of D-Day, code name for the massive Allied invasion of Normandy and thence to Germany and the Nazi occupied countries.

Make a note of this: On June 6, 1998, newspapers and television channels will bear little note of this historic event. Two years ago, December 7 came and went without a reference in our local metropolitan newspaper. Plenty of press, however, on Dec. 7, 1991, 50 years after the Japanese bombed Pearl Harbor and brought this country into World War II -- but hardly remembered 51 years later.

And what made the Normandy invasion so special? Why is it remembered while the anniversaries of the invasions of North Africa, Leyte, Iwo Jima, Guadacanal and Okinawa come and go without mention?

The reason D-Day rings louder than all other World War II bells is because of the massive number of men and women involved. And because the Pacific Islands were small and unknown. And because the Pacific War was more in piecemeal fashion than the European war.

I wonder if the massive Normandy invasion belonged more to General Eisenhower and Field Marshall Alexander, the Allied planners, than to the GIs who fought their way from the English Channel to the interior of Europe? Indeed, wasn't the war for the GI a matter of squad or platoon or company? Wasn't trench warfare more a matter of grief, shock, uncertainty, apprehension, mud, cold, pain, maimed bodies and death? Not so much a matter of the scope and logistics.

Said James J. [Jay-Boy] Sanders '43, who recently returned from a visit to Normandy: "I saw a lot of people get killed back then. A lot of limbs blown off. It's something you never forget. You want to, but you can't."

For my college classmate, Jimmy Fisher of Carthage, Tenn., the war was not the thousands of Pacific miles, but an airplane crashing into the ocean taking his life and those of all crewmen. For Marine Pvt. Pat Parker, one of the all-time great athletes at Castle Heights, the war was a sniper's bullet on Okinawa. For Lt. Bill Sleyster '42, a training accident on a lonely Kentucky road.

Is there any event, though not on the scope of Normandy, significant enough to reawaken this country to the sacrifices in Korea and Vietnam? Probably not. All other military operations, no matter how intense or how horrible, pale in the light of D-Day simply because of its magnitude.

So on June 6, 1994, the golden anniversary of D-Day, I went to Castle Heights and read the names on the War Memorial, a monument to valor which soon will yield to an extension of Castle Heights Avenue.

As I read the names on the plaques, I again was reminded the Heights Class of 1942 was among those suffering the highest number of casualties. They typify a generation of young men who gave the fullest measure in a war that guaranteed the freedom of this nation for at least 50 more years, thus I am listing them:

Lt. Peter D. Diffenbaugh	Lt. Thomas B. Gillespie	Lt. C. E. Grantham
T/5 Clarence Haston	W. Heltzen	A/C Henry F. Heyl
Lt. John B. Johnson	Sgt. Wm. W. Karr	Pfc. Leslie H. Lilenthal
Lt. K.D. Penry	Lt. I. William Sleyster	Lt. J. S. Wiles Jr.

• The original CHMA War Memorial of which JBL writes was located in a traffic circle between the gym and auditorium, and was dedicated May 1, 1982. Brig. Gen. Alonzo J. Walter '45, was dedication speaker. Extension of Castle Heights Avenue North through campus forced its removal. A new Memorial adjacent to Lebanon City Hall [old Main] was dedicated Oct. 11, 1997. The current refurbished Memorial was rededicated Oct. 9, 2010 [page 239]. Two of the memorials were paid for by Academy grads through the Castle Heights National Alumni Association.

Post-Graduates [PGs] and 'spartan' living
• *March, 2006*

In a story by sportswriter Jeff Lockridge written for *The Tennessean*, basketball player Tyler Smith describes his life as a first year post-graduate cadet at Hargrave Military Academy in Chatham, Va.

Tyler Smith is a blue-chip college basketball prospect who needed to hone his skills before moving from high school to the demanding college arena.

Tyler's experience is a story familiar to hundreds of alumni who came to Castle Heights for a fifth high school year, usually for the dual purpose of additional experience in athletics and for an excellent academic environment.

Dick Inman as '49 CHMA post-grad.

In the Lockridge article, Tyler describes taps at 10:00 o'clock, marching to meals, standing at attention, and getting his hair cut as he adjusted to military school life. His primary aim and the school's reason for granting him a scholarship is basketball. But Tyler has learned that other values derived from Hargrave may be more lasting and even more important than basketball.

Dick Inman, a post-graduate at Castle Heights in 1948-49, learned a similar lesson. Recruited for football by legendary Heights coach Stroud Gwynn, Dick almost immediately grasped the range of his opportunities and opened his mind to develop more than his football skills. He was the team leader of Castle Heights' Mid-South Conference champions, and soon became as well an academic leader and a role model for younger cadets.

Tennessee All-America and SEC Legend Bobby Majors was '68 CHMA grad.

Dick graduated from high school at a young age. Eligible for another year of football, he came to Castle Heights the following fall and led the team -- in a season marred by only one defeat -- to a bowl game in Daytona Beach, Fla.

O. E. Philpot Jr., an all-star player at Lebanon High School in 1950-51, elected to attend Castle Heights for football and additional academics in

In a photo [left] taken by JB Leftwich, 1953-54 CHMA post-graduate Earl Cato shows running back skills. Cato, then in California real estate, and Leftwich renew friendship at Heights Homecoming 2000.

1951-52. Like Dick Inman, O. E. immediately filled a void in team leadership which, in contrast to most Heights teams, had few post-graduates.

Coach Gwynn had to deep dip into the ranks of former B-team players in 1951, and was unusually pessimistic about producing a winner. Despite a depth of team talent, O. E. so inspired his teammates that it made a run for the championship. Highlighting the season, Castle Heights defeated previously unbeaten and highly rated Georgia Military Academy 13-6 in a snowstorm on Halloween Day [*page 146*].

And there was Earl Cato, a dazzling runner and all-star player at Tennessee's Hartsville High School in 1952, who came to Heights the next season just to play football. He became a legend at running back. True, Earl had adjustments to make away from an adoring corps of fans in Trousdale County and in competition with a stable of star runners.

Today, Earl Cato is one of the Academy's most loyal alumni, rarely missing a Homecoming and treasuring his experience as a cadet.

There were others – Claude Maynard, Cannon Mays, Billy Smith, Hamlett Halbert and Bobby Majors of the famed Majors football family, to mention a few.

o o o

The boarding cadets, who in most years at Castle Heights far outnumbered the "day boys" -- local Lebanon students who only attended CHMA during the day -- lived in circumstances the world would consider beyond austere. Like the Hargrave environment Jeff Lockridge describes in his newspaper article, boarders at Heights lived in a room containing two each of bunk beds, chairs, tables, lockers and little else. There were no TV sets and use of radios was limited. Cadets were not allowed automobiles. They were allowed two afternoon and one night town leaves per week. A concession was made on Friday nights for cadets with dates – they were allowed out until 10:30.

Conditions were more stringent for cadets delinquent in academics or discipline. Cadets lagging in their grades were required to attend help sessions on Saturday, afternoon sessions on weekdays, and supervised night school. Cadets had to earn the rights for furloughs home [other than Christmas and spring break]. Some accumulated enough merits to leave early on vacation, others spent some vacation days working off demerits assigned for their misdeeds.

Despite rigid regulations, some cadets as might be expected outmaneuvered the system. To get a day off, some would overheat the thermometer near a radiator and spend a day in the school hospital. Record temperature for a cadet was 112 degrees. Other cadets learned to visit the infirmary nurse who freely dispensed Cheracol -- 30 percent alcohol -- for "nagging coughs."

Passing years color the memories of Heights graduates. There likely is no more loyal group of alumni than the former cadets who each year continue to attend Homecoming each October.

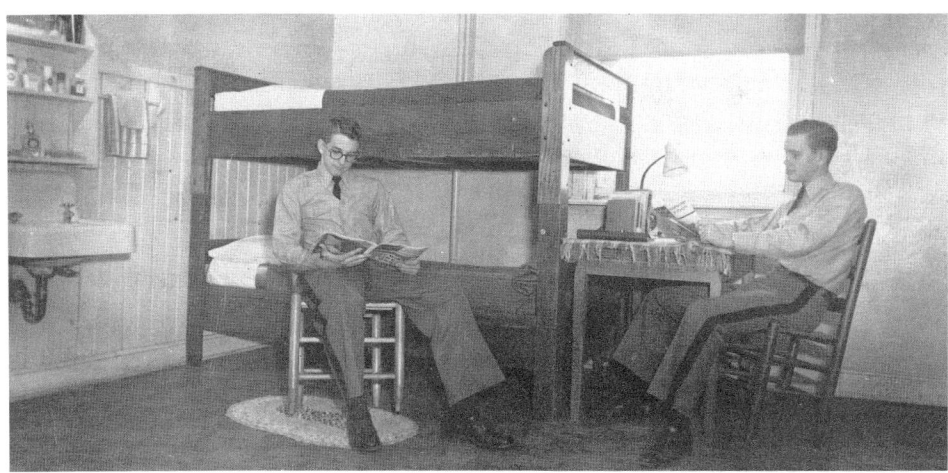

"Spartan" describes this early '50s CHMA barracks room, but cadets added area rugs, wall posters, photographs, record players, radios and small bookcases to "dress up" living quarters. Regardless of a room's motif, there was certainty the weekly SMI -- 10 a.m. Saturday Morning Inspection by cadet and faculty officers -- would find that a quarter could be bounced on each bed's tightly tucked sheets/blanket. And the sink/mirror enabled cadets in each room to take care of personal grooming needs.

Brides, daylilies waken 'years of yore'

• *June, 2010*

Just as countless other oldsters, I am a faithful reader of newspaper obituaries – often turning to the obit page before reading the latest news or sports stories.

This practice led recently to the obit of one of "my" brides. I read with sadness the short biography of a beautiful – and young, when I knew her – woman whose wedding I had photographed in years of yore. She, as were others, was a bride to remember.

In the early years of my teaching career at Castle Heights, school officials decided the Academy needed a photographer. And since I was Public Relations Director, charged with keeping the school's activities in the newspapers, the job fell to me.

The school bought a Speed Graphic, just like the ones used in the old black and white motion pictures shown on television. My previous experience was limited to box cameras. I was totally unprepared to operate a complex Speed Graphic, which could require as many as six adjustments before pressing the shutter button.

I turned to Waldo Seat, owner of Seat's Studio, who took cadet portraits for the school yearbook. Mr. Seat became my mentor and lifelong friend, and often referred brides to me when he had a conflict.

Wedding and industrial photography supplemented the income of my young and growing family, but wedding photography was the most demanding and often the most fun. In two cases, I "shot" five brides from the same family. I must have been pretty good at it since I had repeat customers.

All of this came to mind earlier this month when my daylilies were

Advertisement for Seat's Studio, where cadets went annually for more than 40 years to have "official" photos taken for use in *The Adjutant* and with school news releases. Seat's also took cadet portraits used as gifts to parents, friends.

in full bloom. Daughter Barbara photographed a vast array of blossoms and transferred the pictures to my computer. No film was involved and no long hours in a photo darkroom were required.

With a camera that fit into her pocket, she zoomed in for close-ups and stood back for panoramic views.

My old Nikon camera—with its wide-angle, telephoto and zoom lenses that cost a small fortune—gathers dust in a closet unused for more than two decades. She can photograph with a camera that fits in the palm of her hand a range of scenes that would have required of me all the accessories mentioned above.

Nevertheless, I had the pleasure of photographing a bevy of beautiful brides and seeing their happiness when I delivered the photographs.

But being a bride did not guarantee beauty. One of my brides reminded me more of a character actress than a starlet. I used every lighting technique I knew, but the pictures were true to life. I feared she would reject them and send me home with no return on my investment.

Not so. She was ecstatic. She savored every picture and ordered a galaxy of reprints.

When I did the numbers and added the $$ marks, I changed my mind. She may have been my most beautiful bride.

• Memories of a Photographic Icon

Seat's Studio was a fixture on the Lebanon Public Square decades before I came to Lebanon in 1937, and Waldo Seat was one of the distinct personalities of the small town's persona.

For years, he was the first businessman to open shop each morning, unlocking his front door as early as 6:30 because he wanted to accommodate his customers.

"A lot of people are here at 6:30 to catch rides to their jobs in Nashville, and this is the only time they can drop off their film to be developed and printed," he explained.

In those days, most pictures were shot on roll film for processing. Mr. Seat and Miss Ruby Swann, his assistant of many years, did this on site and sooner than mail-order processors could produce the pictures.

Mr. Seat possessed a vast knowledge of photography, and his pleasure in tutoring was a valuable asset for this unschooled photographer. After Mr. Seat's death, his son-in-law ran the business. Now his grandson is owner and operator. It was perhaps Lebanon's oldest family-operated business. [It closed in 2013.]

CHMA cadets already knew what a syndicated columnist, "Man About Manhattan," described in 1937 about his most mouth-watering travel delights: "It means particularly the ice cream sodas in Shannon's Drugs in Lebanon, Tenn." A cadet hangout, Shannon's offered candy, gum, cigars, cigarettes, magazines and toiletries in addition to the soda fountain booths and tables.

Memories of another Lebanon landmark
• *Excerpt from August, 2010 column*

Years before I arrived in Lebanon in 1937, Shannon's Drug Store was an institution, operating in a building now owned by the Chamber of Commerce.

Each of the Shannon brothers was a distinct personality and each was a "character." Homer was the extrovert, the greeter who stood in the store's front door to entice and welcome customers. A legion of customers regarded him as a personal friend. [The Shannons resisted installing air conditioning because they didn't want their front door closed during warmer months. They regarded a door as a barrier.]

While Homer was the greeter, Harry was the pharmacist.

Harry's passion was the New York Yankees, and baseball was his favorite topic. He had a generous stomach, and he wore his belt well below it. Legend has it that once Harry's pants slid to his ankles when he stretched to reach merchandise on an upper shelf.

The store was a gathering place. The lunch counter, featuring 35-cents plate lunches and tasty sandwiches, attracted a mid-day crowd.

Castle Heights cadets loved Shannon's. They enjoyed the milk shakes especially, and they relished meeting girls there.

A favorite story of the two brothers reveals their teamwork. When a customer arrived with a prescription for a pharmaceutical the store couldn't supply at the time, Homer would engage the customer in conversation while his brother went across the square to Bradshaw's Drug Store and had the prescription filled. He returned, placed it in a Shannon's container, and delivered it to the customer.

Shannon's was an institution, and Lebanon lost a bit of its character when the store eventually closed. Since then and with the proliferation of antique stores on the Square, no other downtown store has developed a following equal to Shannon's.

"Your Health is Our Business"

SHANNON'S

QUALITY DRUGS

Heights yearbook advertisement for Shannon's Drugs, which left family ownership around 1964 and was closed in 1976.

Pondering future archeology 'Dig' sites
• *April, 1987*

There was a time when we boys roamed over a hill and into a valley to visit a long deserted house which stood by a long abandoned lane that spanned about two miles to a public road.

The structure, built on a limestone base, originally was a one-bedroom log cabin into which a kitchen and later a bedroom had been added. A limestone chimney and fireplace heated the 16' x 16' original house and to a lesser degree the bedroom. The cook stove heated the kitchen.

No one in my family remembered the names of any of the house's former occupants, but my grandfather vaguely remembered that in years long past, a family had lived there.

Surrounding the house were oak and hickory trees. A well, long ago caved in, furnished water. A garden provided food. The forest provided fuel. Today, the house is gone, a few decaying logs scattered about and sheets of rusty metal roofing clinging to rotting rafters. The chimney stands, lonesome and almost eerie, harboring memories of those who lived there.

I used to wonder, as we explored the vacant house and pried into the loft, who built this cabin and its lean-to rooms. Was there an air of excitement and anticipation as neighbors gathered to raise the logs for a young bride and groom? Did the couple add the kitchen as soon as they could afford it? Did the children grow up and leave home? Did one of the parents die and the other leave to live with a son or daughter? And did the house remain vacant because it was too far off the beaten path?

Did the builders believe they were building for all eternity? Did they ever imagine that in 1987, only the chimney would remain standing?

In 1877, when Cumberland University officials built Caruthers Hall in Lebanon on a West Main lot, they were building "for all time" a home for the Law School. It probably never occurred to them that the building would stand less than a century, that in 1987 the Lebanon Bank would stand in place of the Law School building, and that in 1987 that bank would sell its property and business to a state banking system.

In 1902, founders of Castle Heights opened its doors and it soon became a recognized military school, reaching its zenith in the years between World War II and the Vietnam War. Major building programs took place prior to World War II and a few years before Vietnam.

In the late 1930s, Castle Heights' officials built Bullard Hall, named for General Robert Lee Bullard of World War I fame, and new and old cadets immediately filled its rooms. It lasted less than one-half century before it fell into disuse, caught fire and burned, and eventually was razed just a few years ago to make way for tennis courts.

The school is mute now. No romping up and down the barracks halls, no slipping off campus after Taps, no anticipating spring vacation, no bullring, no Mid-South Conference champion teams, no valedictory speeches. Do you suppose David Mitchell and I.W.P. Buchanan, as they developed their plans for Castle Heights in the infant years of this century, ever once considered the possibility of a defunct school in 1987?

Nashville's Union Station, built in 1900 and once a bustling transportation center -- hosting CHMA cadets arriving and departing at the beginning and end of each school year -- barely survived and now serves as a hotel and restaurant complex. The 400-room Andrew Jackson Hotel, built in 1925, was demolished in 1971.

Cities in the Mediterranean world -- once thriving commercial centers, with hundreds of thousands of residents -- now are archaeological sites.

How many years before archaeologists probe the remains of the Wilson County Court House or the yet-to-be-built Kroger store?

Castle Heights Missed

To The Editor:

Like many of the cadets before and after my era, I am proud to have Castle Heights Military Academy as part of my educational, emotional and physical heritage! I remember all the good, bad, and tough times — they all seem good now.

The academic experiences were superb. Captain Bradley's chemistry, the math of Captain Leftwich, Captain Stockton's English, history with Captain Bass, Major Fishburn in physics, Captain Stroud Gwynn in athletics — all of these and many more courses and many more men including superior educators from my own family (Colonels John and Kenneth Morgan and Captain Bob Morgan) will never be forgotten by me or by many other Heights cadets. They not only "peeled the crust" from my brain, but taught me how to study and stimulated initiative and motivation. I am sure now I needed this experience greatly.

The emotional support from all these educators was strong, although hard work was expected and demanded by them all.

Discipline, authoritative respect, military understanding and appreciation were all presented and imbedded in a firm but acceptable way. Colonel Dan Ingram, the commandant, was tough, fearful, but fair. I remember old cadet friends with great affection — Stan Harvel, Bill Kleemen, Paul Smotherman, Ron Dawson, Robert Reeves — just to name a few. Even though I haven't seen many of them in years, they are still great friends of mine as they helped mold my life with excellent interpersonal relationships.

I will miss Castle Heights Military Academy. Even though I shed tears when she "retired" recently, I will always have her memories.

James W. Gibson, M.D.
Johnson City, TN.

The sentiments of Dr. James W. Gibson '51, in this Dec. 5, 1986, letter to the *Lebanon Democrat,* were typical of thousands of Heights alums after hearing news of the Academy's closing. Gibson graduated from University of Tennessee College of Medicine in 1957, trained in radiology at Duke University Medical Center, and has specialized for more than 45 years in Diagnostic Radiology in Johnson City, Tenn. He and his wife, Dottie, have two children, three grandchildren.

A true teacher in shadow
of newspaper presses
• *October, 2010*

My friend, George Summers Sr., 84, left this globe last month and there was hardly a mention of the girls and boys he had influenced or his dedication to his profession.

George was plant manager of the *Lebanon Democrat*, but that title falls far short of describing a man of many dimensions whose influence extended far beyond the shop where he worked.

He was a teacher. Not just a teacher, but a teacher deluxe with a genuine love for those he taught.

His mission was not long in revealing itself. He became an amateur printer in the shop of the old *Democrat* after his discharge from the Army in the mid-'40s.

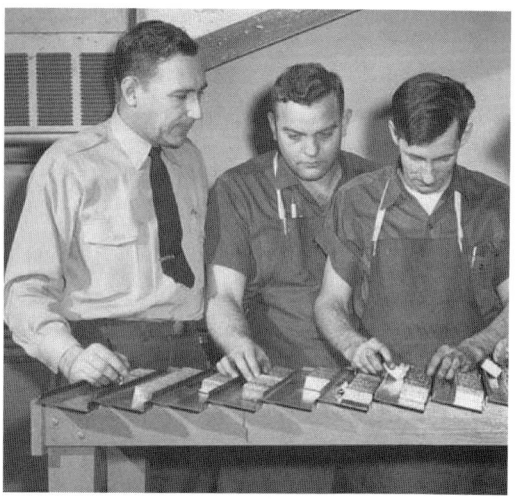

George Summers [center] for more than three decades was primary "hands on" newspaper production teacher as JB Leftwich [left] and *Cavalier* editors went to the *Lebanon Democrat* every third Friday to publish that weekend's edition. Longtime Democrat employee Billy Carr [right] also was instrumental in publication of the student newspaper.

I first took note of George as he helped and taught Castle Heights cadet editors of *The Cavalier*, the Academy's nationally recognized student newspaper. The fledgling editors, as they worked at the *Democrat* every few weeks to produce the next issue, were asking him to "show them" rather than asking for him to do the task, and George would stop his work to teach the eager learners.

Dr. LeRoy Dowdy, currently a college professor and writer/editor of academic books, was one of my *Cavalier* editors. He recalls how George treated the cadet editors "as real newspaper men."

"George Summers was among the last of a breed of workers who built newspapers the old fashioned way – by hand," LeRoy recalls. "He had printer's ink in his veins and molten lead in his character. He always had an encouraging word for staffers even as he taught us the ropes."

Although he had a special affinity for the Heights cadet editors, his fondness for young people knew a wider scope.

Said Lynda Leftwich Newton, who in college was editor of the University of Tennessee's first student daily newspaper:

"In 1960, when I was co-editor of the Lebanon High School student newspaper, the publishing business had not yet been revolutionized by the computer. This meant that we went to the shop at the *Democrat* and worked closely with the people who put the newspaper together.

"George was one of these people. He welcomed us 17-year-old would be journalists. He seemed to enjoy our company. He patiently asked our opinion, and we were never treated as interruptions. I remember George's smile – he was probably amused by our eagerness. These experiences are among my favorite memories of high school."

Another of my student editors, Leonard Bradley Jr., now a Vanderbilt University professor after a career in state government, knew George through their church and also for his help to *Cavalier* editors.

"George was an amazing person, particularly for such a rough and tumble venue as a pressroom," Leonard said. "He took the time to walk us through the technical aspects of how what we all had written would be printed and published."

"In that hectic place where everything was done on a strict time clock, he kept his humor, loved working with kids who were learning and never seemed to be frustrated by our many slip-ups. Quite a tutor, and such a fine man," Bradley continued.

Jim Fall, Heights '55, who edited daily newspapers in Arkansas and Missouri, remembers one particular lesson George taught him.

"I remember his first fast lessons about leads and slugs [pieces of metal] and how to close out a page form, slipping them from his hand like cards from a deck and pounding away with that mallet on his make-up rule. His teachings served me well, especially when I was editor in West Memphis and we were still using hot metal. I doubt there are many around who still even remember that term, much less what it means."

David Hall, Heights '61, who may have been Lebanon's most famous newspaperman in the last half century, reports a special memory:

"Going to *The Democrat* and working with George Summers to put out each issue of *The Cavalier* is one of my enduring memories of neophyte journalism. For all of the advances we have made in newspapers, the days of hot type remain its romantic high point."

But my former editors and I are tardy. We should have said these things to George while he was still here. He deserved to hear them.

The more than 20 cadets in this late '50s Heights Latin-American Club continued the organization's policy of helping new Latin students assimilate, overcoming language and relationship problems, and scheduling social and educational activities.

Column in Spanish ahead of its time
• *November, 2000*

In response to migration of Hispanics to Bedford County, the Shelbyville *Times-Gazette* has initiated a section written in Spanish.

This is an excellent move and an assist to people struggling to adjust to life where their language previously was rarely spoken.

But the *Times-Gazette* was not the first English language newspaper in Tennessee to print stories in Spanish. I believe the first to initiate this practice was *The Cavalier*, student newspaper of Castle Heights.

For years, the Academy attracted large numbers of pupils from the Spanish-speaking countries of this hemisphere. Most of them came from families who realized use of the English language was essential to the future of their children. Many of these cadets came to Heights with varying skills in the use of English. Some knew only a few words.

One boy from Cuba rode a train from Miami to Nashville, then a bus to Lebanon. He knew only two English words: hamburger and Coke.

The school offered no special courses for these cadets who learned to help each other. Teachers were understanding, but most instructors were not prepared to answer their needs.

I was always amazed at how quickly they learned English. Many, but not all, were bright pupils. It was a struggle, but after one semester, they could function to a remarkable degree in a foreign tongue. Indeed, as their years at the school grew in number, some of these cadets came to think in English rather than in Spanish.

The Cavalier offered a column in the '50s in Spanish as a courtesy, a forum for a cadet to express his thoughts in his own language.

All of the Latin American cadets learned to read and speak English. One became salutatorian of his class and delivered an address which upstaged the principal speaker.

The response from the audience was so spontaneous and appreciative that Lt. Gen. Eugene Forester, the commencement speaker, began his speech with a question:

"After the salutatorian's address, what can I say?"

A large number of Cubans attended Castle Heights. After the revolution in Cuba, this came to an end before Castro came to power. During Castro's successful struggle to overthrow the Batista government, the Cuban cadets almost without exception supported Fidel. They thought then he was a messiah. Their minds changed later. One exception was Orlando Segarra, an exceedingly bright Cuban who graduated from Heights with honors.

The Spanish language column in the CHMA newspaper did spawn a few problems. The publication editors did not always know just what they were printing, albeit they would have a third party translate it to them. Nevertheless, nuances often escaped the editors.

There were production problems. It was difficult for type setters to convert Spanish to lead in the old days, or to enter it in the computer in more recent times. Typos often showed up in the correction of typos.

But then, pioneering efforts often are difficult.

Familiarity, amplification trump formal etiquette

• *June 2005*

Did I mention a first dance?

Many former cadets and contemporary females remember dances – formals, that is - at Castle Heights Military Academy, which were usually held in the gymnasium or in the Mitchell House.

I remember most an exercise in etiquette when I was a part of a receiving line, which every cadet and his date had to navigate before joining the action on the dance floor.

Every cadet was taught to present his date to each member of the receiving line, a difficult task for boys who were not steeped in the etiquette of days of yore.

But they learned through the rigid discipline of Mary Fahey, a maiden of unknown years, who supervised the decoration for the Heights dances and who made sure social customs were exercised. Cadets chose not to defy her.

Hosiery flaws did not matter in those functions because the young ladies wore full-length formal dresses, the most elegant attire in their wardrobes.

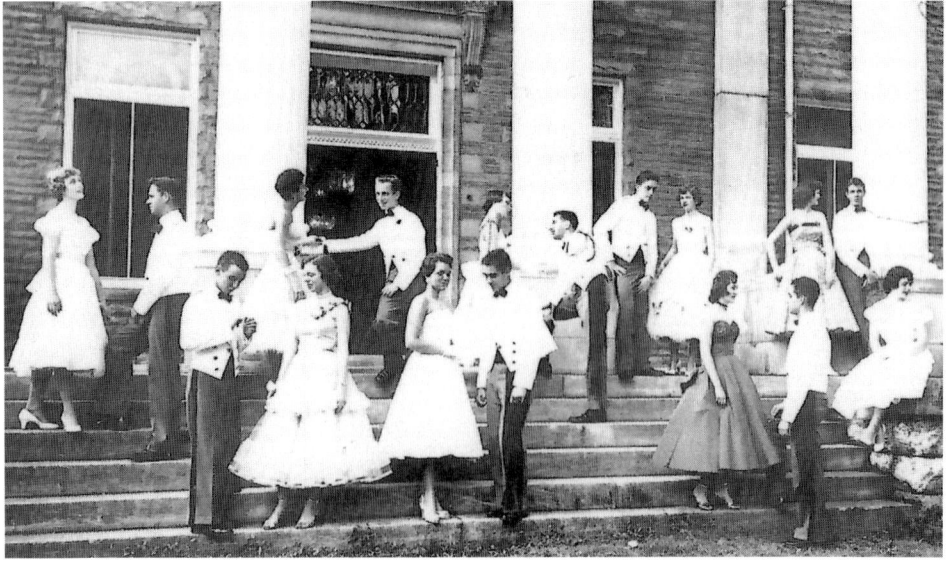

Formal attire and manners once were the order of the day for Castle Heights dances scheduled for the Mitchell House.

Changing styles antiquated formality, and etiquette faded as disco, hip hop and rap replaced waltzes, fox trots and '50s and '60s rock and roll. Heavy metal and disc jockeys displaced Frances Craig's orchestra and the mid-century dance bands. Formality and grace gave way to familiarity and amplification.

Eventually, the gymnasium stubbornly gave way to the wrecker's ball, Mitchell House became headquarters of a national corporation, and Main Building became Lebanon City Hall.

By the Academy's 70th anniversary, music, dress and dancing styles had given way to "familiarity and amplification."

We did not recognize the signals, these changes in mores and etiquette, of formality and courtesy - all precursors of the decline and fall of Castle Heights.

• Ron Blackwood '57 [left], son of one of the original Blackwood Brothers gospel singers, arranged for members to perform at a mid-'50s weekday Heights chapel program. Among the group at that time were [top left] Wally Varner, James Blackwood, Bill Shaw; [bottom] Cecil Blackwood and J. D. Sumner . The Blackwoods sang with Elvis Presley on many of his gospel recordings, as did J. D. Sumner and the Stamps Quartet -- a group he formed in 1965 (with Ron as business manager) after 11 years with the Blackwoods. The Blackwoods have won eight Grammy and 27 Dove awards, sold more than 60 million albums, and are managed by Ron's talent agency. He and his wife Shelley Layne Blackwood have eight children, six grandchildren and two great-grandchildren.

In face of crises, optimism remains
• *April, 1986*

NOTE: Only four months before CHMA was closed, JB Leftwich found positive aspects to write in his column.

Overshadowed by the recent Castle Heights announcement that a zoning change was vital to the school's blueprint for recovering from a severe cash shortage were several events reflecting positively on the Academy.

Among these were the 10-year reevaluation, highlighted by a complimentary report by a visiting team of Southern Association of Colleges and Schools. I watched the members of this team from the day they assembled for a get-acquainted dinner with faculty, administration, students and trustees through an oral report for faculty and others in the Academy auditorium.

I saw the visitors grow comfortable with a school they knew little about, recognize the merits of the Heights program, and finally develop a fondness that showed through an objective report.

These visitors largely were from Tennessee public schools -- Jackson County, Manchester City Schools, White County, Warren County, Harriman City Schools, Roane County, Trousdale County, and Ooltewah High School. Only two, Inge Smith of Harpeth Academy and Dr. John Myers of Father Ryan, were private school educators.

Here are some comments the visitors made:

On the School and Community - "A positive community perception and a high level of interest and support exist."

On the Academic Program - Commendations "for the Advance Placement Program, small classes, a curriculum that stresses the basic academic disciplines, the outstanding counseling program."

On Faculty and Staff - "An environment conducive to teaching and learning is provided."

There were an equal number of recommendations, many requiring dollars. The visitors were thorough and objective—and professional. But when the committee made its recommendations to the Southern Association, it listed no deficiencies.

Col. Jack Little, superintendent, recently received a letter from Dr. John E. Cox, executive secretary of the Tennessee Secondary School Committee of the Southern Association, commending the administration, faculty and staff on the high quality educational program of the Academy.

Hollywood star George Hamilton (center) was guest of honor in spring 1986 for a CHMA benefit dinner and dance. Also welcoming attendees were Mrs. and Mr. Danny Evins '53, Ms. Alana Hamilton Stewart [mother of Hamilton's son, Ashley, who was a Heights Junior School cadet], and Mrs. and Col. Jack Little, Academy Superintendent 1984-86.

Other favorable indicators:

■ **Path to Excellence Campaign.**

This capital funds campaign was launched in October, 1985, with a Phase I goal of $1 million. Maj. Martha Bradshaw, Director of Development at Heights, reports pledges and gifts in this phase have reached a total of more than $800,000. She believes the goal will be reached by July 31, end of the fiscal year.

■ **George Hamilton Benefit Gala.**

More than $31,000 was raised thanks to "An Evening with George Hamilton," star of stage, screen and television [*photo above*]. Alumni, parents, patrons and friends attended the benefit dinner and dance. Hamilton's son, Ashley, attends the Academy, and the actor agreed to the CHMA benefit with proceeds targeted for repair and reopening of the swimming pool, renovation to second floor Ingram Hall, and dining hall improvements.

■ **The Recruitment Campaign.**

More than 45,000 brochures have been sent to a select mailing list of families with children in grades 6-12. Results are coming in. Inquires are well above the number at this period one year ago.

■ **Community Support.**

Despite rumors to the contrary, Lebanon supports Castle Heights financially. Residents of this city always have responded to the needs of its private schools, and this includes Castle Heights. Without Lebanon support and leadership, Heights would have folded in 1974 when the Bernarr Macfadden Foundation withdrew sponsorship.

Despite the financial crunch at this time, Castle Heights has much going for it.

Female cadets at Heights in 1975 -- including the five who enrolled at the beginning of the 1973-74 school year when CHMA changed its all-male policy in effect since 1917 -- in their "uniform of the day" on Mitchell House balcony. Most of the female students from 1973-1986 were from the Lebanon/middle Tennessee area, though several were from out of state and the country.

Yes or No: Girls in military schools
• *April, 1990*

Feminists currently are pushing for a change in policy at Virginia Military Institute in Lexington, Va. -- alma mater of the late, beloved CHMA Commandant Dan T. Ingram -- one of the oldest and greatest of the military schools for the admission of females.

The Justice Department has charged VMI with sex discrimination. Gen. John Knapp, VMI superintendent, believes that within the Virginia college system there is room for all-male, all-female and coed colleges. He, alumni and probably the cadet corps hope to keep the school as an all-male institution.

He is flying against the wind.

In my opinion, VMI would serve the military of this country better if it were allowed to remain a school for men. But there are too many forces against them. True, women have proven themselves in fields once regarded as the domains of the masculine gender. I, for one, praise the progress of women in their fight for equal opportunity.

Feminists claim that female cadets have proven themselves at West Point. I wonder if they face the same rigors that male cadets faced before the Academy became coeducational.

My experience at Castle Heights Military Academy was that the school was better before the girls came, although I voted for their presence before the five pioneers arrived in 1973. It was a matter of timing. The time for girls had come.

Actually the time for girls at Castle Heights came a few years before we voted to accept them. A delegation of parents representing many more girls than the five who broke the gender barrier sought admission for their daughters. We preferred to remain all-male.

Let me note that the girls in general were fine cadets. They were good students, good athletes and good with the military aspects. And that is just the point. After the girls came, many of the boys backed off and let the girls take the lead. They chose not to compete against the girls. Such is the teen-age male syndrome.

The proponents of coed military schools sometimes argue that it is not "normal" for the genders to be separated. Maybe so. But there were thousands of cadets at Castle Heights who found and enjoyed contacts with the opposite gender, matured, married and lived normal lives.

I am sad to witness the demise of the all-girl and all-boy schools. My granddaughter, Missy Newton, is a graduate of Wright School for Girls in Mobile, Ala. The education she received there prepared her for the college discipline. She hit the ground running in college and never stopped. And so did many of her classmates.

Her brother, Andy, is a senior at UMS, formerly University Military School. This, too, was a fine single-gender school, but probably not the equal of Wright. Two years after Missy graduated, the two schools combined, abandoning the Wright campus for the UMS facility. The school now is UMS-Wright.

It is my perception that the coed school, albeit an excellent institution, is below the caliber of either Wright or UMS prior to their merger.

I am sorry that they merged. Many factors entered this blending, including economics. Tuitions went up and enrollment fell. Their merger may have been a matter of necessity.

But the merger meant an end to many long-standing traditions. Things changed. Indeed, some things changed for the better.

Of course, in the heyday of Castle Heights, there were some cadets who would have preferred coed education. I remember John Mincemoyer who attended Heights for a number of years. One day he came running up to me and, with mock excitement, announced:

"Sir, I just found out."

"Found out what, Mincemoyer?"

"I just found out there are schools where boys and girls go to school together."

John was pretending he had been deprived of this information and had been at Castle Heights so long he had had no opportunity to find

Four of the six members of the 1985-86 final cadet staff, headed by Battalion Commander Stephen Werst, were women: Capt. Makiko Takeda, S-2 officer; Maj. Karen Haas, S-3; and Capt. Karen Henkel, S-4. Not shown are Maj. Laura Barnes, executive officer, and Capt. John Anderson, S-1.

out about coed schools.

And whereas John Mincemoyer pretended he wanted to attend a coed school, most of the boys preferred Heights as it was. Indeed, some of the boys did not return "after the girls came."

Whatever the outcome of the VMI dilemma, the admission of girls should not force the institution to change its traditions. Old rigors should remain and old customs should prevail. If the girls want to attend VMI, they should be prepared to accept and participate in honored customs, including the tradition dictating that new cadets have their heads shaved.

• Girls served in many leadership positions at Heights 1973-86, and earned valedictorian and salutatorian academic honors. In the last year of Heights operation, 1985-86, two of the four company commanders were females, and of that school year's Battalion Staff, four of the six officers were young women.

• Waving signs that read "Men of Quality Respect Women's Equality" and "Better Late than Never," women of all ages stood on the steps of the U. S. Supreme Court in June, 1996, to celebrate the Court's 7-1 ruling in United States v. Virginia [No. 94-1941] which held the male-only admissions policy of the Virginia Military Institute violates the equal protection clause of the Fourteenth Amendment and that Virginia's creation of Virginia Women's Institution for Leadership [VWIL] at the private, all-female Mary Baldwin College was inadequate to remedy the violation. Justice Clarence Thomas did not participate because his son attends VMI.

Of catcalls, 'Sacred Ground,' profanity...

JB Leftwich served as advisor to the Academy's chapter of Quill and Scroll, an international honorary society for high school journalists. Members of the 1958-59 unit revised *The Volley Student Handbook*. Among highlights:

- The **'Circle of Sacred Ground'** is dedicated to the Senior classes of Castle Heights, and is to be trodden on by "old men" only. No first-year men are allowed to walk through its center or otherwise "profane" it. If an old man asks you to walk through it, he is exercising a right he does not possess.

- **Catcalls**, or wolf whistles as they are more commonly called, are out of place on the Heights campus when another cadet is walking his girl.

- **Sheet Decorations:** A tradition to old cadets but new to freshmen, for it is unique at Heights. Before many of the games, and especially Homecoming, the barracks will be covered with multi-colored sheets with witty slogans and humorous cartoons, urging Heights teams to victory.

- **Freshman Dip:** Soon after the first wearing of "whites," the Commandant will announce Freshman Dip. In view of the fact that the new men (by this time of year) have met their obligations and have been accepted, they will be thrown into the pool. This is one of the more enjoyable traditions of the Academy, but if rough-housing gets out of hand, the Dip will be halted.

- **Freshmen will serve as window and hall orderlies.** No new man is exempt from this tradition. Each freshman will serve his turn, sweeping down the halls twice daily before CQs and closing windows as instructed to do so on cold mornings before reveille.

- **It is traditional for freshmen to carry old men's laundry.** The new men will not be asked to carry more than two laundries aside from their own.

- **Bragging** or otherwise entertaining the old cadets with tales of your prowess, adventures or experiences is frowned upon and you will be less popular as a new cadet if you practice this.

- In the entire history of the world, here has never been a good excuse offered for **any use of profanity**. It is a practice which always has been frowned upon by cultured people, and its use automatically conveys the impression to others that its user is unable to express himself in good English. Visitors and parents find its use obnoxious and odious. Do not reflect discredit on your character and on your school by indulging in the use of profanity.

- **Rules from 1913 handbook:**
  1) "In order to avoid misunderstanding, we call attention to the fact an extra charge of 15 cents per meal will be made for meals sent to rooms."
  2) "Each boy must bring one rug about 3 X 6, six napkins, one napkin ring."
  3) "No student will be allowed to: A) Smoke cigarettes under any circumstances, the penalty being expulsion; B) Chew tobacco without written consent of his parents."

Chapter Two
Faculty & Staff

"As a general rule, teachers teach more by what they are than by what they say."

-Unknown

"The mediocre teacher tells. The good teacher explains. The superior teacher demonstrates. The great teacher inspires."

-Author William A. Ward

THE DRILL:
By the time JB Leftwich retired from CHMA 38 years after he first stepped on campus in 1941, he had -- by his own admission -- become close friends or served with some of the most extraordinary educators ever to manage a classroom. There was no greater tribute JB could pay a peer than to say, "He [she] was a teacher." The majority of the more than 8,000 Castle Heights alumni can readily name one or perhaps two Academy faculty that made a positive, permanent impact -- and not just because of what he/she taught in the classroom but because of who he/she was as an individual. Many great educators taught at Heights, supported by dedicated men and women serving on the staff, and JB was proud to tell about them.

Overleaf Photo:
Heights' faculty changed with the times from '40s and '50s to the mid-'80s, but excellence was a common thread.

Photo Credit: '50s and '80s *Adjutant* yearbooks

Faded fame obscures Heights' benefactor

• *June, 2003*

He was famous on two continents, an international icon, an eccentric, a visionary, a promoter, a publisher, a writer, and body builder deluxe.

He was well ahead of his time as a physical culturist, a health promoter, a fighter for freedom of speech and a disciple of a changing attitude toward sex.

His magazines were tame measured by today's standards, but lurid in the Victorian world of the early Twentieth Century. He owned and published a daily newspaper in New York City, *The Evening Graphic*. It was unofficially called the "Evening Pornographic," albeit its content was far milder than today's market checkout tabloids.

Born in 1868 as Bernard Adlophis McFadden, he decided in the mid-1890s after moving to New York that "Bernarr Macfadden" better suited his new physical culture emphasis and changed image.

He disdained alcohol and tobacco, usually slept on the floor, vigorously exercised his scalp, and rigidly exercised his eyes. As a young man, he began to lose his hair and his eyesight. When he died at age 87, he had a lush mane and did not wear eyeglasses.

He was a frequent visitor to Lebanon.

In 1928, Castle Heights Military Academy had fallen on hard times and was fighting for survival. Providentially, Bernarr Macfadden stepped in, bought the school, built a new barracks, a new gymnasium and a new auditorium. With an infusion of capital, the school thrived until changing attitudes and inflation struck in the Seventies.

Macfadden usually came to the Academy for commencement. A flamboyant showman, he once jumped out of an airplane and landed near campus. He left commencement ceremonies by jumping from the stage.

On stage, he would tell daring jokes to the commencement audience much to the dismay of Col. Harry L. Armstrong, the prim and proper superintendent of the Academy, who was visibly embarrassed.

While a teacher at Castle Heights, I knew Bernarr Macfadden and I interviewed him for newspaper stories during his visits. He loved the attention.

He was born Bernard Adolphis McFadden, August 16, 1868, to a farm family in Mill Spring, Mo. Both of his parents died before he reached his teens, and he moved from relative to relative until he struck out on his own. Because he was frail, he worked to build his body into muscular perfection.

Among those at 1939 banquet for dedication of CHMA's Bullard Hall (from left): Col. H.L. Armstrong, American Legion National Commander Raymond Kelly, Tennessee Governor Prentice Cooper, Bernarr Macfadden and Gen. Robert Lee Bullard.

In 1899, he began *Physical Culture*, a monthly magazine that survived for 50 years. Using stories submitted for *Physical Culture*, he began a new magazine called *True Story* that peaked at three million circulation and was widely read, often covertly, by women -- and men -- nationwide. Compared to language in today's publications, its stories were tame -- though titillating in early and mid-Twentieth Century.

He was a visionary. In the '30s, he advocated a federal department of health that would not come until much later. He did not believe medicine was effective. He advocated strict diet, plenty of sleep, fresh air, regular exercise. He was a precursor in changing attitudes toward sex. Although far afield in some cases, many of his health principles gained wide acceptance and endured.

At 80, he married his fourth wife, Johnnie Lee McKinney, 44-year-old health consultant/lecturer. The marriage lasted four years. During this marriage, he ran for governor of Florida. At the end of his life, he had squandered a fortune. His wealth at one time had been estimated at $20 million, probably the equivalent of $300 million of today's dollars. He died October 12, 1955.

During his long and flamboyant life, his name recognition in this country was only slightly less than Joe Louis and Franklin Roosevelt. Now, two generations after his death, he is almost forgotten, a mere postscript in accelerating history.

Three buildings on the Castle Heights campus bore his name. Only one, the auditorium, still stands.

For those of us who knew him, it is almost inconceivable that the current generation has no clue about him, that his glory is a faded flower, a testimony to fleeting fame.

She reigned supreme in President's home
• *September, 1997*

While well merited attention is focused on the renovation of the Main Building of Castle Heights, the restoration of the President's Home has not received the attention it deserves.

John [Lebanon native and Heights alum] and Betty Burch have done a superb job in bringing a building, once headed toward the point of no return, back to a state more elegant than it was in the past. This building now is the home of Rademacher's restaurant which brings a special touch of class to Lebanon's array of eating establishments.

When I joined the Castle Heights faculty in the fall of 1941, the building was the residence of Col. Harry L. Armstrong, president of the school, and his wife, Mildred Tomlinson Armstrong. On a modest scale, but still a residence of distinction, it was the Heights castle presided over by a queen who wielded power in the Hilltop fiefdom.

Mildred Armstrong may not have viewed herself as royalty but it was our perception she regarded herself as a cut above the status of faculty wife. From her aerie on the second floor she issued orders concerning the other wives who, although they were not employees of the Academy, generally executed their delegated responsibilities with little complaint.

Neither did we teachers complain about the order of things. In that age of job appreciation, we accepted additional duties, as did our wives, in good spirit.

Mildred Armstrong held herself aloof from the faculty and staff. Indeed, we teachers joked about the power behind the throne who at least was the peer of the president. Colonel Armstrong also was a reserved person, an intellectual who ran the school and did not mingle with the hirelings. We -- at least, I -- were somewhat awed by him and never attempted familiarity.

Mrs. Armstrong did not enjoy good health -- some said she enjoyed bad health -- during my years, and in her last decade apparently relaxed her reign. Or so it seemed. One thing we knew: she was strictly anti-alcohol. And so was the Colonel. I suspect she may be resting somewhat uncomfortably in Cedars of Lebanon Cemetery now that there is a bar in her former home.

She died in 1957, leaving a distraught husband who regarded life without her as a bleak state -- until a widow from Louisville, Ky., Mrs. Joseph A. Radamacher, showed up to enroll her son -- Bill [now deceased], who graduated in 1961. Romance flared and in due course there were wedding plans.

I was school photographer, and when Colonel and his lady love decided to marry, I was asked to go along and photograph the wedding. Virgil Hastings, a dignified black employee who frequently served at Academy social affairs, and one other person I can no longer identify made the trek to Louisville. The only incident I remember is stopping at a roadside restaurant where the white members of the party ate at a table while Virgil ate in the car.

My most vivid memory of the wedding was the champagne. Colonel had laid aside his antipathy toward alcohol. Following the ceremony, he said to me: "Major, would you propose a toast?" I don't remember my toast, but I think what I said pleased him.

The marriage endured, but the new Mrs. Armstrong was not a clone of Mildred as Colonel had hoped she would be. He retired as Heights' president and moved into his bride's home. His glory days when he lived in the President's Home on campus were not to be duplicated.

Back to John and Betty Burch's restaurant. The food is good. The atmosphere is pleasant. The building is stately. And while Mildred Armstrong bans the building from her hauntings, the restaurant offers Lebanon distinct alternative dining.

• Vacant for more than 10 years after Heights' 1986 closing, the President's Home opened as Rademacher's Restaurant in 1997. A few years later, Dan Evins '53, Cracker Barrel Restaurants chain CEO, bought the property and remodeled/reopened it again as Rademacher's. New management subsequently took over and operated it as Castle Heights Chop House [closed in July, 2013, due to the economy]. [Both restaurants featured throughout the two-story building hundreds of photographs and mementos of the Academy, its cadets and faculty, and Homecoming celebrations were held in each.] In 2014, the facility reopened as an Italian restaurant, Sonny's on Castle Heights.

• The restaurant was named for Pete Rademacher, 1948 Heights grad who during an eight-year amateur boxing career had a 72-7 record -- including four Seattle Golden Gloves championships, U.S. Amateur Championship, Chicago Golden Gloves, and the All-Army and Armed Forces Services championships. In 1956, he captured a gold medal, heavyweight division, in the Melbourne Olympics. [He also attended college, playing for Washington State as an offensive lineman.] In 1957, in his first professional bout, Rademacher lured Heavyweight Champion Floyd Patterson into a title match. He dropped Patterson in round two, but Patterson won by KO in round six. Other professional fights included bouts with Zora Folley, Brian London, George Chuvalo, Archie Moore and Carl "Bobo" Olson. He retired from a business career in 1987 as president of McNeil Corporation, Akron, Ohio. In 1996, Rademacher and two daughters helped carry the Olympic torch on streets of Cleveland. He has served on Heights National Alumni Association Board of Directors more than 25 years.

The end of an era

• *July, 2004*

Ironically, we wait until it's too late, until friends or family members pass on, before we speak or write the words of praise they deserved while life energized their bodies. After their deaths, we are inspired to eulogize. As Shakespeare did not write, we come to praise Caesar, not to bury him.

And so it was with Leonard Bradley, one of the best friends I ever had. He died earlier this month. Why didn't I say to him these words? "Leonard, I want you to know how much I admire you, how much your friendship means, what a great teacher and administrator you were."

I can answer the question. Because it would have embarrassed the heck out of him. Indeed, he never sought praise. He sought to perform life's tasks earnestly and honestly. He was willfully independent, strong willed and achievement oriented. He was one of the few people I have known who found the job he loved and excelled in meeting its challenges.

He knew his priorities – family, church, friends and professional duties. Embarrassment notwithstanding, he deserved to hear what I have written here.

Recognized as an outstanding headmaster and administrator during his three decades at Heights, Lt. Col. Leonard K. Bradley was just as frequently referenced by graduates for his teaching skills in chemistry.

We used to joke, he and I, about our funerals. We reasoned there would be no "standing room only" services for us because we had attended the funerals of the ones who would have attended our funerals if they had survived.

The saddest deaths are the ones out of sequence, but this rationalization does not lessen the impact in the loss of an old friend.

More than 60 years ago – in the 1941-42 school year—Leonard Bradley and I joined the teaching staff of Castle Heights, thus beginning an association that lasted more than three decades at the Academy. In the mid-Seventies, he left and, in effect, became the father of Friendship Christian School. He deserved more recognition for this achievement than he received.

During his tenure at Castle Heights, he went from the classroom, where he

Named headmaster in 1958, Colonel Bradley oversaw changes to aid faculty and cadets in better preparing for the competitive college admissions situation developing in the 1960s-1970s.

taught chemistry, to the administrative staff, where he served for many years as headmaster, a position equivalent to dean in many schools. He developed and expanded sound academic principles and stern but fair discipline, enhancing the Academy's scholastic reputation.

He was a staunch defender of his teaching staff, most of whom regarded him as a personal friend. He adroitly resolved teacher-student conflicts, assuring the teacher of his support and counseling the cadet. When teachers were admonished, he offered sound advice in the privacy of his office.

As a direct consequence of his support, many of us were better at our jobs. One of my responsibilities was director of student publications. Leonard – Colonel Bradley – arranged my teaching schedule to allow maximum time for this activity. He was directly responsible for the national honors these publications received each year.

He loved his job. When the call came from his church to head a new Christian school, he first turned it down. But his church was persistent, the challenge tempting, so ultimately he left Castle Heights for Friendship School and a career that lasted until his retirement.

o o o

Though restrained and seldom prone to revealing his emotions, his pride in his family however understated was foremost in his thoughts. He and his wife, Mary Ann Bryan Bradley, who died in 1995, had five sons and a daughter, each of whom achieved remarkable goals [*page 241*].

I have known many fine educators during my long career of teaching. Leonard Bradley would rank high in the short list of best in his field. He took no short cuts in preparing his pupils. He always supported his teachers, but each teacher knew his expectations. He and private education were a perfect fit.

Other great educators are on the scene. More will appear, but there likely will never be another Leonard Bradley. [*Yearbook Dedication, page 293*]

Trite as the phrase may be, an era has ended.

Leonard and Mary Ann Bradley [sister of Elizabeth Donnell, wife of Lt. Col. Lindsey Donnell] were married more than 55 years when she died in 1995. She also worked at CHMA for many years as an administrative assistant.

o o o

How did Castle Heights cadets regard him?

I have a BS in biology, chemistry and medical technology, and much of this I owe to the background given me by Colonel Bradley. After 50 years, I still have my textbook and still refer to the notes in the margin.
Jim W. Legg '55/Medical Technologist

Colonel Bradley was a grand gentleman and a superb teacher. He helped to make Heights what it was and provided me with a basis for future successes.
Edward A. O'Neal '54/Retired Captain, United States Navy

He was such a gentle and soft-spoken man who set an example for good conduct. As a teacher he was patient and made sure every student understood the subject at hand.
Stan Harvill '51/Retired Air Force officer

As chemistry teacher he stimulated a love of science and as headmaster he was a stern watchdog for academic standards. Colonel Bradley

Cadets rarely saw the humorous side of any faculty member – though some were skillful at using humor in their classrooms -- but Majors Leonard Bradley [right], Tom Harris and JB Leftwich were among those willing in the '50s to "let their hairs down" in Lebanon Lions Club skits and musicals held in Macfadden Auditorium.

was a role model for all that is good, decent and noble in the teaching and molding of young minds.

Robin Berrington '58/Cultural Attaché, American Embassy

Colonel Bradley stood forward at Castle Heights as a teacher and leader who knew that education was most lasting when it stood on discipline and responsibility. He was a stalwart among many fine men at a great school.

David Hall '61/Newspapers Editor-In-Chief

Colonel Bradley was a low key, intelligent conversationalist, compelling us to listen well before responding. The cadet corps was, indeed, fortunate to have this fine teacher and administrator at Heights.

Bob Cleveland '59/Computer Company Official

I was never a good chemistry student but managed to pass Colonel Bradley's chemistry course with little more than a "get by" grade. But at the University of Missouri, in a required chemistry class, I rarely opened my textbook and made an "A." He was a great teacher.

Jim Fall '55/Executive Director, Montana Newspaper Association

Classroom wizard, coach, teacher

• *April, 2006*

The death of Merlin Sanders earlier this week marked the end of a teaching career punctuated with greatness and accented with humor tapped from a vast reservoir of subject knowledge.

Remembered as "Colonel Sanders" by hundreds of Castle Heights cadets who passed through his classes, Merlin Sanders created a learning atmosphere where students absorbed a body of knowledge that sent them on a quest for more.

He could teach many subjects but enjoyed most mathematics, then physics and chemistry. He enlivened his lectures with dry comment and off-the-wall humor that cemented students' attention. He remained in his classroom long after class hours, offering struggling pupils additional assistance.

Col. Merlin Sanders sense of humor endeared him to cadets in the classroom and to athletes on teams he coached during his 12 years at Castle Heights.

Merlin Sanders ranks high among the great teachers I knew, either as a pupil or in more than three decades as a fellow teacher. He was so good as an educator, Castle Heights promoted him to commandant, placing him in a position where he functioned well but was never happy.

Later, he went to Cumberland University where he recruited students and once again filled a position he didn't enjoy. After these sidetracks, he returned to the classroom.

Colonel Sanders not only was a classroom teacher, he was a coach. Though inexperienced in the sport, he took over the wrestling team at Castle Heights, read texts on the subject, relied on senior wrestlers' willingness to teach beginners, and produced conference champions.

Three words capsule his life: He was a teacher.

• Earned his AB, Henderson State Teachers College; MA, Peabody College. He joined Heights in 1958, teaching algebra, chemistry, serving as head coach of freshman football and wrestling, assistant track coach. Named Cumberland University Director of Admissions, 1970. [*Yearbook Dedication, page 304*]

'Tough love' for the troublemakers, underdogs

• *August, 2010*

She could be unbending or resilient, distant or loving, cranky or understanding.

But in one arena, she never varied. Her passion for the Castle Heights cadets was unswerving and intense.

To be more specific, her most intense passion was for the cadet "underdog," and to paint an accurate picture, her goal in life was to redeem the troublemaker. Except for football players whom she loved, she did not spend much time with highly rated cadets.

She came to Castle Heights as the commandant's secretary in 1941, after a career at Shannon's drugstore where cadets often sought her counsel. To many cadets, who thrived through her tough love, she was a mother-in-absentia.

"Miss Fahey" was a familiar site at football games and other sports events throughout her 30-year career.

Superintendent Lt. Col. Ralph Lucas presents Mary Fahey with insignia after promoting her to "Colonel" during 1971 Homecoming festivities.

Ted Lavit '57, came to Castle Heights in the second grade and, in effect, grew up on the campus. Mary Fahey "adopted" him. Says Ted:

"It's hard to imagine a day in the life of a cadet without contact with Mary Fahey. She was in the dining room at every meal and was the eyes and ears of the commandant and superintendent. She was the postmistress, Academy social secretary, and as secretary to Col. D.T. Ingram was present each time a cadet answered a report before the commandant.

"The first time the word 'tacky'

took root with me was when Mary Fahey, instead of placing a letter from my girlfriend, Rita Ianarella [Brooklyn, New York] in my mailbox, handed it to me with the back side up pointing to lipstick, glaring at me and at the same time uttering: 'That's tacky'. Sometimes a cadet would receive his mail by special delivery from Mary Fahey without paying the extra postage."

From a 1970 issue of *The Cavalier*:

"Just start listening to the problems of 500 teen-age boys and you're well on your way to spinsterhood," Miss Fahey said. She "retired" in 1968, but stayed on in just about the same capacity in which she has served the Academy for more than 25 years -- continuing as postmistress, secretary to the superintendent, and an on-the-spot combination of Ann Landers and Dear Abby.

Cadets, whom she regards as "her boys," somehow end up telling Fahey about their troubles -- not that she always lends a sympathetic ear. She is just as likely to give them a tongue-lashing if she thinks their attitude merits it.

She admits no partiality, but neither does she deny a soft spot for Academy athletes. Fahey is their number one fan, seldom missing a game on the road or at home. She lives in an apartment in the gymnasium, and usually "knows the score" about all of the players.

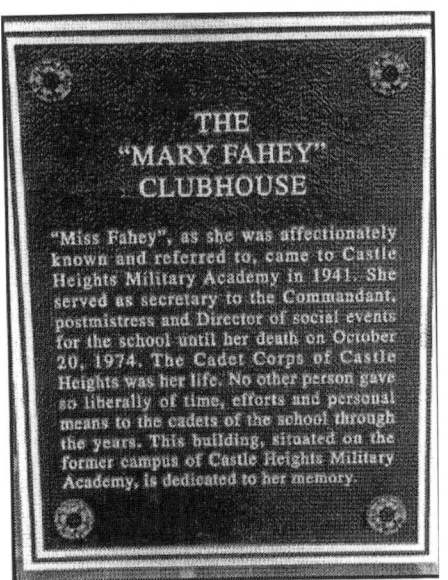

THE "MARY FAHEY" CLUBHOUSE

"Miss Fahey", as she was affectionately known and referred to, came to Castle Heights Military Academy in 1941. She served as secretary to the Commandant, postmistress and Director of social events for the school until her death on October 20, 1974. The Cadet Corps of Castle Heights was her life. No other person gave so liberally of time, efforts and personal means to the cadets of the school through the years. This building, situated on the former campus of Castle Heights Military Academy, is dedicated to her memory.

Mary Fahey lent to the character of Castle Heights. Many cadets changed their ways and graduated because of her tough love. And the football team knew it had no greater fan.

Her memory is honored in Academy Place, a real estate development behind Lebanon City Hall [the old "Main], where the clubhouse is named for her [plaque (left) outside main entrance]. [*Yearbook Dedication, page 287*]

• Academy Place features one-, two- and three-bedroom condominiums, and the main street through the project is Armstrong Drive. There are 11 courts [short streets] in the development, all named in honor of Heights faculty: Baker, Bradley, Donnell, Gwynn, Hale, Hosier, Hurd, Ingram, Leftwich, Phillips and Wooten. CHMA grad Danny Evins '53 was involved in the project, thus the Academy names associated with it.

'Leave a few bushes unshaken'
• *July, 1996*

Major R. Kenneth Morgan Jr., veteran teacher and one-time head-master of the school that bore his name, brought to Castle Heights in 1955 a store of wisdom and knowledge that almost immediately made him a favorite of both teachers and cadets.

He is remembered by alums for his chapel talks where he used "ripping up and down the big road" instead of "raising hell."

Those were the days when social mores were more rigid and conduct of young people was expected to be more circumspect, prompting strict supervision of campus social events -- especially when members of the opposite gender were on campus.

One night during a formal dance, R. Kenneth and I were assigned to patrol the area surrounding the gymnasium and auditorium just to make sure no embarrassing episodes episoded. He and I strolled leisurely on a pleasant spring night, chatting and occasionally walking behind the gym where the dance was underway.

During intermission when the cadets were expected to escort their dates to the mess hall for ice cream and cake, the possibilities of mild indiscretions increased, but R. Kenneth, now in his latter years as a schoolman, seemed to take no notice.

"Don't you think we should step up our patrolling?" I asked.

"No," he said. "I think we should leave a few bushes unshaken."

He was right, you know. Over-supervision is just as harmful as laxness.

Maj. R. Kenneth Morgan Jr. was one of the Morgan family members with major impact on Tennessee prep school education.

•After earning AB from Vanderbilt, R. Kenneth Morgan Jr. served as headmaster at Morgan School for Boys [closed in 1950] started by his father in 1885. He taught at Heights until his 1968 death. A big Kentucky Derby fan, he reportedly attended for many years. [*Yearbook Dedication, page 302*] Kenneth's brother, John, was Junior School Headmaster from 1950 to his 1962 passing. Kenneth's son, Bob -- now living in Gallatin, Tenn. -- was Junior School instructor 1956-62, and Senior School 1962-69.

Lest we forget those that fix things

• *August, 1983*

James Michener, in his novel, *Space*, creates a lead character he names Dieter Kolff and places him at Peenemunde -- on Germany's Baltic Sea coast and World War II site of development and production of the V-2 rocket -- as a contemporary of Wernher von Braun in the German rocket program.

Dieter, as described by Michener, was considered a German national asset because he could "fix things." Although uneducated, Kolff had an "almost mystical sense of what an engine could do or not do."

In many ways, Luther Musice, who died in Lebanon last week, was like Dieter Kolff, because he, too, could fix things. I first became aware of Luther's capacity for "fixing things" while we both were employed at Castle Heights, and he was a member of the maintenance crew.

At some point in the 1970s, he retired from Heights to become trouble-shooter for rental property we own or manage, and -- through his genius from keeping things running -- to make it possible to expand. He knew where every clean-out plug, every fuse panel and every spare part were. He understood electricity, was a good plumber, painter and carpenter.

But he never quite understood that I didn't understand. The obvious to him was obscure to me. Sometimes he would ask my opinion about a perplexing problem, and as often as not the solution would come to him as he vocalized it.

Luther Musice graduated from no school, perhaps never read a book, and probably never pondered philosophical concepts. But he was innately smart and although he knew how to do many things, he was intelligent enough to know what he could not do.

He was more than just intelligent. He understood responsibility. If you told him to do something, you did not have to followup.

More than two years ago - on New Year's Eve - the heating circuit malfunctioned in an apartment during a cold night. I never knew Luther's plans for celebrating the holiday, but I do know he dropped his plans and celebrated in the basement correcting the problem.

There must be many untutored geniuses in this country and in other countries who, unlike the fictional Dieter Kolff, lived their lives in anonymity, fixing things which may have perplexed even highly educated experts. No person is more important than the person who can fix things.The world needs Dieter Kolffs and Luther Musices if for nothing else to teach us not to equate education with intelligence.

'Little All-America' born to teach

• *September, 1992*

He had been away from the Cumberland University campus for more than a year when I arrived in 1937 for four years of college, but his mythical presence was felt almost as if he were still present.

"In the 100 years of Cumberland football, no other individual has so captured the imagination of those who have followed the campaigns of the Bulldogs on the gridiron," wrote historian G. Frank Burns.

Of all the great football players produced in Wilson County -- Hoyal Johnson, Clifton Tribble, Harold Greer, Joe Gwynn Atkinson, to name a few (and to fail to remember some just as great) -- no other name evokes emotion and passion like the name of Lindsey Donnell.

"It was in 1936 that Donnell led the Bulldogs to a spectacular championship season, winning Little All-America honors for himself and setting a national record of 1,500 yards gained," writes Burns. Donnell held this record until O. J. Simpson broke it.

There is little doubt Lindsey Donnell also could have made millions if he had come along in this era of high salaried athletes and lucrative endorsements -- and, if he had chosen to play pro football.

Fundamentally, he was a mathematics teacher. His was an incisive grasp of the structure of mathematics. He taught not only problem solv-

Heights cadets knew Major/Colonel Lindsey Donnell as junior school headmaster, a football/track/soccer/tennis coach, athletic director, and/or head of the math department. And as an educator whose chief concern was welfare of the cadets.

Lindsey Donnell's accomplishments at Cumberland University are honored by naming of the soccer stadium and by presentation of an annual award in his name to the outstanding CU student-athlete.

ing, but the beauty and poetry of math. I know. I, too, taught math at Heights, and when I encountered a tough one, I called on Lindsey.

But back to football. I never saw him play. But I saw him coach some of the great backfields Heights fielded in the '40s. Once during practice session of the fabled team of 1943, he was not making his point. "Center the ball to me," he said to center Bascom Cooksey. "I am going to run one play. Hit me! Don't let me through."

Bascom centered the ball and Lindsey was gone -- right through a great defensive team on a 50-yard touchdown run. Lindsey was an athlete. Nobody converted an idea into athletic action better than he. His physical coordination was phenomenal.

Saturday at Cumberland University, friends and admirers will gather to name the school's new stadium for a football legend -- a legend building just one year after his graduation.

Unfortunately, Lindsey Donnell who is now incapacitated will not be present. But for his old teammates, his family and his host of admirers, this event is a fitting tribute to a man who was even more than a great football player.

He was a teacher.

Lindsey Donnell (second left) was vital part of football staff of Coach Stroud Gwynn (right). Others were Ralph Lucas, Frank North.

* Earned AB, Cumberland University; MA, Peabody College. Joined CHMA in 1937, teaching math and serving as soccer and "B" football head coach, assistant varsity football coach. He and his wife Elizabeth [sister of Mary Ann Bradley] were married in 1937, for more than 35 years. They had a son, Mark -- '64 Heights grad, salutatorian, "Most Likely to Succeed" -- who became a physician, but died in 1993; and six daughters (all still living): Lynn [Freeman], Elizabeth [Nelms], Ellen [Barlament], Mary Ann [Wyatt], Robin [Maynard] and Susan [Fisher]. Elizabeth passed in 1974, Lindsey in 1993. [*Yearbook Dedication, page 296*]

When *reading* was the 'national pastime'
• *Spring, 1973*

Back in the "good old days" when times were bad and you didn't have a television set (no matter, there were no TV stations), an automobile (too expensive), or even a radio (no TVA electricity, and battery sets were too high), your principal source of diversion was reading.

You read everything - Tarzan, Zane Grey, Jack London, newspapers, the Bible, *True Confessions* magazine.

There were no paperbacks so you bought reprints, usually at Christmas, and assigned them to various members of the family as gifts. And when they finished, there was a waiting list of friends and neighbors.

There were no bookmobiles or community libraries in our neighborhood, so you borrowed and read and re-read until the books disintegrated.

It was in this environment of isolation from modern transportation and communication (we did have a four-party, self-installed telephone system) that I determined to write for a newspaper or magazine or anybody that would publish my project.

Mrs. D.T. Ingram presents honorary Ingram saber to Cadet Capt. Buddy Sloan at October 1971 Homecoming celebration.

Most of all, I wanted to author books. I never made it.

Many of my old associates did, and I am proud of them. There was William O. Steele (plain old barbed-pen Bill Steele then), who turned from lampooning coaches during our college days to writing adventure stories for young people. Bill is the most published of the group, a clever writer then and now.

There was Hugh Walker, an associate at the *Democrat* during the pre-war days, authority on Middle Tennessee history, who drew from his reservoir of knowledge to write *Tennessee Tales*.

There was Virginia Prewitt, who labored with me on the old *Cumberland Collegian*, and who went on to journalistic achievement in South America and non-fiction books on Latin-American subjects.

And there was Mildred Ingram -- to be accurate, Mildred Rebecca Prewett Ingram. Mildred and I shared an office during the '40s, marking the beginning of an enduring friendship.

It was not always evident Mildred was due star billing in the remarkable Ingram household because of the merited stardom of her husband, the late Col. D.T. Ingram, Heights commandant and a legend in his own time. And because of a beautiful daughter and two handsome sons.

Nevertheless, the ingredients of stardom were awaiting expression, emerging in short stories in *The New Yorker, Seventeen* and *Town & Country,* and in two novels which enjoyed more than modest sales.

Interestingly, Mildred's talents first were recognized outside of her immediate area. Generous praise by reviewers of her first novel [*If Passion Flies*, 1945] was followed with the same treatment of her second book [*Light as The Morning*, 1954] -- both written under the pen name Bowen Ingram.

Then came an unproductive period during which her husband was long ill and subsequently died [April, 1969], and finally a return to writing.

And now we have *Milbry*, a beautiful but brief autobiography of a little girl growing up in a by-gone era of Middle Tennessee. It is told in simple but beautiful prose, in dignity and in good taste, and in language which has no need for x-rated words.

Col. Ralph Lucas awards Heights varsity letter to Mrs. D. T. Ingram during 1971 Homecoming festivities.

The story has its own brand of excitement and adventure, but largely it's Mildred Ingram's skilled writing and capacity for telling a story without false note or forced situation which carry it.

Perhaps some motion picture producer will recognize the book's potential as a vehicle for the screen, but its timing may be wrong.

There seems to be little audience for G-rated movies.

• William O. Steele [1917-79] was a native of Franklin, Tenn., and wrote more than 35 historical adventure story books -- most from his home in Signal Mountain. Two of his most notable are *The Perilous Road* and *Winter Danger*, winners, respectively, of the 1959 "Newberry Honor" and 1962 "Lewis Carroll Shelf Award."

• Mildred Rebecca Prewett was born in 1904 in Gordonsville, Tenn., educated in public and private schools in Gordonsville and Memphis, and attended Cumberland University law school and School of Arts. She was a reporter for the *Lebanon Banner*, married D. T. Ingram in 1925, and had novels published in 1945, 1954 and 1972 under the Bowen pen name. She died in March, 1980. Approximately 2,000 items [almost 15 cubic feet] -- including hundreds of Colonel Ingram and CHMA artifacts -- are included in "The Bowen Ingram Papers (1856-1978)" maintained by the Tennessee State Library and Archives.

'No longer hangs the fluted shade'
• *August, 1994*

I am old enough
[But not too old]
To love the golden,
Not the gold.

Col. Paul Wooten was a CHMA treasure for 30-plus years.

This verse is from a just published book of poetry written by the late Paul Wooten, compiled and published by his wife Lillian Wooten, and entitled, *No Longer Hangs the Fluted Shade.*

Paul Wooten may have been Wilson County's most published poet with verse printed in *The Saturday Evening Post, Boy's Life* and other nationally distributed periodicals. Indeed, he may have been this county's only poet, since all that rhymes is not poetry.

G. Frank Burns writes: "Paul Wooten is one of the few poets I have known, and his poetry is magic of the truest sort." Wilson County writer and editor Dixon Merritt said: "There are many versifiers, but few poets."

Who was this poet who walked among us until his death in 1986? Was he some head-in-the-clouds esthete? An intellectual? A buried-in-books scholar? In truth he was all of the above -- at times. Like most poets, he was much more.

He was an outdoorsman, a dedicated fisherman, a golfer who sometimes hit over the lake on Hunter's Point Number 7, a baseball buff, a musician with skills on the piano and saxophone, a licensed pilot, a veteran of World War II, a linguist, assistant commandant at Castle Heights and teacher of literature, husband and father.

We were friends, golfing buddies. Our families once took a Florida vacation together. A camping vacation. He was a teacher with few peers. My son, Jim, described him as one of the greatest teachers he ever had. He loved literature, and his love transmitted to his pupils -- despite resistance in some cases.

Paul Wooten loved nature and deplored all things plastic. He disliked hills gashed by highways and rural scenes marred by lighted billboards. He wrote:

My senses quite abhor the sight
And feel so strongly slighted
To see a light that shines at night
Yet really isn't lighted.

He had a wry sense of humor. He also could kid himself. Said he in a parody of familiar lines appearing in many text-books:

Out of the Debt that covers me --
Black is the Pit from bill to bill --
I've never had a balanced Budget.
Never have, and never will.

Readers will be impressed with the diversity of his moods. He was Poe, introspective and brooding. He was Housman, contemplative and melancholy. He was Wordsworth, overjoyed with the beauty of nature. He was Ogden Nash, twisting wry humor out of the commonplace.

Most of all, he was Paul Wooten, unique and profound and funny, delighting baseball fans with the story of "Tenderfoot Teal" who was supposed to lift a team from the cellar and into the pennant race, and tickling all of us with the story "Archibald the Rabbit," who had a proclivity for procreation.

He battled sham and pretense. He hated all things plastic. He punctured pomposity. He was an environmentalist long before the word became overworked. Overhearing a landowner disparage a hillside, he mused: "I half-way thought I owned that hill."

The measure of his greatness emerges in a few excerpts from some of his newspaper columns:

- "The first dawn of December, out of the creek, came in all white and silver, with scattered touches of faint gold. Frozen mist turned trees into clouds of smoky gray, and thin ice lay around the reeds in the shallows."

- "Something, probably a rabbit, stirred up a halo of old raindrops in a patch of tall grass and a couple of crows flapped black rags across the muddy road. Three wild ducks (Mergansers, I think) came barreling down the creek in tight formation, low over the water -- and a kingfisher waited on the tip of a thorn tree near the back and watched the wind go by."

- "A freight train blew its imitation-freight-train whistle some- where near a downtown crossing. I thought maybe it would hurry and get there before I had to go on. If the windows of the caboose were open, that would be a sure sign of spring -- but the train didn't come in time for me to see. Those cabooses are probably air-conditioned now, anyway..."

That his poems are not in textbooks is a pity, but the publication of this volume of his poetry may drop enough rose petals to send back a modest number of echoes.

Guest Column [*page 190*] and Yearbook Dedications [*pages 292 and 303*].

Snow on the Hilltop was infrequent, but when it did fall and stick, cadets knew how to handle it.

Preacher's tenets serve us well

• *May, 1996*

One of my favorite people from my long stint at Castle Heights is John Henry "Preacher" Garnett Sr., who during his latter years at the Academy drove the school bus.

Preacher, now 87, has lots of preaching stories banked in his memory. One of his favorite is the Sunday he baptized 22 converts.

'Neither rain nor sleet nor snow....' deterred John Henry Garnett from his bus driving duties.

Baptism in his church means every thread and every hair of the convert is wet. Immersion. Totally saturated. And so was Preacher, by the time he immersed No. 22.

Many cadets, including graduates from 1967 through the Academy's closing in 1986, remember him fondly -- as a "good man," "all kindness all the time," "I have such sweet memories of him," "very friendly and talkative with those of us who rode on his bus," and perhaps the most telling: "I was wearing a CHMA sweatshirt and he stopped me on the street to talk. Really big guy with a preacher's face. I mean really big guy!"

A cadet favorite: John Henry 'Preacher' Garnett.

The last time I saw Preacher, he demonstrated his love with a bear-hug. When Preacher, about 6-foot-3 and lots of muscular pounds on his frame, hugs you, you know you have been hugged.

Says Preacher: "When you are kind to people and treat them nice and love them, they're likely to be kind to you and love you and treat you nice.

He's right, you know.

Librarian who loved limericks
• *March, 2008*

Private schools in days of yore attracted characters, both pupils and teachers, and Castle Heights throughout its rich and illustrious history attracted its share.

The cadet corps usually was peppered with characters – and here, we mean interesting personalities – but so was the faculty, many of whom have been profiled in other columns.

I never learned what the C and the H stood for, and it mattered not because to his fellow teachers and to the cadets, he was "Uncle Peter," a term of affection coined by the cadets who never used it in addressing him.

For more than 25 years, Maj. C. H. Hurd served as Heights librarian, using his word skills to write limericks and endear himself to thousands of cadets.

Maj. C.H. Hurd, knowledgeable in literature and lore, was the CHMA librarian. This was a job he loved, and he was content to spend the academic hours at his library desk. Other times, he retreated to his room on Second Division [in lay terms, second floor] Main Building, where he presided over energized teen-age boys.

He never claimed to be a disciplinarian and deferred most of that chore to the cadet division officer on his floor. His division was not problem-free. Just as on other divisions or floors, problems developed. But his system worked pretty well.

Major Hurd was married, and he and wife lived long lives happily apart. He visited her in Nashville just as she occasionally visited him at Castle Heights. They appeared congenial and pleasant together, but they just chose to live separately.

Major Hurd earned his BS in library science from Peabody College, and an MA from Vanderbilt. He joined CHMA in 1942.

A lover of limericks, he spent hours reading, writing and memorizing them. But his passion was sophisticated word puzzles, several cuts above the daily newspaper crossword puzzle.

Major Hurd and Headmaster Leonard Bradley, during Hurd's latter years at Castle Heights, were great friends, and Bradley inherited his friend's limerick collection, neatly typed on small index cards. Leonard

A sharp wit and quick tongue helped Maj. C. H. Hurd [center, shirt, tie at a '50s dorm Christmas party] control "the usual suspects" who lived during 25-plus years on Second Main, for which he was in-residence faculty supervisor.

Jr., later inherited the collection.

In turn, Leonard Jr., deposited a packet of limericks with me. Here's a sample:

> *There was a young sinner named Chet,*
> *Who liked to pet, gamble and bet;*
> > *And he prayed every day*
> > *"Take my sins all away,*
> *But, Lord, please don't do it just yet."*

Teachers came and went at Castle Heights, but Hurd was among a throng who came and stayed. During his tenure at the Academy, a generously overweight young teacher joined the staff, and he and Hurd became friends, but Hurd could not resist writing this limerick:

> *There once was a guy named Herb Kaiser*
> *Who, from what I have heard, was a sizer.*
> > *From his front to his back*
> > *He was like a hay stack.*
> *When he puffed, he would send forth a geyser.*

I don't know if Major Hurd shared this limerick with Herb Kaiser, but I do know they remained friends. To the librarian's dismay, his rotund friend left Heights to teach at Baylor in Chattanooga, where he reportedly reduced his rotundity.

Nobody was aware Major Hurd enjoyed an occasional nip until after his death, when his room was cleared of many years' accumulation of pack-rat personal items, including a few empty bottles.

Said Leonard Jr.: "Maybe his wry humor was rye humor."

Former cadet Bob Cleveland '59, remembers Hurd had a special greeting for cadets who were infrequent library visitors.

"I was sometimes delinquent in use of the library, and when I showed up, he congratulated me on finding my way to the library door," he said.

But the best Hurd story was created by cadet Robin Berrington, editor of the 1958 yearbook and a friend of Hurd. Robin decided the book should be dedicated to the librarian.

Robin also thought Major Hurd, still a captain after years of service, deserved a promotion. He discussed the idea with the headmaster and eventually approached Col. Harry L. Armstrong, Academy president, who gave the scheme his blessing.

Berrington's scenario concluded when he presented the honoree an advanced copy of the yearbook during General Assembly where he read the dedication [*page 295*], and promoted Captain Hurd to major.

Hurd was the only faculty officer in Academy history promoted to a higher military rank by a cadet.

Camping in another century
• *April, 2006*

Jonas Scott Coverdale was the first CHMA Junior School Headmaster and founded the Hy-Lake Summer Camp for Boys in 1931.

In 1942, six months after Pearl Harbor, we finished our first year at Castle Heights and moved into summer jobs at Camp Hy-Lake, a boys' camp on the Caney Fork River near Quebeck, Tenn.

It was to be a different experience – a different life-style – for both my wife and me. I was a senior camp staffer and she became secretary to Jonas Coverdale, owner/operator of the successful program. Coverdale – "Covey" to his friends – was headmaster of the Castle Heights Junior School during the academic year. Most of his camp staff came from Heights faculty and senior classes.

Campers came from Nashville, Lebanon and other Middle Tennessee locales. Some came from out of state. A few Heights cadets from foreign countries attended Hy-Lake because they were in this country for the entire year. Heights then had no summer school.

Covey was a dynamic personality. His drive and spirit were contagious, creating a cohesive atmosphere. Paul Redick, formerly a Cumberland University football star and at that time a Heights instructor, was the camp's second in command. Like Covey, Paul was a great story teller with a talent for weaving fact and fiction.

Overnight trips were camp features. We would load the juniors or intermediates or seniors into the camp bus and head for more primitive sites where we would set up for a night or two. A favorite haunt was Fall Creek Falls State Park [about 90 miles southeast of Lebanon], which then had none of the modern accommodations that characterize it today.

On other trips, there were even fewer ac-

Maj. John Sweatt started at CHMA in 1943, later heading the Science Department, and was a Camp Hy-Lake counselor.

commodations. We slept on folding cots, dipped our water from a spring, swam in the river, and ate from a huge pot of stew, labeled "Covey's Specialty." After supper, we gathered around the campfire to hear Covey's and Paul's stories, laced with supernatural features the two master story-tellers made believable.

Among the junior campers was a little guy named Tommy Lowe '50, a Lebanon boy who would grow up and help found the Cracker Barrel Restaurants chain. Tommy knew the ghost stories were mostly fiction, but he had trouble separating fiction from fact. When bedtime came, I found Tommy's cot next to mine. Since the scene of one of the ghost stories was near by, he opted to take no chances.

My porous memory recalls some of the staff of my era – Alan Swasey, C. V. Baker, Emmett Strickland, Brice and Tom Harris, Barnett Gamble, Robert Hosier, John L. Sweatt and Lindsley McDonald.

Maj. C. V. Baker -- Heights math instructor since 1945, Director of Intramural Athletics and assistant football coach -- was among Camp Hy-Lake staff.

These were great teachers and counselors.

John Sweatt not only was a superior biology teacher, he was a gifted musician. Tom Harris, affectionately called "Commando," was one of the most popular teachers at Heights. Robert Hosier, known for his dry humor, coached champion swimming teams at Heights. C. V. Baker, a coach of champion football teams in Nashville, was a gifted teacher of mathematics to underachieving pupils at Heights -- where he also served as intramural sports program director and an assistant football coach. Lindsley McDonald was probably Lebanon's greatest artist. Barnett Gamble, principal of Lebanon's McClain School at the time, moved on to higher positions in Huntsville, Ala.

Emmett Strickland was from Nashville, where he was basketball coach at West High School and en route to the Tennessee Sports Hall of Fame. Beginning in 1943, he took West to six consecutive state tournaments, winning the championship in 1944, 1946 and 1948.

Junior staffers who come to mind are Buddy Walker, James Elrod, Carlos Izzaguirre and Tandy Wilson -- whose mother was camp nurse. Buddy gained fame by diving from a high bridge over the Caney Fork into the river below.

Covey's wife, Gertrude, was dietician. She and her talented cooks

Celebrity visitor to Camp Hy-Lake in the late '30s was Fielding Yost (left), University of Michigan athletic director and 25-year head football coach [six national championships, 10 Big Ten titles, 165-29-10 career record, winner 49-0 over Stanford in first bowl game ever played (1902 Rose)]. Looking on are Hy-Lake founder and CHMA administrator Jonas Coverdale and camp junior staffer Carlos "Izzy" Izzaguirre, Heights athletic legend [*page 143*].

guaranteed super meals . . . and happy campers.

We returned the following year to Hy-Lake for a second season, along with a two-month-old daughter [Lynda] who became a camp pet. In 1944, Castle Heights began a summer program which terminated our connection with Camp Hy-Lake. (Hy-Lake was a nice place for reading. I remember an article in *Life* magazine about an army officer promoted from colonel to major general. His name: Dwight D. Eisenhower.)

Among pleasant memories of a lifetime were our summers at Camp Hy-Lake. There, we were part of a community, indeed, a part of a family. As with many families, time and separation dissolved close ties and blurred events we experienced and enjoyed in those halcyon days.

'Commando' brought experience, originality to classroom
• *April, 1992*

A recent column asking for remembrances of great Castle Heights teachers brought some fine results.

Hamlet Halbert '52, now of Lebanon, remembers with affection and humor Tom Harris, teacher of English at CHMA for a number of years before transferring to Cumberland University.

Although a major in the Academy's system of rank, the veteran of World War II was already a Navy lieutenant commander when he came to Heights in 1945.

Nobody called him "Major" Harris. In his early years, he was Commander Harris but as time passed, he became "Commando." All of the teachers at Heights had nicknames. Tom's was one of the best and most affectionate.

Vanderbilt University grad and World War II Navy Lieutenant Commander Tom Harris made English "fun" for more than 20 years in a CHMA classroom.

The cadets in Commando's classes soon learned to expect the unexpected. They loved his classes and they loved him because life in his classroom was one interesting experience after another. This is not to imply Tom Harris substituted entertainment for substance. Tom knew his subject, and his pupils learned the subject. They probably studied a little harder just to please him.

"He was a great and imaginative English teacher," said one Heights alum, "and stressed the importance of being able to write effectively. One of the most helpful things he taught us, though, was ' the three-initial sign-off.'

" Commando said once we began our professional careers, we were going to be required time and again to initial reports, documents and forms. So he had us link the initials of our first, middle and last names -- like JLS -- and practice writing them over and over. Man, I can't tell

Supervisor of the Heights Tiger Squadron of the Civil Air Patrol, Maj. Tom Harris helped more than 1,000 cadets -- meeting three times a week in the CAP classroom or at Lebanon Municipal Airport -- have access to ground school instruction and actual flying time. Some cadets received their private licenses.

you the number of times I've had to do that the last 35 years, and every time I do, I think of Major Harris."

Because of his military flight experience, Major Harris supervised the Heights' Civil Air Patrol Tiger Squadron. In the late '50s, the unit had more than 60 members and continued its ranking as the largest and most active CAP unit in the country. Many cadets received flight instruction [including navigation, engineering, communications and meteorology] from Lebanon Airport personnel, and -- as did 16 students in 1957 -- eventually received their pilots' licenses.

In his classroom were aids used in CAP instruction. "Few students have studied Shakespeare with a mock airplane hanging above them," said Jim Legg '55.

Tom Harris was a personality, a character worthy of a central role in a book. [*Yearbook Dedication, page 289*]

He heard the music of a different flutist

• *September, 1995*

He marched in his own parade.

He was his own muse.

He heard the music of a different flutist.

He climbed the down staircase.

He swam against the current.

He knew the conventions and therefore knew when he was unconventional -- which was much of the time.

His life reads better as a column than as a news story. He would not fit as a fictional character. Too unconventional. Only in real life was there such a character.

He was tight, stingy, a skinflint who would not install a cooling system, who endured the cold of winter without heat. But his stinginess applied only to himself.

Capt. Norman Cleveland, CHMA faculty 1952-53.

He was generous, compassionate, caring with others. Especially with his family -- his nephews and nieces whom he loved.

He developed skill in athletics, especially in tennis.

He learned to play golf, using a putter so unconventional that this club had its own name.

He would not accept gifts without compensation. Without overcompensation. The slightest favor would bring a check -- through the mail for dinner at a restaurant.

His pride was in his career in education. Special joy was in the pupils he taught, the lives he influenced, the character he helped to shape.

He developed his own theology, defying the gods of providence and even the God of Abraham and Jacob. He came to terms with himself and in all likelihood with the Deity of the Universe.

He possessed a high intelligence. His penetrating insight was uniquely keen. He was an intellectual -- a Henry David Thoreau without a Walden Pond.

He loved the written word, and he loved writing the word. He enjoyed those who wrote the words.

Indeed, he was unique.

"I am not crazy," he once said. "I am an eccentric."

Few argued the issue. He was -- well, he was different. And those who knew him accepted the difference and enjoyed him for what he was. A genuine eccentric. A personality for some future biographer to capture. A character in a Broadway play. A challenge for the most talent-ed actor.

He would not have me paint him as he was not. What you saw was what you got. Above all, he was honest with others and with himself. More than with most, with his own self he was true.

• Norman Cleveland [1921-1995] •

His earthly remains reside in an urn in a Lebanon cemetery. All that is left of him. At least on this planet. Who knows what other planet may become the habitat of the spirit of this unique man?

Perhaps he will reside on a planet that will better recognize his un-usual talents, his gift of intellect, his compassion for those about him.

During the Eighteenth Century, Thomas Gray pondered over the people buried in a country graveyard in England. Who were these un-known people in an obscure cemetery? What genes of greatness once ran through their veins? Were there undeveloped geniuses, prime min-isters, poets among them?

Perhaps in a more prosaic vein in a small town cemetery in Leba-non, Tenn., a future poet will muse as he or she stands above the grave that was new last week. Maybe he or she will voice what many thought in this town with Norman's passing. Maybe the future poet will write:

"In August, 1995, the community became a bit duller on the day this man died."

• BA, Cumberland University; MA, Peabody College. Bomber crew during World War II, and served in Korean War as Air Force Master Sergeant. On CHMA faculty 1952-53, subsequently teaching at New Mexico Military Institute as well as other prep schools. Retired in Lebanon, Tenn., running unsuccessfully for Superintendent of Schools. Periodically attended Cumberland baseball games with Heights' Maj. Lindsey Don-nell. Unsubstantiated rumor has it he once allowed [while sitting in passenger seat] a 14-year-old nephew at Heights to drive his Thunderbird to and from Nashville.

Portrait of 'iron discipline'

• *May, 2010*

Former cadets and a dwindling corps of Castle Heights career teachers bade farewell to one their most colorful members Monday when final services were conducted for Bobby Todd, age 79.

To some cadets, he was Captain Todd. To others he was Major. To all who knew him at the Academy where he joined the faculty in 1952, he was a portrait of iron discipline, pragmatic concern and dogmatic determination to instill in his pupils the rudiments of the English language and his principles of living.

Some pupils were disdainful, while others became his disciples. And in the years that followed, most acknowledged they learned from Bobby Todd.

Capt. Bobby Todd, CHMA faculty 1959.

Though an exponent of rigorous exercise, an admirer of rippling muscles and a proponent of daily walks long before walking became faddish, he could be mindful of less disciplined cadets burdened with doubt and uncertain in purpose.

These words by Myron McClellan '58, Denver, Colo., who credits Bobby Todd with a life reversal, are revealing:

"I was recently asked who the major influences in my life have been, and the first person I mentioned was Bobby Todd. He was the first adult male who made me feel as if I mattered as a human being, as if I counted, not for my talents as a musician or as a good student, but just as a person.

"I feel his concern changed my life. In fact, I have often thought it may have saved my life. He held me in high regard when I was the least certain that I had any value at all. I am so happy that, many years later, I was able to call him and thank him for the blessing he gave me when I was 12 years old, and that has lasted throughout my life. He will always be a true hero to me"

Another facet of the character of Bobby Todd was revealed during an encounter he had with Sam Hatcher '66.

"One of my best (worst) memories of Captain Todd occurred late one night on third floor Main. I had guard duty and was gathering reports or doing some official function. All was seemingly quiet, when Captain Todd suddenly appeared from a dark corner, taking me to the floor with a hand-to-hand combat move and shouting 'Hatcher, what are you doing on my floor [where he was in-resident faculty supervisor]?'

"As cadets, we had to respect Bobby Todd because for the most part we were scared to death of him. In truth, he was an excellent teacher. While he taught subjects and verbs in the classroom, he taught the importance of "yes sir" and "no sir" outside the classroom. He was a master of discipline and a valued teacher in lessons in life."

Rob Hosier '63, president of the Heights National Alumni Association, recalls Bobby Todd as an outstanding instructor.

"He was certainly one of the most colorful members of an outstanding faculty. He truly cared for the cadets," Hosier said.

Terry Hawkins, Dumas, Ark., class of '70, said he tried to "steer clear of Captain Todd."

"Like many cadets, I made sure not to get in Captain Todd's way or in his bad graces. He was feared by some, but respected by all. I never had him as a classroom teacher, but when I was a senior, he called me out in Chapel one day because the floor of Bullard Hall that I was supposed to be keeping clean, orderly and in line – well, it wasn't. I was embarrassed. He was right. Lesson learned."

Don Ash '73, learned a lesson in the Todd classroom on setting goals and obtaining objectives.

"I had Major Todd for sophomore English. At the beginning of each grading period, he would give us a grade we should achieve for that time period. He gave me a 94 once, and I begged for a lower goal. He said, 'Donnie, goals should never be easy. You will be amazed how you can surpass expectations if you work harder than you thought possible'."

Bobby Todd made a believer out of Don Ash, who now is a veteran cir-

Members of the Heights Class of '59 joined with Maj. Bobby Todd [ramrod straight, center] during Homecoming 1969 festivities. The 1959 seniors considered Todd one of their favorite faculty, and after his 2010 passing created a plaque in his honor which will hang in the CHMA Alumni Museum & Archives.

cuit court judge in neighboring Rutherford County.

John Hoover, Clearwater, Fla., may have caught the essence when he described his former teacher as "a rock of a man."

The 1974 Castle Heights yearbook, in its dedication [*page 311*], described Bobby Todd's impact on his students: "In his 22 years at Heights, he has been an important influence in the lives of numerous students."

The persona of Bobby Todd was etched in black and white – there were no gray areas. He demanded performance from his pupils, but no more than he demanded from himself.

In summary of his life at Castle Heights, he was a member of a unique tribe of teachers, each distinctive and each engraving his own distinctive creed on decades of cadets.

And in a company of unique Castle Heights teachers, none was more distinctive or iconic than Bobby Todd.

• Another classic Bobby Todd story:

In 1963 and 1964, the son of U.S. Senator Albert Gore of Tennessee -- Albert Gore Jr. -- attended Castle Heights summer sessions to take college prep courses. Also enrolled those two summers was Barbara Leftwich [now Barbara Froula of Knoxville, Tenn.], one of two daughters of JB and Jo Doris Leftwich.

"I had classes with Al in both 1963 and 1964," Barbara said, "but we became friends the second summer when we both took Spanish. Capt. Jerry Hurst -- four-sport athlete at Middle Tennessee and known as 'Big John' (6'8") at Heights -- was our teacher, and Al called me 'Teacher's Pet' because my grades were slightly higher than his. It was a friendly competition.

"One day Al was trying to get my attention, and he whistled at me from across The Circle," she continued. "Apparently Captain Todd heard him, and gave him demerits and Al had to walk the bullring. Dad told me his Mother said he needed to be home 'working tobacco.' I don't think Al wanted to be treated differently than other students, but he never whistled at me again. I wonder if about 15 other boys on that bullring brag about walking off demerits with a future U.S. vice president?"

• Earned his AB from Middle Tennessee State College, and was member of Heights faculty 1952 – 1978. Married Sabra Woodall of Lebanon in mid-1960s, and they had one son, Bobby Jr., Murfreesboro, Tenn.

Cadence about to change for 'celestial cadets'
• *July 2007*

When the definitive history of Castle Heights is finally written, I hope the historian writes a chapter on the fine men who ran the Military Department, indeed, the teachers who taught more than military science and tactics.

These men, sent to the Academy on rotation by the United States Army, were not trained in schools of education to become teachers. They were trained on the drill fields, in the barracks, and in many cases on the battlefields. They were teachers nonpareil, especially the sergeants, who brought special knowledge – and often special flavor – to the cadets.

U. S. Army Sgt. Major John S. Richards, Heights Military Department 1964-74.

The non-commissioned officers were in the trenches with the cadets where they made telling impressions. Few sergeants had as much impact on the cadets as did Sgt. Maj. John S. Richards.

He was unique – by definition, incomparable. And maybe the quality that made him unique, in addition to dedication, first-hand knowledge in the military and a keen intelligence, was character – and color. He was a colorful character.

He could chew out a cadet and simultaneously make the boy feel better about himself. He would crunch a wrongdoer, and later defend him when he was in a crisis.

One example concern is a cadet whose offense endangered his remaining in the corps. The discipline committee was on the verge of dismissing him from the Academy. Sergeant Major Richards served on the committee, and believed in strict discipline. But what was best for the boy weighed heavily in his mind.

On the night before the committee met, he called the cadet to his office and told him he was about to get his fanny kicked out of school. (Here, I confess "fanny" may not be an accurate translation.) Richards

The Heights Military Department coached the Academy's rifle team for military school competitions -- such as the Third Army Shoulder-to-Shoulder, Mid-South and Tennessee Trophy matches, won by the 1969 CHMA team.

then prescribed a procedure that could possibly keep him in school. First, he addressed attitude, telling the cadet if he truly hoped to stave off dismissal, he had to be humble.

"But you darn sure better be sincere in everything you say, and you had better be prepared to take whatever punishment you get. Furthermore, you've got to be a model. One blink and you're gone."

A contrite defendant appeared next day and begged for another chance. The committee voted severe punishment but not capital punishment. That boy, Louis Washburn, now a probation officer in Nashville, graduated from Heights and made a success in life.

A tough old Army sergeant was due the credit.

Lt. Col. [Ret] William Waters, a native of Lebanon and a graduate of Castle Heights, termed John Richards "a soldier's soldier."

"Throughout my military career, I met many command sergeant majors, but none left me with the lasting impression like the very first one I had the privilege of knowing. There are people you never forget."

Often gruff, John Richards also had an expansive sense of humor.

Military Department personnel assigned to CHMA in the early '60s included [seated] Capt. William MacMillan, Lt. Col. George E. Wright, Lt. Michael Bardis. Standing: Sgt. Earl Gentry, SFC Richard Shields, M/Sgt. Henry Mayberry, Capt. Stanley Hobbs, SFC J. C. Taylor

Weapons training was a Military Department task, as was coaching the CHMA drill team -- which participated in parades, ceremonies and tournaments throughout the Mid-South and was defending 1971 champions of the Fancy Drill Competition held at University of Tennessee-Martin. Primary Department focus was training of the corps for the annual spring Third Army Military Inspection to determine whether the Academy would retain its Honor School Junior ROTC rating first attained in 1937.

His son, Conrad, told his dad he had been promoted to lieutenant at Heights. Richards carefully examined his son's head, and said: "I've always heard lieutenants had holes in their heads. I just wanted to check."

In the early 1950s, Korea erupted into a major conflict and the U.S. forces were again engaged in battle. John Richards served three years and won two Bronze Stars, a Combat Infantry Badge, and the Army Commendation Medal with four oak leaf clusters.

He was proud of his record at Heights, where he built a reputation for fairness and toughness. Beneath his rough veneer, many cadets detected a tenderness that never conflicted with his persona but instead complimented it. At Castle Heights, he fit perfectly into the unique atmosphere that made the Academy one of the country's best military schools. He innately understood his role, and his performance of duty still embellishes the lives of the cadets he taught, disciplined and loved.

Early in his career, he met Fay Lewis and fell in love. Their marriage of more than 50 years and their two children—Conrad of Atlanta, and Janice Raney of Lebanon—were sources of pride. He also relished his role of grandfather and great-grandfather.

John Richards died last week after a short bout with liver cancer.

At his funeral, one Heights alumnus said: "If there's a celestial ROTC, those cadet angels better be prepared to march to a different cadence. Sergeant Major Richards is about to take over."

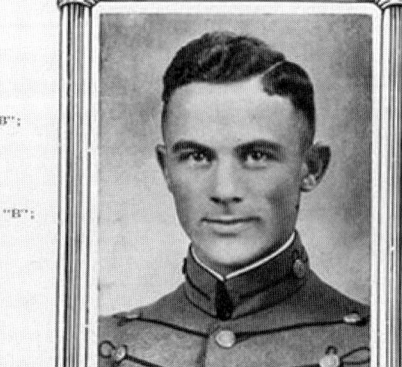

Fourth Class:

  Private Company "B";
  Football Squad.

Third Class:

  Corporal Company "B";
  Varsity Football;
  Varsity Baseball.

Second Class:

  Sergeant Company "D";
  Varsity Football;
  Captain Baseball;
  Treasurer Richmond
    Club;
  Marshal Final Ball.

First Class:

  Private Company "C";
  Varsity Football;
  Varsity Baseball;
  Treasurer Richmond
    Club;
  Marshal Final German.

Dan Ingram

DANIEL TAYLOR INGRAM, A.B.
Richmond, Va.

Born 1898. Matriculated 1917.
Artillery
"Dan," "Dan'l," "Ingrance"

E came from McGuire's School in Richmond, and the only things that could be held against him were that he had such nice curly hair and a pair of lovely eyes. Four years haven't changed his hair, but the difference is readily noticeable in those eyes. He has not been able to avoid the women, and the soulful expression in them has given way to one of complete indifference which is entirely assumed, notwithstanding his intimacy with Sam Mason.

He was a meek and lowly rat, but when Mose Goodman took him into his Marines he changed. Oh, how he changed. Being somewhat of an artillery shark, he became Peerk's veritable shadow, and was a battery commander at Camp Knox because of his wonderful ability(?).

But these are minor accomplishments. He has been the fastest halfback on the football team for three years, and to say that he is fast is putting it lightly. He's just too fast. He started at third base on the baseball team, but had too much speed in putting them over to first. So the coachees let him pitch because the catcher had a bigger glove. In addition to captaining the nine of '20, he pitched a no-hit, no-run game, and his three-base hits have broken up quite a number of interesting games. However, you'd never know him for a star off the field, because he is not the kind that needs advertising. He lets his work do it for him.

Dan's athletic fame is overshadowed only by his reputation as a man who says what he thinks and thinks what he says. If he goes to Suffolk to live he will probably enter the fish business— but that is his own affair. He deserted Chemistry for the Arts, for the "Hay" called and would not be denied. And so whatever you do or wherever you are, Dan, our best wishes go with you and you can't lose, for it isn't in you.   "You're damn right!"

From 1921 *BOMB*, Virginia Military Institute yearbook

84

'Only Legend I ever met'

• *Written for 1971* Lebanon Democrat *supplement commemorating CHMA's 70th Anniversary.*

I was just out of college and starting my first job as a teacher at Castle Heights.

I was completely ignorant of military matters. (I wasn't sure whether the cadets were supposed to salute me, or I was supposed to salute them.)

And I was embarrassed. I didn't have a complete uniform so I showed up for the opening of school wearing officer's pants, white shirt, khaki tie, leather belt and fairly fancy tan shoes. I was hatless, a cardinal sin.

Representing the best of Virginia Military Institute and Castle Heights Military Academy was Major/Colonel Dan T. Ingram, Academy Commandant 1929-63, and Superintendent 1963-65.

As I was standing in the halls of Main Building, a little man dressed nattily in correct military attire passed me, turned, glared, then spoke: "Hey, buoy, I want to see you in my office."

I was 21 years old, looked younger, and desperately longed to appear more mature. I suddenly felt as if I were 12.

"Buoy, why aren't you in uniform?," he wanted to know.

"I – I don't have one yet," I managed.

"Well get one. And another thing, buoy, why are you wearing officer's trousers?"

"Sir, I am an officer."

"You! An officer?"

He couldn't believe it and I had serious doubts myself. I thought about telling him it was all a mistake.

That was my first encounter with Maj. Daniel Taylor [D. T.] Ingram,

Something seldom seen by Castle Heights cadets: a smiling Col. D. T. Ingram -- here with alumni during a CHMA Homecoming celebration.

then commandant of Castle Heights, and undoubtedly my most unforgettable character.

Colonel Ingram died April 17, 1969, at age 70.

His death marked the end of an era at Castle Heights, but the legend of D. T. Ingram lives and grows, destined to reach proportions larger, but no greater, than the man who served Castle Heights from 1921 until illness forced his retirement.

Eventually, after I grew up a little, we became good friends. I learned more about him and his relation to Heights. I learned he stuck it out during the Depression and worked for little or no salary to help the Academy.

He was so good as commandant [1928-63] that he remained stuck with the job until two years before he semi-retired. Opportunity finally opened to his becoming superintendent, and he served two years in that position.

I was never a cadet at Heights, so I missed that special relationship which developed between Colonel Ingram and his "boys."

"When you were a cadet, you respected him, feared him a little," said Ernest Pellegrin '48, now an attorney in Gallatin, Tenn. "But when you were a man, you loved him. Not only because he was an intelligent, witty, affectionate, kind, dignified man, but because he was proof 'Southern Gentlemen' was not just a romantic legend, but really existed in truth."

Roger Davis '58, Hollywood TV and motion picture actor, wrote:

"I never saw his flaws – I never looked for them. He was fair without being naïve. One could not give of himself more for the benefit of others than did our beloved commandant."

Jay Cleveland Jr. '55, would like to follow in Colonel Ingram's footsteps. Now back in college, after several years working in other fields, he plans to become a teacher.

"Colonel Ingram always has been my example of a most unforgettable living memory, legend, example, and man.

"He seems to have left the world as quietly as he used to stroll Heights walkways. Because of his quiet dignity, and so many other qualities impossible to describe, it is impossible for him to slip from my memory and thoughts," Cleveland continued. [Jay served as CHMA Commandant eight years.]

Married in 1925, D. T. and Mildred Prewett Ingram -- and their daughter, Alice, and sons Dan Jr. '47 and John '52 -- were the Academy's "First Family" for more than 40 years. Joseph P. Wiegers (left), son-in-law of Bernarr Macfadden and his successor as Macfadden Foundation head, had a son, Dan, who is a 1956 CHMA grad.

Leonard K. Bradley Jr. '58, State of Tennessee agencies official, remembers Colonel Ingram from the time he [Bradley] was a little boy.

"The school probably has more of Colonel Ingram in it than of any other man. Heights is built on the lives of such men," Bradley said.

Joesph P. Wiegers, Bernarr Macfadden Foundation chairman, said during the funeral: "It is only the outstanding man who possesses that rare gift of understanding that makes a young man, comprehend the value of authority` and to accept an older man's judgment as justified. Colonel Ingram was that kind of disciplinarian, and his boys loved him for it.

"Castle Heights was fortunate to have Colonel Ingram as a leader. We believe Heights will be a living monument to his memory," Wiegers said.

Tennessee Governor Buford Ellington said in a telegram: "I am sure the example he set will long continue to influence and inspire many."

Bob Cleveland '59, former Peace Corps member now working for IBM, said: "He was the only legend I ever met."

I believe Heights alumni everywhere agree. He was not the "Mr. Chips" of Castle Heights. Mr. Chips was merely a product of fiction. Colonel Ingram was bigger than life. [*Yearbook Dedication, page 286*]

Chapter Three
Cadets

"Let us remind you that the boys of today,
your boy among them, will be the men of
tomorrow. Civilization is in a critical period.
Tremendous problems must be solved by this
next generation. There will be a great need for
clear thinking and clean living."

-CHMA Catalogue, Late 1940s

THE DRILL:
As noted by the tributes in Chapter Nine, JB Leftwich endeared himself to Heights cadets because of his genuine interest in and concern about them. Whether mentoring editors of *The Cavalier* and *The Adjutant*, guiding math students through theories of Pythagorean, or capturing cadet accomplishments by way of skilled photography, JBL's "job" was the students. Nowhere is this more evident than the pride, love and admiration shown in his columns on Heights grads.

Overleaf Photo: Cadets "march in review" during 1970s full-dress formal Sunday parade

Photo Credit: JB Leftwich

Heights' 'Cum Honore,' Castro prisoner

• *October, 1989*

Orlando Segarra '59 -- Cum Honore [highest CHMA graduating honor]; Latin-American Club President, member of the Round Table Council, newspaper and yearbook staffs, Quill & Scroll, three consecutive years zero demerits -- accepted this plaque during Homecoming festivities Saturday as classmates and other alumni stood in lingering applause for one of the Academy's outstanding graduates.

Orlando Segarra, Havana, Cuba, who in 1959 soon was to return to his homeland and the beginning of the Fidel Castro oppressive regime.

Orlando "Landy" Segarra, the only Cuban of several in the Academy at the time who recognized the menace of Castro. "He will ruin my country," he told me as he prepared to depart Castle Heights.

Orlando Segarra, who opposed Castro and spent almost 20 years in Cuba as a political prisoner, managed to get out of the island country in 1987, and move to Panama before finally arriving in Miami and sanctu-

Orlando Segarra [center] was one of eight 1959 graduates designated for the Academy's highest honor -- with [from left] J. R. Wilson, R. W. Cleveland, C. O. Bringle, H. V. Whitten, J. C. Castro and H. C. Woods. [B. L. Burney not in photo].

ary of his father's home. But before he was sent to prison, he was able to send his wife, two children and other family members to freedom.

Orlando Segarra [right] and Paul Holsen, '59 Heights grads at 50th anniversary class reunion

Segarra brought most of his miseries on himself. He was a counter-revolutionary activist and a saboteur, but he was sent to prison on trumped-up charges.

"I did a lot of things and was never caught," he said. "But I was innocent of the charges they lodged against me and I never admitted guilt. You can't imagine being a Cuban political prisoner."

I can only try, but my mind will not come to grips with the horrors he endured.

"At first, political prisoners wore clothing different from the criminals, but this did not last. We were mixed in the prison population with murderers and rapists. You can imagine how that was."

No, I could not, so he described incidents I do not care to print. He lived a nightmare, often stripped and beaten. His ribs were broken. He was placed in solitary confinement, once for a 21-day stint, naked and battered, and forced to subsist on bread and water. He served his three-week punishment in a little cell in total darkness.

"You can't imagine being alone in darkness for 21 days."

I could not imagine such conditions for 21 hours.

There was a brief exchange of letters when he returned to Cuba after his 1959 graduation. Once he told me not to write on CHMA letterheads because of "military" in the school's name. Abruptly, the correspondence halted, and I did not hear from him for more than 30 years.

"Early in my prison years, I met a guard who treated me kindly, but he was a low-ranking official. Years passed, and I was transferred near Havana where I discovered this guard had moved up the ladder to become prison warden.

"He called me aside to outline a proposal, but I told him I did not want to get into anything that would raise my hope of freedom. He wanted me to become a liaison between prisoners and the administration. For almost five years, the prisoners brought their problems to me and I went to the officials. I was able to work out a program that later was adopted and implemented in all of the prisons."

Was every day the same? Were there no pleasures?

"We learned to survive. Sometimes we created problems for the Castro regime. There were small triumphs. I enjoyed teaching English to some prisoners. This lasted until the authorities found out about it and I was punished -- beaten. English, you know was prohibited."

The day finally came when he was told he was to be set free. "That was a great day, but I was too numb to appreciate it," he said.

Then to Panama and subsequently to Miami. While he was in prison, his wife divorced him, assuming he would never be freed. He has remarried since coming to this country.

Segarra is now white haired and emotionally scarred. He has difficulty sleeping and his dreams often are nightmares. But he is unbroken.

"Do you know what kept me going during the roughest times? Remembering things I learned at Castle Heights. I am dead serious. My years here were the best of my life.

"What disturbs me most in this country is the way Americans take their country for granted, the way Americans abuse the privilege of being Americans, the lack of patriotism of many Americans. I just don't understand why people think patriotism is corny."

Coming from another, this sentiment might be suspect. Not from Orlando Segarra.

• One of Segarra's close friends at Heights was Paul J. Holsen II of La Cieba, Honduras, who entered Heights Junior School in 1952, and also was Class of '59. He graduated as a sergeant, and was squadron commander of the CHMA Civil Air Patrol -- which he joined to learn how to fly [following in footsteps of his cousin, John, a pilot for TACA Airlines, and his father, who was in World War I and went on to fly for the Army Air Corps, retiring as Major in 1939]. Holsen after leaving The Hilltop had a career as a pilot for the CIA's Air America. "Landy" resumed contact with Holsen after his release from prison, and the two have come to many CHMA Homecomings since the 1990s. Excerpts from Holsen's account:

"Every year Heights received many new cadets from Cuba, Puerto Rico and a few from Venezuela, but none of us were allowed to take ROTC...One Cuban [Landy] stood out to me, a small guy in stature but always with a big smile and a heart just as big. I recall when Fidel Castro visited New York, and was treated as a hero. Landy told me and Major Leftwich, 'He's no good.' ...[After Segarra's release], I made arrangements to get him to Miami and to our home in Fort Myers, Fla. Over a matter of time, Landy told me he'd gone back to Cuba after Heights and joined and helped form underground movements. He also was night manager of the famed Nacional Hotel where Castro had a penthouse. Each morning around 0400, El Che Guevara would come and play poker or have coffee with Segarra. Guevara learned Landy was fluent in English, and called on him to translate into Spanish service manuals that came with a large shipment of Leyland British buses....One night just after Fidel left his penthouse, an explosive device went off. As hotel manager, Landy was sentenced to 30 years in prison. ...Landy lives in Miami today [2014], and has health issues, including only one eye, but we speak daily."

He waited tables to avoid tuba toting
• *October, 1995*

Charlie Cook's business card says, "Consultant Et Al Ltd.," but whatever Charlie's credentials these waning years of the 20th Century, he is remembered by fellow cadets at Castle Heights as "Cajun," the substitute tailback who ran wild in 1943 against Montgomery Bell Academy.

On three consecutive possessions and running behind the second team line, Cajun dashed 49, 70 and 55 yards in that memorable game as CMHA defeated the rated MBA team 53-0.

Wherever former cadets of the early '40s gather, they discuss Cajun Cook's remarkable feat that autumn afternoon more than 50 years ago. Castle Heights had the game won early in the second half, and Coach Stroud Gwynn pulled Pat Parker, one of the Academy's greatest athletes from the game.

Charles Cook as '44 senior.

Cajun rarely misses a Castle Heights Homecoming. He loved when he was a cadet in 1938, and continued to love it his senior year of 1943-44, and to this day.

Oddly, Cajun came to CHMA to be a member of the military band, not to play football. His is an interesting tale:

In 1938, my Mama wanted me to be in the Byrd High School Band in Shreveport, La. She found out they had no base clarinets, so she bought me one. Never mind I could not play one then or ever. I simply couldn't play any musical instrument.

She hired a music teacher to instruct me, but this effort failed.

Through political maneuvering, I was put into the band in Shreveport. Since I couldn't play a thing, I made a deal to carry the tuba. I was given a band uniform and told not to make any noise. I marched along carrying the tuba and my Mama was happy.

Captain Bomar [later Tennessee Lt. Gov. James Bomar and subsequently president of Rotary International, but at the time a CHMA instructor] recruited me in Shreveport. Mama told him I played the base clarinet so I got a scholarship to play in the Castle Heights band.

I came to Heights knowing that at the first band practice Captain [Virgil] Medcalf would find out I couldn't play the damn thing. I was operating under a false pretense, and I had a big problem.

I arrived at Height two days before school opened, trying to figure out

Though Charles Cook was never a member, the CHMA band -- and Drill Team -- was noted for its annual participation in the Memphis, Tenn., Cotton Carnival parade, and on-campus concerts during the academic year.

what to do. I was between a rock and a very hard place. I was scared to death.

I went to Major Ingram, Commandant, and told him I had this problem. I had this band scholarship and I couldn't play a musical instrument, and I had to have a scholarship to stay in school. I told him I would do anything to stay.

Major Ingram went to Mr. E.L. Martin in the business office, and they figured out I could be a waiter -- the waiters' waiter. I would serve the cadet waiters who ate after the cadets finished. I kept that scholarship all the way through Heights. My last year, I was headwaiter. [Also battalion commander.]

My parents never knew I played not one note in the band. They were happy thinking I was a band member. I had survived the first of many problems I got myself into while I was at Heights.

I always appreciated Major Ingram. He has had a great influence on my life. A man not to be forgotten. Tough but fair.

Castle Heights Military Academy prepared me for what I did in life. Heights had been my family all of these years. When Heights closed, I felt as if my family had passed away.

And, Mama. She died thinking I played base clarinet in the Heights band.

Students willing to wait cadet and faculty tables three times a day and weekends received meals and 25¢ per meal, 50¢ at the formal dance intermissions. Maximum paid weekly was $3, with balance going to tuition. Three-to-four cadets each year earned "head waiter" status and 35¢ per meal to oversee the "long white line."

Serendipity day to honor CHMA idol

• *October, 2006*

Wednesday was a serendipity day sandwiched between two weather fronts that dominated the landscape before and after.

That was Wednesday of last week, a date set earlier for a visit by three teammates and a teacher to the grave of Pat Parker, dynamo of the 1943 Castle Heights Mid-South Conference champions in football.

Lacey Fields [Ashland City, Tenn.], Bill Burnett [Milan,Tenn.] and Bascom Cookesy [Lebanon] joined me in planning the nostalgic journey to the tomb of a Castle Heights icon [a native of Lafayette, Tenn.] where he was buried after falling on Okinawa in World War II.

Lacey was an end, Bill a guard, and Bascom, who did not make the trip because

Pat Parker
as '44 senior.

of an unexpected medical appointment, was the center. They, along with other stellar linemen and blocking back Bone Rodgers, created the openings that enabled Pat Parker to race to prep football glory.

Pat Parker was much more than an athlete who starred in four sports. He became the moral leader of the cadet corps, so idolized that his ego could have bulged had his character been molded of weaker materials. Instead of viewing himself as something apart, he deemed it an honor to play with such talented teammates.

Pep rallies embarrassed him. He would stand before the cadet corps, blush, scratch his backside, and struggle for words. In a lopsided victory over a favored opponent and late in the game, he yielded to his backup and disappeared. The cadets, hoping to hoist him to their shoulders, found him in his room doing homework assignments.

He joined the US Marine Corps after graduation, and soon was shipped to the Pacific, where he fell to a sniper's bullet.

At the Lafayette cemetery, we were joined by Heights alumni James Chamberlain '48 of Lafayette and Jim Roberts '46 of Murfreesboro, who attended the Academy after World War II and were schoolmates of Murray Parker, Pat's brother. [Murray, now deceased, was a 1946 CHMA grad.] Rounding out the group was Jerry Greenway, *Macon County Times* editor, who melded comfortably into the party.

Pat Parker was a four-sport athlete at Heights -- basketball, football, baseball and track -- after starring for two years on Macon County, Tenn., High School squads. He was a member of the 1942 CHMA Mid-South basketball championship team, and earned the Most Valuable Player trophy in the 1943 M-S tournament (though Heights was not the winning team). His gridiron skills helped lead the Tigers to the 1943 M-S football championship, and him to a place on the All Mid-South team.

In the cemetery, James led us to Pat's grave. It was not the scene I had anticipated. Pat's body was first buried in a family plot, and later transferred to its present site where he rests with his mother, two brothers and other family members.

Nearby is the grave of Dr. Edgar "Bully" Bratton, who played with Pat on the 1942 Heights team and later at the University of Georgia.

We clustered around Pat's grave and told Pat Parker stories. Pat ran 70 yards for a touchdown against Baylor while the players stopped action and gawked, was one Bill Burnett recalled. "Bob Page and Bascom Cooksey opened a hole in the Baylor line and Pat exploded through. Bill was downfield looking for an absent Baylor safety to block as Pat dashed into the end zone.

"The referee had whistled a foul, the defense just stopped action, and Pat was gone," Bill said. "Baylor was offsides, so the play stood."

Each of us said a short prayer, and Bill placed flowers on Pat's grave. Then we headed for Macon County High School where Pat was a pupil for two years. There, in a wall display, are Pat Parker pictures, sweater letters, newspaper stories and jersey number 95 he wore as a Heights player. The jersey, which earlier was displayed at Castle Heights, was donated to the Lafayette school when the Academy closed.

Pat's cousin, James Young Carter, a teacher at the high school, joined us at the trophy case and answered questions about his kinsman.

The football field at the Lafayette school is Pat Parker Field. The Castle Heights field should have been named for Pat, but red tape and a remote owner of the school thwarted efforts to effect the change. Later the field was named appropriately Stroud Gwynn Field, honoring a coach with a 25-year tenure.

Our sentimental journey was not to mourn the players' star teammate and my pupil. We were there to honor the memory of a cadet who entered our lives and in memory still resides there.

He was magnetic, but unaware of his rare talent. He was never a high-ranking cadet officer, but he was a moral compass that directed a cadet corps. Not only was he a star athlete, he was a landmark cadet.

His attributes were humility and graciousness, traits that burnished a sterling character. His presence lingered long after his tragic death and his fingerprints marked the Academy as long as it endured.

From *The Cavalier*, September 28, 1945:

"This is a hard story to write because it stamps 'finis' on the career of one of Castle Heights' greatest athletes and most beloved alumnus. This is the story of a gentleman -- a boy who always 'went the extra mile' and always did a little more than his part. This is the story of a boy who was loved by all who knew him...Three years ago, a blonde kid from Lafayette, Tenn., took the pigskin and ran circles around a Baylor team that lost only one game...When the year was over, he had made a record that placed him on the All Mid-South football team. But that was not all. He led the basketball team and was named MVP. He was a star on the track team, played baseball as well, and earned four letters....Pat Parker was easily the most popular cadet in 1943-44, the year he graduated. ...His fellow cadets elected him to the Honor Council, put him in the Heights-Y and DeMolay, and elected him a senior class officer. He graduated Cum Honore. Following graduation, he gave his all just as he did when he carried the ball for Heights. Pvt. John P. Parker, US Marine Corps, was killed in action on Okinawa last summer. He personified 'character' and 'Castle Heights.'"

Another Heights' 'Soldier' passes

• *September, 1999*

Lt. Col. [Ret.] Ernest L. Brown, Wilson County's most decorated World War II serviceman, died Saturday night at his home in San Antonio, Texas, following an extended illness.

Colonel Brown, who grew up in Wilson County and graduated from Castle Heights Military Academy in 1938, received the Distinguished Service Cross, the Silver Star, the Bronze Star and the Purple Heart with two oak leaf clusters, all for service in the Philippines and in the Bataan Campaign of December, 1941-February, 1942.

Ernest L. Brown as '38 senior.

He was wounded three times during the campaign and in the following years as a prisoner of war of the Japanese.

At age 22, he was one of the youngest captains in the Army. He was taken prisoner in Bataan and survived the infamous Death March to Camp O'Donnell -- an 80-mile march that began in April, 1942, following the three-month Battle of Bataan, and involved conservatively 70,000 Filipino and American prisoners of war. Later, Colonel Brown sustained injuries in two attacks by US Army Air Force bombers while he and other prisoners were being transported on Japanese ships.

He endured more than three years of captivity, emerging as an Army major after Russian troops brought deliverance. Subsequently, he was promoted to lieutenant colonel.

After retiring from the Army, he owned and operated an automobile agency in San Antonio.

While growing up in Lebanon, he lived with J. Bill Frame, former editor of *The Democrat*, and Bessie Lee Brown Frame, his aunt. His only survivor in Lebanon is Laura Lee Frame Mingledorff, a first cousin.

Tennessee: birthplace of journalists

• *April, 1986*

Few states can match Tennessee in the production of journalists

That contention was graphically illustrated last week when writers with Tennessee roots convened in Nashville for "Journalists' Reunion Homecoming '86." Many of them, a vast number, are alumni of *The Nashville Tennessean*, and many of them were trained under Coleman Harwell, *Tennessean* editor from 1948 to 1959, and now age 80.

Among the writers Harwell hired and later sent to larger assignments were David Halberstam, who won a Pulitzer Prize for his coverage of the Vietnam War for *The New York Times*; Tom Wicker, associate editor of *The New York Times*; Fred Graham, CBS News correspondent; Creed Black, chairman and publisher of *The Herald Leader*, Lexington, Ky.; Wallace Westfield, NBC producer.

Under John Seigenthaler, *The Tennessean* continues its tradition as an incubator of national journalists. These include Jim Squires, editor of the *Chicago Tribune*; David Hall, editor of *The Denver Post*; and Frank Sutherland, managing editor of the Hattiesburg, Miss., *American*.

Three of the newsmen returning for "Homecoming '86" began their journalistic careers at Castle Heights where they were editors of *The Cavalier* -- which for 40 years was dominate among the state's high school newspapers. Few high school newspapers produced more good writers during that span than did *The Cavalier*.

The three *Cavalier* alumni who returned for the Journalists' Reunion festivities were Hall, Sutherland and John Means of *The Washington Post*. Of the three, Hall was the most serious journalist while at Heights. During his 1961 senior year, as editor-in-chief, *The Cavalier* won highest honors in state and national contests, including being selected as one of the nation's six best high school newspapers. He won journalism scholarships to the University of Tennessee, edited the UT student newspaper

The Cavalier was distributed every third Saturday in the mess hall, prior to cadet arrival, and students spent the bulk of meal time reading about themselves, classmates, faculty, sports, recent activities and upcoming events.

and was instrumental in converting it into a daily publication. [A Lebanon girl, who just happened to be named Lynda Leftwich, was the first editor of the UT daily newspaper. And another former *Cavalier* editor, Stan Huguenin '59, worked with Hall and Leftwich on the UT *Orange + White*, serving as managing editor.]

CHMA editors David Hall '61, Stan Huguenin '59, and L.K. Bradley Jr. '58 [Sports] joined with 'Coach' JB Leftwich for 1969 Homecoming activities.

Johnny Means '44 was an irrepressible and sometimes irreverent writer for *The Cavalier*, but he was imaginative and talented. He is a grandson of O.N. Smith, one of the "founders" of Castle Heights.

Frank Sutherland '62 was a feature writer serving under LeRoy Dowdy, editor-in-chief of the 1961-1962 *Cavalier*. Frank sometimes did his assignment with flourish, sometimes did his assignment, and sometimes didn't bother. Once when Frank either made a token effort or didn't do his assignment, LeRoy wrote or rewrote Frank's story but gave Frank a by-line. Frank entered one of these in a state contest and won first prize.

David, deadly serious about his editorship, abolished the gossip column -- called *Spillway*, and written anonymously by a cadet bylined "Flying Saucer" -- much to the displeasure of the cadet corps. A delegation confronted David outside my office and David, his face almost the color of his red hair, refused to bend. Despite threats and attempted intimidation, the gossip column remained out of *The Cavalier*, and the controversial issue gradually faded.

There were many other fine writers on *The Cavalier*, many the equal of ones already mentioned. To name a few -- and to omit others just as good but who do not come readily to mind: Edward McClellan, PhD., Indiana University; Albert Smith, publisher of a string of Kentucky newspapers; Chuck Ward, one of Tulsa's leading architects [*page 166*]; Bob Bailey, PhD., Rockwell International; Tom Bailey, PhD., design engineer with TRW Corp.; Gordon Baskett, international printer.

One of the best business managers *The Cavalier* ever had was a cadet named Sam Hatcher '66. [He launched and built Main Street Media in Lebanon into a holding company for suburban news and lifestyle publications -- including the twice-weekly *The Wilson Post* newspaper. He stepped down as *Post* publisher in 2013, after sale of MSM.]

'Cavalier' Editors Have a Tradition To Keep

Other Schools Look Hungrily At Awards

By
JACQUELINE SHARBOROUGH

Cadets who are editors of "the Cavalier," school newspaper of Castle Heights Military academy in Lebanon, have a problem on their hands.

They've got to keep up the award-winning precedent set by past editors, or face the fact that they've let hundreds of students and alumni down.

"The boys are always willing to try something they think will make the paper better," said Maj. J. B. Leftwich, advisor. "It may be a new column, or new make-up, anything that will be an improvement."

Sharborough

The merits of the newspaper will be up for ratings again this week at the convention of the University of Tennessee High School Press association. The meeting will be held at the Andrew Jackson hotel from Thursday night through Saturday.

Other schools can well afford to cast an envious eye at "the Cavalier" record. It has won 22 consecutive ratings of All-American from the National Scholastic Press association, seven consecutive medalist ratings from the Columbia University Scholastic Press association, as well as winning an All-Tennessee rating from the University of Tennessee for a number of years.

Outside Help Praised

The current editors give credit to a number of people outside the editorial staff for their help in keeping the newspaper on top.

"The administration is very co-operative, sometimes holding back stories until we have printed them in the paper," said Ed McClellan, 17, editor-in-chief and son of Dr. and Mrs. G. O. McClellan of West Hamlin, W. Va.

"The printers go out of their way to help us, too. We come out on Saturday morning and they frequently will hold up the presses until late Friday night if we have a good story breaking," he said.

Major Leftwich is quick to give praise to the staff for its work.

It's a pleased staff of "The Cavalier" that holds an impromptu editorial conference to look at the latest edition of the Castle Heights Military academy newspaper. Meeting at the cannon to discuss their "baby" are, from left, Robin Bennington, associate editor; Leonard Bradley Jr., sports editor; Maj. J. B. Leftwich, advisor; Ed McClellan, editor, and Myron McClellan, associate editor.

—Staff colorphoto by Howard Cooper

most of which is done in their leisure time.

All on Honor Roll

"Our boys have to be top students, or they would not have the time to put on the newspaper that it requires," he said. "All of them are honor roll members. When other boys are studying, our staffers are digging up stories and writing them."

For his own work advisor, the Columbia Press association has announced it will present the major with a gold key in recognition of the job he has done.

Myron McClellan, 16, brother of the current editor, will follow fraternal footsteps and take over the top editing job next year. Myron is associate editor now, as is Robin Barrington, 16, son of Mr. and Mrs. William R. Barrington of Rocky River, Ohio. The sports editor is Leonard Bradley Jr., son of Mr. and Mrs. Leonard Bradley of Lebanon.

"The Cavalier" is published every three weeks. The editors feel their highest honor has come from alumni who subscribe to the paper from as far away as Arabia and South America.

As Myron said:

"You might say the sun never sets on 'The Cavalier.'"

The Nashville Tennessean in 1957 reported on historically high journalism standards maintained by the *Cavalier* editors and staff -- under Maj. JB Leftwich's tutelage -- and its many state and national awards as a result.

• Traditionally, Spillway was written anonymously by "Flying Saucer" periodically during a school year, and referenced various cadets and their latest girlfriends, and occasionally even those of single faculty, plus rumors of cadet mischief. Toward end-of-year graduation ceremonies, identity of that year's FS was revealed, and he was tracked down and thrown fully clothed into the Academy pool. ["Flying Saucer" in 1956-57: Ted Lavit [*page 233*]. In 1958-59, concerned about high school newspaper judges' criteria, *Cavalier* editors, with strong JBL encouragement, decided to print Spillway as a separate insert so it would not appear in issues submitted for judging.

High School no indicator of future success
• *June, 1998*

Of all the arenas of achievement, high school may be the worst place for predicting future successes or failures. Being an honor student or even valedictorian is no guarantee of success in the so-called "real world." Being a C student is no guarantee of failure. Successes in the real world are a mix of former high school achievers and non-achievers.

Alonzo Walter as '45 senior.

In my early years of teaching, I remember marking Cadet John Doe, who never mastered Algebra II, as on the track to failure. A few years later, Dr. John Doe showed up at Homecoming.

Alonzo "Lon" Walter, class of '45, was a nice, likable cadet at Castle Heights Military Academy, capable of more than he produced and often in low gear when he should have been revving up the scholastic ratio. He caused teachers and administrators no trouble. Except for his sunny and gregarious disposition, he easily could have simply melded into the corps and faded into the bracket of "normal boy with considerable potential."

Lon moved through the Heights military program, making no great splash and earning no stripes. Nobody thought of him as a future cadet major or colonel. But he was bright, so he was accepted to the Virginia Military Institute, alma mater of fabled Col. D. T. Ingram, Castle Heights commandant. True to form, Lon blended into the VMI cadet corps, and was passed over for promotions. Nevertheless, he did graduate as a "distinguished cadet," and as such was commissioned a second lieutenant in the United States Air Force.

Said Lon: "I was a private for four years at VMI, but I did manage to become sports editor of the cadet newspaper and yearbook. There may be some connection between the amount of time I applied to these extracurricular activities and my lack of success in receiving rank in the cadet corps. After carrying a rifle for six years -- two at Castle Heights and four at VMI -- I was finally a second lieutenant."

Lon progressed through the Air Force flying school and graduated as a fighter pilot just two days before the Korean War began. Piloting the F-86 Sabre, he flew with some of the great aces of World War II.

"I was a near miss," he writes.

After Korea, he progressed through Air Force programs and schools, tested new fighter armament, and flew the newest fighter aircraft. He was selected as a candidate astronaut in the Project Mercury program. He made it to the final 32, but was not selected to be an astronaut.

Another "near miss," he writes.

And, guess what? Lon Walter was receiving promotions during his career.

But Brigadier General Alonzo Walter? Yes, promoted to general in July, 1974. Hard to believe for someone who spent six years as a military school private.

• BS, Virginia Military Institute, 1949; MS, US Air Force Institute of Technology; Air Command & Staff College, 1961; Air War College, 1966. Flew 48 combat missions in Korean War [including wingman for WWII and Korean War ace Gabby Gabreski]. Base posts included Randolph, Eglin, Maxwell, Edwards, Hickam. Assignments: Headquarters Space Systems Division; Headquarters, USAir Force; US Air Force Academy; Aerospace Studies Institute; XXIV Corps Air Liaison Officer/Direct Air Support Center Director, Da Nang, Vietnam; Commander, 31st Tactical Fighter Wing, Homestead; Deputy Director/Operations, U.S. European Command, Stuttgart, Germany. Honors include Parachute Wings; Legion of Merit, two oak leaf clusters; Air Medal, four oak leaf clusters; Distinguished Unit Citation, oak leaf cluster; Republic of Vietnam Gallantry Cross with gold star. Command Pilot Brig. Gen. Alonzo J. Walter Jr. [upper right] retired June, 1979.

• Walter and wife Doris [AF nurse, commissioned officer], had two daughters -- Beverly and Terry. In 1974, Terry [right] was commissioned USAF Second Lieutenant. In 1989, she married USAF Lt. Col. Donald F. Gabreski [son of Colonel Gabreski of WWII and Korean War service], and they have two sons. Retired in 2010 as Lieutenant General, having served as highest-ranking active duty USAF woman officer. She was Vice Commander, Air Force Material Command, Wright-Patterson AFB. Honors include: Master Aircraft Maintenance Badge, Parachute Wings, Air Force Distinguished Service Medal, Legion of Merit [bronze oak leaf cluster], National Defense Service Medal [two bronze stars], and Joint Service Commendation Medal (oak leaf cluster).

'Me gustaria ofrecerles un cordial saludo…'

• *September, 2002*

It was commencement for the Castle Heights Military Academy class of 1979, and the salutatorian was behind the lectern beginning a speech required of the class member finishing second in the academic standings. Just another schoolboy speech, we thought.

"Me gustaria ofrecerles un cordial saludo al superintente, miembros de la facultad, padres, visitantes, y mas importante a la clase graduanda que hoy, 27 de Mayo de 1979, celebrara la graduacion de la ultima clase de los Setena."

Abruptly, the audience of seniors, underclassmen, parents and others were alert.

Victor Tarano as '79 senior.

Was salutatorian Victor Tarano, a Puerto Rican, going to deliver his address in Spanish? If they had not been shocked at Victor's opening sentence, the seniors would have looked at each other knowingly. But they were quiet, rapt in their attention. Instinctively, they and the audience in general knew this was no ordinary salutatory address. The speaker was magnetic. The listeners' eyes were glued to this almost hypnotic cadet who suddenly had emerged from the seniors' ranks.

"I would like to offer a friendly greeting," said Victor, translating his opening remarks.

He then repeated his salute to the superintendent, faculty, visitors and classmates on that Sunday morning, May 27, 1979.

Seated behind Victor on the Macfadden Auditorium stage were administrators of the school along with Lt. Gen. Eugene Forester, the Watertown native who at the time commanded one of the United States armies. It was a coup to attract a speaker of the distinction of General Forester. All of us anticipated his address.

For the next few minutes, the General and all others in the building forgot prestige and achievements and focused on an 18-year-old cadet who spoke English as a second language.

"When I came to Heights three years ago, my goal was to develop myself in body and in spirit so I could be able to serve mankind," he said. "This was quite a challenge because I had to learn a new language and adapt to a new society. By using God as my guide, I was never disappointed," he said.

In a less charged atmosphere, this would have signaled another sermon, and many cadet eyes would have glazed. Not so this day. The cadets leaned forward so as not to miss a word. But it was not only the words Victor delivered, it was the magnetism of the speaker himself. Indeed, as much the messenger as the message.

One of the amazing aspects of this dramatic slice of time rested in the persona of the speaker who until that moment had never been a "big man on campus." There were many biographies in the yearbook longer than Victor's.

"I became interested in the Bible which I used as a source of advice whenever I needed one. I especially enjoyed the occasion when I felt that a particular passage was written especially for me

"In Ecclesiastics, I discovered a passage that applies to all of us in this class: 'Young man, it's wonderful to be young. Enjoy every minute of it; do all you want to do; take in everything, but you must give an account to God for everything you do.'"

I watched the cadets. There were no eyes rolling, no slouching, no whispering. Actually, some heads were nodding ascent.

Victor eased the tension: "I don't want to sound like a Sunday School teacher," he said. "But if you would listen to this last passage from Romans, you could possible find inspiration to re-direct your life's efforts: *Don't copy the behavior and customs of this world, but be a new and different person with a fresh newness in all you do and think. Then you can learn from your own experience how His ways satisfy you.*'

"We are living in a society where institutions are changing. As a result of mounting problems, our values are changing. But no matter what happens in our country, our young people have to take a leading role in bringing back true values: truth, morality, justice, love, honesty, sincerity and peace."

Then he thanked his teachers. "Their efforts in the formation of our character were not in vain." He concluded with: "May God bless us all."

After a brief moment of silence, as if the audience expected more, applause probably unequaled any other cadet speech erupted.

The audience knew the peak of the program had passed. There was sympathetic applause when General Forester was introduced. He immediately recognized that an earnest and sincere young man had unintentionally upstaged him.

"After the salutatorian's address, what can I say?" General Forester asked. Then he delivered what at another time and place would have been a stirring address. Because of his poise in recognizing the drama just played out, his audience was both polite and appreciative.

These words have been spoken by others before and after that day in May. Reading them now, I realize that however true and emphatic they are and whatever the impact they had that commencement day, they are not the same on paper as they were when Victor Torano delivered them.

May 27, 1979, was a day when words and sincerity melded, when the eternal truths echoed with new meaning as a boy in a Castle Heights uniform spoke to his classmates.

It was an interval in time that still resonates in the minds of those who experienced it.

Col. Victor Torano, circa 2000.

• Earned BS, Tulane University; medical degree Universidad Central del Caribe; Adult Psychiatry Residency, Boston University Medical Center; Addiction Psychiatry Fellowship, Massachusetts General Hospital, 1996; Flight Surgeon, Aerospace Medicine, 2005; Air War College, 2009. Duty at Fort Jackson, S.C., and Puerto Rico's Muniz Air National Guard Base. Colonel Torano works for Puerto Rico Mental Health and Substance Abuse Administration and as a hospitals consultant. Awards include Meritorious Service Medal, National Defense Service Medal, Global War on Terrorism Service Medal. He and his wife, Dr. Vionnette E. Pagan, have two children.

• **2014 Report from Colonel Torano:**
"I've been able to return to each '79 class reunion. I attended in 1999 with my fiancée, and in 2009 with my two children. At Heights, I was close to Col. Jay P. Cleveland, commandant at the time; Headmaster Col. Gene Hale, and Major Dixon Ward. I pretty much just studied, stayed out of trouble, and was involved in sports. Being away from home, I found solace in reading the Bible, as it provided strength and comfort. My Salutatorian speech -- which I wrote and had Colonel Cleveland review [he suggested some changes] -- brought some attention, and the theme resonated with the audience. At the 2009 class reunion, I introduced myself to Colonel Leftwich, and he was eager to tell everyone of the speech and the impact it had caused."

Cannon pranks, walking the 'bullring'
• *November, 1993*

One of the great traditions born and nurtured during my long stay at Castle Heights focused on the cannon which usually, but not always, was chained to the flagpole immediately in front of Main Building.

Frequently, during the course of an academic year, cadets would give it a new covering of paint -- always more imaginative than drab olive -- during the small hours of the morning. As a result, the cannon bore many coats as the years rolled by.

Lt. Col. D. T. Ingram, for generations commandant and in charge of cadet discipline, surprisingly took a rather detached view of the prank.

"If they were not painting the cannon, they would be painting something else," he would say. "We'll catch most of them, anyway."

As the years rolled by and spray paint became readily available, the cadets, as did pupils in other schools, targeted other things -- such as the football field press box and brick walls.

One morning, Lt. Col. Ralph Lucas, long time coach and Superintendent in his latter years at Heights, walked out of the front door in Bullard Hall right into the cannon aimed at his family apartment.

Another year, members of one class stole the cannon, loaded it onto a lowboy, and transported it to Nashville where they parked it in front of the studios of WLAC-TV. They wanted to be on television, they said.

They were on TV, and subsequently they were on the Heights bullring.

While on the subject of the bullring, let me add another item to my recent "Class of 1943" column. Bill Pankey had a conflict and was unable to attend the annual Homecoming reunion October 16-17, so he showed up here about one week later in search of anyone with a connection to the Academy during the early '40s.

Bill's nickname while at Heights was "Bullring" Pankey, a name he earned for his frequent assignment of penalty tours. "There's probably still a circular rut I wore in the ground walking the bullring," he said.

• The regular bullring, around which cadets marched off their demerits, was located in the vicinity of The Armory [and the watchful eyes of military staff] near one of two official "buttholes" -- outdoor locations where smoking was permitted. [The second smoking area was at a rear corner of Bullard Hall barracks.] The ring was identified by a circular worn dirt path in a grassy area. Penalty tours on special occasions -- early evening, weekends, prior to holiday leaves, post-graduation -- were moved to the flagpole circle in front of Main, making it easier for cadets on daily guard duty [stationed in Main] to keep track of the penalty tourees.

**Bill Pankey Jr.
as '43 senior.**

One day, Bill bought some apples for snacks during CQ [Call-to-Quarters, or study period]. The apples gave him other ideas. He went to Baird and Saftly Hardware Store on the public square where he bought a segment of dynamite fuse. Not dynamite, just the fuse.

Back in his room, he used shoe sole dye and carefully blackened a couple of apples. Then he removed the stems and replaced them with the fuses. During the break between Call to Quarters, he lit the fuses and casually rolled the apples down the barracks stairway as cadets were returning to their rooms.

Needless to say, all Hades broke loose.

Bill's schemes were more innovative than his plans to escape detection. It took little imagination from the division officers to conduct an inspection and discover the cadet with shoe polish stains on his hands.

And, needless to say, D. T. Ingram displayed little humor in dealing with the culprit.

It was back to the bullring for old Pankey.

Pankey, as did so many of the cadets who walked the bullring, turned out all right. He served in World War II, went to college, married, reared a family and enjoyed a career in art. He now is retired from Walgreen Drug Co., where he served as art director. His wife died recently, ending a marriage of more than 40 years.

Cannon enticing even to non-cadets
• *October, 1997*

[As noted above], administrative officials and military support staff took a dim view of the cadets' tampering with the cannon's paint job. Occasionally, the culprits were apprehended. They paid stiff penalties.

And, needless to say, stiff penalties did not stop the pranking.

As time evolved, instead of splashes of paint hastily administered, the cadets became bolder and more creative. Once it appeared in candy-stripe decor. Indeed, the splashers were often scorned for their lack of daring. It was considered somewhat cowardly to pour a can of paint over the cannon or simply to spray paint splotches.

The class of perpetrators also evolved. Some of the Academy's most honored cadets later admitted -- or bragged -- they had painted the cannon.

Originally inclined to "hit and run" the Heights cannon with splashes of paint, cadets by the late '50s had become more willing to risk discovery by taking time to "decorate" with stripes and other designs.

Somewhere along the line, even "town boys" [not cadets] reportedly got into the act and slipped on campus and to paint. I don't know this to be true and the reports may be greatly enlarged, but occasionally a respected citizen of this town will drop hints.

Even Lebanon Mayor Don Fox, greatly admired by Castle Heights alumni because of his role in restoring Main Building [*page 224*], hints that as a Lebanon teen, he may have thought of stealing the cannon. Or so he reported during recent Homecoming Day activities. In fact, his yen to steal it evidently persisted.

In a talk at the Saturday alumni luncheon, he said, "Last night I called three or four city employees to help me steal the cannon [now located in front of alumni headquarters]. We were just ready to get it when the door of the alumni house opened and Susan Hosier [National Heights Alumni Association administrator] stepped out."

I am not sure whether the mayor, just as so many others have bragged about stealing the cannon, was boasting or if, indeed, he did make a latter day effort to realize his boyhood dreams.

I do know that when Mayor Fox made the statement, Susan stood up and took a bow.

• The best-known Heights cannon, and one now located at the Ingram Alumni House, actually was the second one to serve as the CHMA icon. Reportedly the first was melted during WWII, for use as scrap metal. The more permanent cannon was a pre-World War I three-inch Hotwitzer manufactured in 1902.

Annual Spring inspections by visiting US Army officers were held to determine Castle Heights status as an "honor school," first awarded to the Academy in 1937. Officers inspected all buildings and facilities, visited military classes, and reviewed cadets in the barracks and in ranks during a formal parade.

Starting things off with a bang

• *September, 2006*

To say Castle Heights cadets were "challenged" during their stay at the school is understating the ingenuity and performance of thousands of boys who passed through its portals.

Not only in the classrooms and on the athletics fields were they subject to challenge, they often felt they were dared to outwit their superior officers and their instructors.

An example of cadet ingenuity involves John Granville '54, who came to the Academy from Abilene, Texas, at the beginning of his junior year, and Tony Turney from Dallas, who also entered Heights in the 11th grade. These two rarely knew a challenge they didn't meet head on. Their chemistry generated an exploit so daring that had their identities been uncovered, their CHMA future would have been endangered.

They were gifted with fertile minds and surging imagination, ingredients leading to one of the Academy's most interesting federal inspections. As background, let me explain one of the most critical and intense annual events on the Academy calendar. Each year, a team of Army officers was sent to military schools such as Castle Heights to evaluate its military program and, if the school scored high, award the coveted "Honor School" distinction. Winning the honor each year was vital.

The award was a tradition at Castle Heights, but the school's Reserved Officers Training Corps [ROTC] officials as well as Academy administrators -- and the Corps of Cadets -- were always "up tight" when Federal Inspection rolled around each spring.

Preparations for annual inspections included practice parades with cadet officers checking for correct procedures, review of small unit tactics, and students' knowledge of the General Orders -- and, after the Granville/Turney "incident," policing of grounds to check for out-of-place soft drink bottles.

It was against this backdrop that the Granville-Turney duo executed their coup de grâce. Here is the story in the words of John Granville, a recent visitor to the campus of the now extinct military school:

"As Col. Leonard Bradley taught me in chemistry, gunpowder is very unstable. Unaware of this fact at the time, my roommate, T. 'Texas Tony' Turney, and I were producing it by mixing salt-peter, powdered sulphur and activated charcoal in our room on second floor of Main. These ingredients were available at the drug store in town, as was dynamite fuse at the hardware store.

"This was a long time ago and I can't remember the proportions, but the mixture is by weight, not volume. Since we didn't have scales, getting just the right mixture required some experimentation. Early versions were made in ink bottle sizes, tossed out our window in the dead of night, until we had a fairly reliable product.

"In time, we produced one using a Coke bottle heavily wrapped with adhesive tape. We tossed this baby out one night, and it landed in the hedge around the circle in front of Main -- actually on some bare ground where there was a break in the hedge that people used as a short cut.

"This was during study hour and our product seemed to be another dud. We were looking out our window hoping for a delayed explosion when 'Uncle Peter' [Librarian Capt. C. H. Hurd] started back to Main from the library and walked right over our bomb. Fortunately it was a true dud and we retrieved it in the middle of the night. The incident frightened us enough, however, that we redoubled our Quality Control effort to include burning a small quantity of our product to test its efficacy before incorporating it in the finished product.

"The final product was complete in time for use on the Sunday night when the US Army officers were present for the annual federal inspection. The explosion occurred during their kickoff meeting prior to reviewing the CHMA operation next day.

One of most dramatic segments of Heights parades, whether for annual inspection or spring Sundays for townsfolk and visitors, was first sighting of battalion commander and staff -- followed by band and companies of cadets -- as they leave the Hilltop and proceed down tree-lined main drive before turning sharply to lead the corps onto the football field for maneuvers and drills.

"The explosion rattled the visiting committee and sent Academy officials seeking culprits and damage. They found neither. Puzzled cadets erupted from their rooms and stormed to windows and doors.

"As Col. D. T. Ingram said in assembly Monday, Academy officials hoped to get the Inspection 'off with a bang,' but not the type of bang experienced the night before.

"In spite of the excitement, Heights was accredited for another year. I can't remember whether we were found out or not. It's hard to keep a secret like that!"

As I recall, the identities of the Big Bang perpetrators never were discovered, the culprits graduated and went on to distinguished careers,

John graduated from Heights in 1954, entered and graduated from the United States Naval Academy, transferred to the Air Force [before the Air Force Academy produced graduates], later earned an MBA and enjoyed a successful business career.

Who knows, his bent for daring may have factored into his successful career.

Has it really been that long?

• *June, 1986*

This is the story of three ladies, two graduation exercises, and the compression of time.

There she was, Jean MacArthur, 87, widow of one of America's military geniuses, poised and articulate, presenting the Douglas MacArthur Award to Cadet Lt. Col. Stephen Werst [cadet corps battalion commander] during the Castle Heights Military Academy awards night program in May for this year's graduating class.

Jean MacArthur, 87, widow of Gen. Douglas MacArthur, presented the Heights annual award named in his honor during May, 1986, commencement exercises to Battalion Commander Stephen H. Werst. Those attending did not yet know these would be the Academy's last graduation festivities.

Cadet Werst and other cadets and their families were reaching out and touching history, spanning the years from World War II -- even from WWI, for Douglas MacArthur was an officer in the first great war.

Most of the cadets' parents were small children or infants or even unborn when Jean MacArthur returned shortly after World War II to Murfreesboro, her home town. CHMA's cadet corps was transported to Murfreesboro to see the native Tennessean and her famous husband. I remember standing on the flat roof of a building with Ernie Keller of radio station WSM -- Nashville "home of the Grand Ole Opry" since 1925 -- as he described the events.

Was all of this really from 40 years ago?

All of us discover the compression of time and its erratic but unrelenting march, adding years that seem like only weeks to our lifetimes. And each of us as we mature asks the inevitable question, "Has it been that many years?"

Jean MacArthur, who lives in New York City and was in Middle Tennessee last week visiting a sister in Murfreesboro, appeared younger than her 87 years. "It's a real honor for me and the school," said Cadet Werst. Said Mrs. MacArthur. "This gives me the greatest possible pleasure."

And then there was the graduation exercise itself with Makiko Takeda delivering the valedictory. There was a bit of irony, unmentioned of course, that Makiko, a citizen of Japan, won the highest academic honor at Castle Heights and was featured on the commencement program on the same weekend that Jean MacArthur was on campus.

Makiko Takeda of Japan was the 1986 class valedictorian, and one of four females on the Academy's six-member cadet staff.

It was General of the Army Douglas MacArthur who was one of the chief instruments in the defeat of Japan. The preamble to the award praised the general, calling him "conqueror of Japan, liberator of the Philippines and protector of Australia."

Makiko Takeda earned an academic average of 96.075 in difficult subjects to finish first in her class, one step higher than Salutatorian Werst. And Makiko became a bit Americanized during her years at Castle Heights, participating in athletics and in the glee club where she joined in the singing of "The Star Spangled Banner."

She delivered her valedictory in perfect English, and she was heartily applauded for she was popular with her fellow students. She has been accepted at Vanderbilt University.

And the third lady?

She was participating in graduation ceremonies of the Julius T. Wright School for Girls in Mobile, Ala., where 40 pretty girls in identical white dresses sat on the stage bathed in light from theater floodlights. Among them were six National Merit semifinalists.

She is Melissa Leigh Newton, one of our five granddaughters, now 17 -- within a month of my age when I graduated from high school 49 years ago -- and one of those spotlighted at Wright School last week.

Has it been almost 18 years since Missy arrived - and to a degree, took command of our lives? Undoubtedly for her the time-span of these years was much greater than for her grandparents. We were hardly used to her being in high school, and now she is headed for Birmingham Southern College in pursuit of a career in medicine.

Lebanon, Heights' rosters of Generals 'impressive'

• *May, 2002*

The headline in the newspaper read: "Lord takes command."

Your first thought is, "great, this is wonderful," then you realize you are reading an Air Force base publication and the subject of the story is not the Lord, but Gen. Lance Lord, who grew up in Lebanon [son of Oscar and Patti Lord]. The general now is the new commander of AFSPC (which the base newspaper did not spell out but which means Air Force Space Program Command -- I think).

Gen. Lance Lord, Heights '64.

The new four-star general attended and graduated from Castle Heights in 1964, where he played football and was a cadet leader, en route to a degree from Oberlin College in Ohio and then into the US Air Force. During his distinguished career, he was in the mid-90s the Director of Plans, Headquarters Air Force Space Command in Colorado.

A second current Air Force officer with a Heights connection: Maj. Gen. John Bradley. He was born in Lebanon, grew up on the Academy campus where his father, Leonard Bradley, was headmaster; graduated from Heights in 1963, then the University of Tennessee where he was in Air Force ROTC. General Bradley is now deputy commander, Joint Task Force-Computer Network Operations, U. S. Space Command, Arlington, Va. [He retired in 2008 as Lieutenant General, with more than 7,000 hours in fighter aircraft.]

Lt. Gen. John Bradley, Heights '63.

And there is another general, born in Lebanon, with a Heights connection.

Maj. Gen. John J. Ryneska -- West Point class of 1968 -- is deputy commanding general, 18th Airborne Corps, Ft. Bragg, N. C. He may be the least known of the local corps of generals. He was born here while his father, Lt. Col. Joseph. Ryneska, was Professor of Military Science and Tactics [PMS+T] at Castle Heights [1946-48]. Colonel Ryneska served in the South Pacific under CHMA alum Maj. Gen. William H. Arnold.

General Wesley Clark, who attended Heights in 1959-60 and was a swimmer on Coach/Maj. Robert B. Hosier's team, is now retired after serving as commander of NATO forces during the action which led to the fall of Slobadan Milosavic, the Serbian president of Yugoslavia.

Brig. Gen. Sandra Gregory Bradley.

General Clark was a center of political controversy which led to his early retirement and aborted a career that some thought would lead to head of the Joint Chiefs of Staff.

Yet still another high ranking Air Force officer with a Lebanon connection -- on the list awaiting Congressional approval for promotion to general -- is Col. Sandra Gregory. She never lived in Lebanon, but is the wife of US Air Force Col. Thomas Bradley [John Bradley's brother], who is a 1969 graduate of Heights. *[Colonel Gregory got Senate confirmation in 2002, and was made Brig. General in 2003. She retired in 2006 with more than 29 years' active service.]*

A footnote to Lance Lord's Lebanon connection: His grandfather owned and operated for many years a variety store, then known as a Five and Ten, on the northeast corner of the Lebanon Square. His uncle, Buddy Welty, continued the operation until a few years before his death.

• Up until the 1960s, Castle Heights' highest ranking alumnus in military service was Lt. Gen. William H. Arnold. A native of Dyersburg, Tenn., General Arnold graduated from CHMA in 1920 "with honors" before going to West Point, where he ranked high in the 1924 class. He commanded the American Division in the Philippines during the Korean war. He wore the Legion of Merit with Oak Leaf Cluster, two Bronze Stars, Air Medal, Silver Star, and the Distinguished Service Medal [including two for WWII]. In 1945 in a message to Heights cadets: "What you learn today will be of inestimable benefit to you tomorrow and all the years to come. Some day, in the field of battle or field of human endeavor, those things will be required." He died in 1976.

A good story and often repeated
• *June, 1996*

A stranger, age about 66, stood before me in my office, sent there by someone who knew I knew some of the story of Castle Heights Military Academy.

"Are you JB Leftwich?" he asked, after identifying himself as a former cadet.

I acknowledged my identity, but obviously he didn't remember me. That was all right, I didn't remember him, either.

"My name is Tom McKenna, Heights Class of 1948," he said.

I remembered the name, not the person. Tom had come to Castle Heights for his senior year only, graduated and disappeared from the Academy's mailing list.

He asked about Dan Kendall, D. T. Ingram, Harry Armstrong -- all chief administrators during his brief stint at Heights.

All dead, I told him.

Lindsey Donnell, Ernest Stockton?

Both deceased.

His classmates, Charlie Steen and Art Shemwell?

They, too.

Tom had come to Castle Heights because his academics needed reinforcement.

"Never failed anything, but didn't make the grades my parents thought I was capable of making," he said. Then he looked away, remembering: "Castle Heights did a lot for me. I went from a C student to an A student. Even challenged the valedictorian and salutatorian."

It's an old story, repeated many times to those of us who had the good fortune to teach at Heights. We saw the improvement over and over. I suspect that we never quite understood how our methods worked, but they did. Not always, of course, but enough to give us bragging rights. I think the Academy just provided the right academic environment for many boys. And later, girls.

What makes this story interesting to me is a column I had just finished on the very subject Tom and I discussed ….about how so many boys got their bearings on the Heights Hilltop. About how the school stressed first academics, then athletics, then military, and so on. About how Heights was not training boys for military service.

"I supposed you are retired now," I said. "But from what?"

"The United States Army," he said. "I am a retired lieutenant colonel."

Earl Major '61, now a retired captain, had a distinguished career in the Navy. He is a son of Helen Major of Lebanon, and the late Will Earl Major.

Two 1962 Heights graduates from Lebanon advanced to the rank of commander in the Navy. James R. Jewell Jr., son of Jimmy and Estelle Jewell of Lebanon, is now retired. LeRoy Dowdy, son of Emmy Lou Dowdy and the late Roy Dowdy of Lebanon, remains in the Navy reserves.

One other Heights alumnus of that general era merits mention. Lt. Commander John Sweatt '59, son of the late Heights educator John L. and Mary Dee Sweatt, also is now retired from the Navy.

• After a 28-year US Army career, Thomas P. McKenna retired as a Lieutenant Colonel in 1975. In 2011, at 82, he published *Kontum: The Battle to Save South Vietnam* [a 1972 battle in which he participated], and in 2013 it was named winner of the William E. Colby Award for "significant contribution to the public's understanding of intelligence operations, military history or international affairs." [Previous Colby winners include James Bradley's *Flags of Our Fathers*]. After graduating from CHMA in 1948, McKenna joined the 82nd Airborne Division then under command of Lt. Col. William Westmoreland, chief of staff; he graduated from West Point in 1953, and became a career Army infantry officer, serving more than eight years abroad. He graduated from the Command & General Staff College in 1970, and in 1971 earned an MA, University of Kansas. Service decorations include Combat Infantry Badge, Legion of Merit, four Silver Stars (two for valor), Purple Heart, Meritorious Service Medal, two Commendation Medals, Vietnamese Gallantry Cross [with silver star] and South African Parachute Wings. He lives in Stowe, Vt., with his wife, Ann. In 2014, McKenna published a second book, *From Vicksburg to Cedar Creek*, an account of a Civil War regiment in which his grandfather served.

The dawn of an old 'New Day'
• *January, 1997*

During the more than a decade since Castle Heights closed its doors in 1986, most of us have dreamed of a miracle that would save the Mitchell House, the flagship of Lebanon mansions and once the nerve center of the Academy's junior school.

Dan Evins as '53 senior.

There have been short-lived attempts to generate funds and sponsors who would dig deep and restore the historic house. Many of us have engaged in wishful thinking . . . . and wistful thinking. Realistically, most of us thought it was a lost cause. And most of us hated to see it deteriorate day by day.

"The best thing that could happen to Mitchell House would be a giant sinkhole," I frequently said. "I just wish the earth would swallow it and magically grass would start growing where it once stood."

Comes now to the rescue Dan Evins, Heights class of '53, Lebanon's own and president and co-founder of the Cracker Barrel, Lebanon's home-grown national restaurant empire -- probably the only combination willing and capable of performing the miracle required to restore Mitchell House to the beauty and prominence it enjoyed in days of yore.

There is more.

The package purchased by Cracker Barrel includes Macfadden Auditorium, the once magnificent site of cadet assemblies, school-produced Gilbert and Sullivan operettas, commencement exercises, and countless community activities.

I have a personal attachment to the Auditorium. When I began teaching at Heights in September, 1941, that facility was still under construction. It was completed during Christmas break and when classes resumed, I was assigned Classroom 5 in the basement.

Indeed, I saw Macfadden Auditorium born and I saw it dying. I hope to be present for its resurrection.

Without Dan Evins, there would be no hope of either's resurrection.

Dan was a champion wrestler at Heights, and later assisted Capt. Merlin Sanders in coaching the team. And still later, he was Chairman of the Board of the Castle Heights Foundation, an organization formed to buy the Academy and nurture it for 12 years after the Bernarr Macfadden Foundation floundered in 1974. (*Continued page 123*)

The Mitchell House by 1997, empty for a decade, suffered severe water damage and overall interior and exterior decay. Project architect Mike Manous said, "[the building] was in horrible shape. Neglect and years the school was so strapped for maintenance funding [put] the structure on a long, slow decline from the very day it was finished."

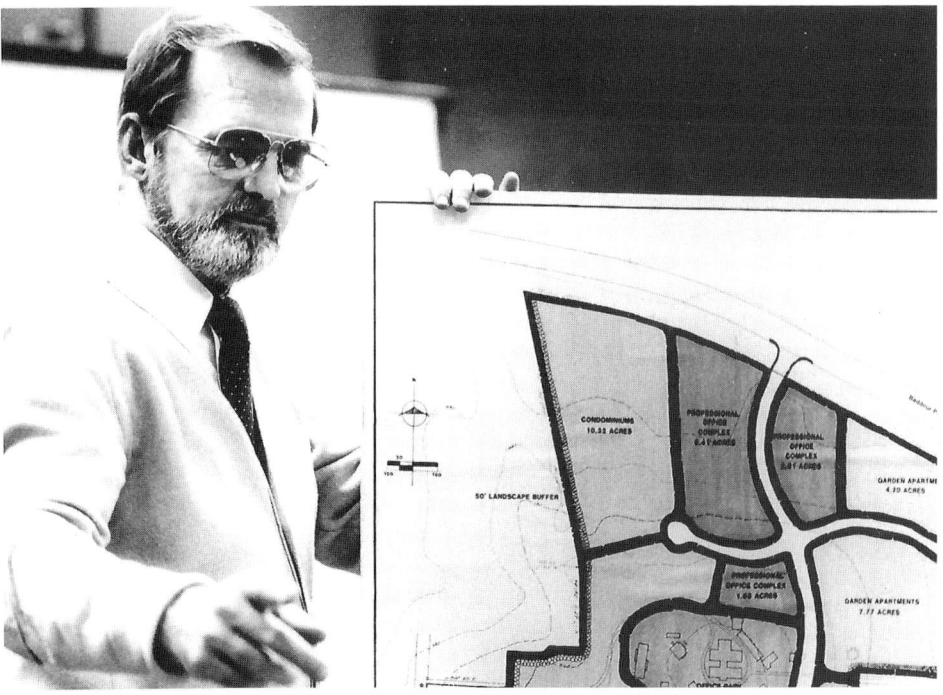

Dan Evins '53 as chairman of the Castle Heights Foundation, which bought the Academy in 1974 from the Macfadden Foundation, requested in the mid-80s zoning changes to make the Heights campus more valuable to increase its loan value -- an effort that, while approved, did not provide sufficient funding. Evins and his corporation saved The Hilltop's Mitchell House, restoring it by late 1998 to serve as CBRL Group Inc.'s executive offices.

Restoration of the Mitchell House by Dan Evins '53 to serve as CBRL Group, Inc., corporate headquarters features several tributes to Castle Heights and its history, including brick courtyard with every grads' name and the CHMA seal. Built 1906-10 by David and Elizabeth Mitchell as a family residence, the house served from 1936-86 as the home of CHMA's Junior School [or the "Goober School," as known by Senior School students] -- where some cadets lived and attended classes.

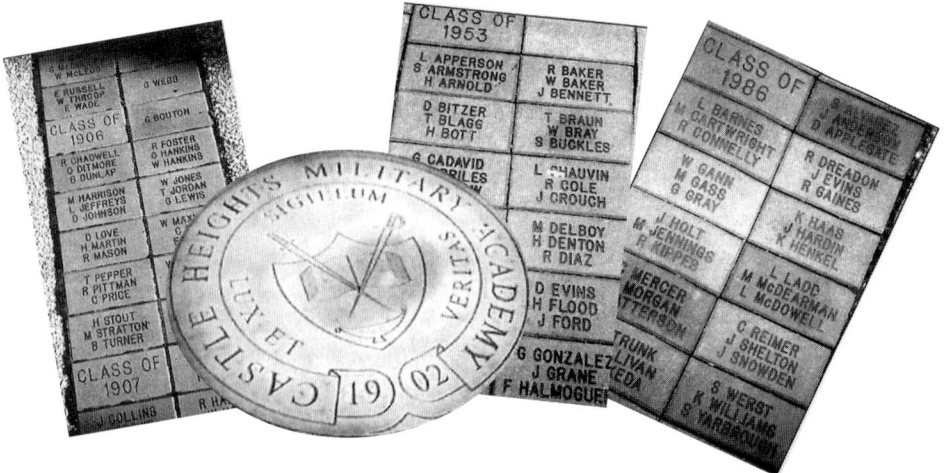

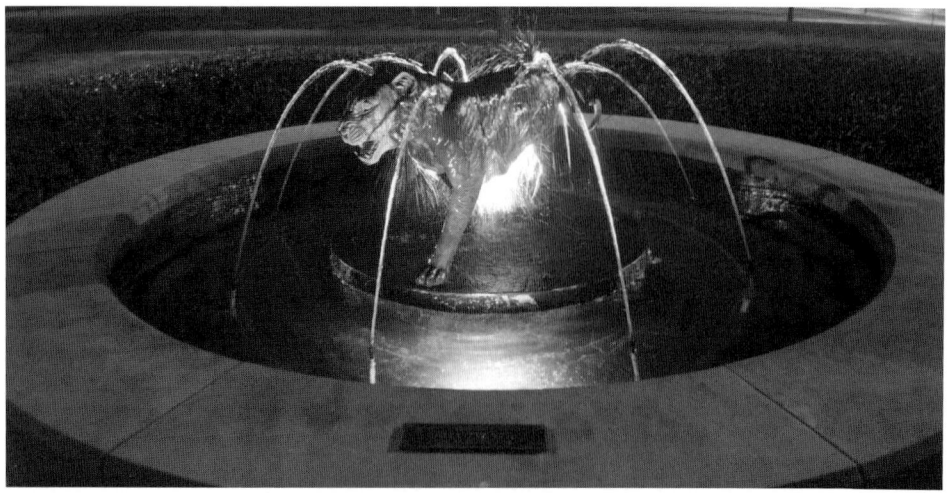

Lawn fountain featuring CHMA tiger mascot now at Mitchell House.

Though not always a welcomed activity by cadets, the Sunday spring afternoon formal parades were a Lebanon attraction and offered the Castle Heights corps the opportunity to show off its military routines -- including the award-winning drill team procedures and sounds of the CHMA band.

It was Evins' sad duty to officiate at the 1986 funeral of the Academy. After it became evident no miracle was going to save it from collapse, Dan and the Board made the decision to close its doors.

This was agonizing. I know. I was a member of the Board during many of the years it fought impending demise. The final decision was especially difficult for Dan Evins, the gritty wrestling champion who doesn't yield without a fight. There probably were some who wanted to kill the messenger when word the Academy would close reached the public. No one regretted the final decision more than those who made it. No one worked harder than Dan Evins to avoid the conditions that dictated that decision.

And now to the delight of every Castle Heights alumnus and of the residents of this community, two great old buildings may be saved. Coupled with Buchanan Hall [CHMA's Main, as it was known, now the proud Lebanon City Hall], the proposed restorations will preserve much of the heart of the Academy complex.

All three buildings will serve residents of this city and county.

I can think of nothing more exciting than this recent announcement. Our community owes its gratitude to Cracker Barrel.

And to Danny Evins.

• The "new" Mitchell House reopened in 1997 includes on the east lawn the CHMA Memorial Gardens featuring engraved brick pavers with the names of every CHMA graduate from 1905-1986 -- surrounding the school seal. Also prominent is a large fountain with a metal tiger, representing the Academy mascot.

• As for Macfadden Auditorium, no attempt was made to restore it due to remodeling cost projections and physical conditions. Efforts by CBRL Group, Inc. to sell the structure continued for more than a decade until 2010, when it was demolished.

Somber thoughts on Memorial Day
• *May, 2010*

An email from Charles Baird Jr. '65, my friend and a former student, prompted sober thoughts Monday as millions of Americans observed Memorial Day.

The email included a web address for the Vietnam Memorial Wall. The author of the website has entered by states all of the fatalities in this country's last of the four extensive wars of the previous century. Clicking on a state and selecting a town or city easily accessed the site.

This I did, and found the name of SFC Clyde Ward '55.

His nickname was "Coppie," and he was an undersized football player who made the Heights team of 1954, and who yearned for an appointment to the United States Military Academy and an Army career.

Coppie never made it to West Point, but he enlisted in the U. S. Army and fought in Vietnam, where he was fatally wounded May 21, 1967. He was 30 years old.

Seven from Lebanon are listed on the site, including Ward and two of our daughter Barbara's Lebanon High School classmates: SP4 Jerry Lancaster and CPL Terry Dillard.

Thus I was prompted Monday on Memorial Day to visit the Castle Heights War Memorial located on the campus immediately in front of Main Building, now Lebanon City Hall.

I read the names of alumni who fell in three wars, remembering most of them as lively and sometimes mischievous cadets, typical of their generations and, in some cases, members of my generation.

There was Leslie Lilenthal, son of the CEO of the Tennessee Valley Authority, at Heights only during his senior year, who made an impression on the corps and on the faculty with his robust sense of humor and his ability to laugh at himself. Leslie was a casualty of World War II.

There was William Sleyster, Leslie's classmate, a Mid-South Conference wrestling champion, who died when a vehicle struck him as he marched in ranks while in training. Bill

William Sleyster as '42 senior.

was in one of my algebra classes, but his mind was not entirely focused on math. There usually was a bit of mischief lurking in his brain cells.

There was Capt. LeGrand Brown, son of two Heights teachers, who served in Vietnam, contracted a deadly disease and died after the war.

And Thane Hooker, battalion commander and *The Cavalier* editor who was in the Army before Pearl Harbor, survived the famed Death March in the Philippines but later was killed by enemy fire.

Other names on the Heights Memorial revived contemplative thoughts and evoked melancholy just as poignant. But passing decades eroded memories, and faces matching some names did not come to mind.

My thoughts wandered to my own classmates, boys entering adulthood in my senior class at Cumberland University who soon after graduation donned military uniforms. I thought of Jimmy Fisher of Carthage, one of the finest basketball talents in the country when he played for the Bulldogs. Jimmy died in the Pacific Theater when a transport plane with him aboard crashed.

And Joe Raymond Carter, a fine athlete and sports editor of the CU student newspaper I edited. My fading memory could not recall the circumstances of his wartime death.

And Joe Wright, close friend and a Wilson County native who joined the Army Air Force and died in an airplane crash in this country.

Most of the boys in my own high school class served in the armed forces during World War II. Remarkably, not one of them was a World War II fatality.

Memorial Day is a federal holiday first enacted to honor Union soldiers after the Civil War, but extended later to honor American veterans of all wars. It originally was known as Decoration Day. When I was a lad, it had been extended to honor veterans and non-veterans alike.

In my youth, Decoration Day was a festive occasion for kids and a reunion for families who gathered at cemeteries, brought picnic food and enjoyed visits and renewals. Anticipation among young people was as keen for Decoration Day as for Independence Day.

On this particular Memorial Day, my somber mood needed a transfusion from the more festive mood of my youth's Decoration Days.

Remembering Jerry, other vital Tennessee journalists

• Published *February, 2000*

The death of few newspaper writers has affected readers as deeply as did the January death of Jerry Thompson whose blue collar column, "Thompson's Station," was a longtime feature of the *Nashville Tennessean*. Most of his readers felt as if they knew him personally, and some, including me, did. He died after a 12-year battle with cancer.

Jerry became a staff member during my tenure as a state correspondent for the Nashville newspaper. For a brief period, he was in charge of the state news desk and rode herd on all of us part-time reporters; he also helped train Al Gore as a reporter. Thompson won a Pulitzer Prize nomination for his 16-month 1979-80 undercover investigative report of the Ku Klux Klan.

The affection his associates at *The Tennessean* felt for Jerry was similar to the feeling they felt for the late Herman Eskew who, as city editor, trained many of the current crew. Herman, a close personal friend who lived all of his life in Lebanon and graduated from Heights and Cumberland University, was as much teacher as journalist. Among those he taught on the staff was young reporter Jim Squires, who later became editor of the *Chicago Tribune*. Russ Finney was another boss. He was a good newspaperman, but loved to nit-pick. If I wrote "simultaneous," Russ would change it to, "at the same time."

This became a game. At every opportunity, I would write either "simultaneous" or "at the same time," and it would always come out in the opposite. Finally, I caught on that he had caught on to the ruse and was changing the word or phrase because I expected it of him. Another thing: I was paid well, often more than I deserved. In the early years, I clipped and pasted together all stories I wrote and sent the "string" to my editor who sent me a check. Hence, the word "stringer" for us non-staffers. My pay in the early part of my stint was 10 cents per inch, and $3.00 per picture. It was fair pay. Later, I billed on an hourly rate. My bills were never questioned.

In many ways, I was fortunate. I loved working for a good newspaper, and I loved teaching. Though newspapering was sometimes boring. I spent one Christmas Day in the Wilson County jail (office, that is) waiting for a well known prisoner to arrive. I endured many long sessions of boards, commissions, councils and committees.

It also could be exhilarating. There was nothing more gratifying than seeing your story on page one. And there was nothing more pleasing than knowing the staffers who went on to fame. Or those who remained with *The Tennessean*.

Like Thompson in Nashville, editors of the *Lebanon Democrat* have had an important impact on this community. The ones I knew were unique each in his own way. The legendary Dixon Merritt was a nationally respected journalist who is best remembered for what he termed a trivial piece but was secretly proud of and is known universally as "the Pelican Limerick."

J. Bill Frame was a mover and shaker in the community who left during the prime of his career to fight in a world war. He returned to motivate and initiate many movements which led to progress and improvement in Lebanon.

G. Frank Burns also had two careers -- in journalism and in education. He retired from the *Democrat*, earned his Ph.D. and taught in two universities. As a historian, he may know more about Lebanon and Wilson County than any other person in the history of this area.

Carl Wallace -- Maj. Gen. Carl Wallace who served in Korea -- became editor when the newspaper changed hands about 30 years ago. He brought the publication into the modern era, changing it to a daily newspaper with an aggressive quest for the news. He was gifted at developing news sources and news stories which often jarred and energized the community. Carl was instrumental in 1974 in forming the Castle Heights Foundation which bought the Academy from the Bernarr Macfadden Foundation and kept the school open 12 more years.

Maj. Gen. Carl Wallace, Tennessee Adjutant General 1975-81, was vital to CHMA mid-'70s survival and a key *Lebanon Democrat* editor.

Wallace was appointed State of Tennessee Adjutant General in 1975, serving in that position until 1981. Upon retirement on 1991, he was appointed the first Chancellor of Cumberland University, his alma mater.

PAUL ULBRICH
Wrestling
Winner, 157 pound class

RANDY THORNTON
Swimming
Winner, 100 Yard Butterfly

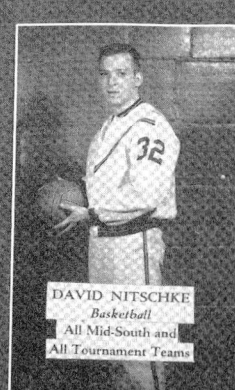

DAVID NITSCHKE
Basketball
All Mid-South and
All Tournament Teams

CROCKETT CARR
Basketball
All Tournament Team

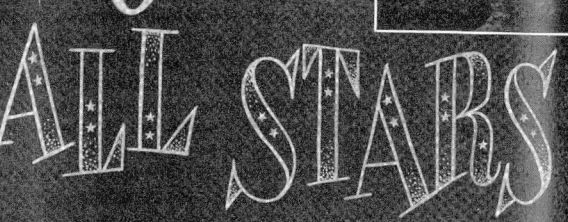

JOSH NUNN
Basketball
All Mid-South Team

Mid-South
ALL STARS

BOBBY HAYNES
Football
All Mid-South Guard

BUTCH RUSSO
Wrestling
Winner, 167 pound class

JIMMY WILSON
Track, 1958
Winner, 100 yard dash

Chapter Four
Athletics

"Every boy will some day be a man; and it should be his one ambition to be a strong man -- strong in mind and body. With such a physical equipment as a beginning, he should be able to reach this highest possible development mentally, morally and spiritually."
                                    - Bernarr Macfadden

THE DRILL:
JB Leftwich loved sports, and took pleasure in photographing and writing about the coaches, athletes and teams of Castle Heights Military Academy. And during his 38 years on The Hilltop, athletics were an important and winning part of the cadet experience. As a member of the Mid-South Athletics Conference, Heights teams excelled in football, basketball, swimming and wrestling, and each year fielded competitive squads in cross country, soccer, track, baseball, golf and tennis.

Overleaf Photo:
Exemplifying annual CHMA team and individual accomplishments are these 1958-59 Mid-South Conference All-Stars.

Photo Credit:
Individual *Adjutant* photos by JB Leftwich

A cure for walking monotony
• *October, 1987*

The walking fad — and a desire to prolong our years — has caught up with me and my wife, so on a regular basis we grind the cinders of what used to be the Castle Heights track, which circled the school's football field.

For us, this is familiar territory; for 38 years I was a member of the Academy staff and one of the most ardent fans of the school's teams.

One day, as we walked, my wife suggested we walk half of the laps in one direction, then reverse the pattern for the last half.

"It might help break the monotony," she said with good reason.

"But it's not monotonous," I said. "See that spot over there? That's where Earl Cato began a 90-yard touchdown run in 1953. I was on the sideline with a camera, and Earl cut across field so I could take his picture. He did this more than once, you know.

"And that spot? That's where Pat Parker in 1942 took the second half kickoff and ran 84 yards for a touchdown. The game was scoreless up to that point, but we went on to beat Baylor 26-0 in what was considered an upset victory.

"And there? That's where Forest Atkins gathered in a punt and ran 52 yards for a touchdown in 1951 against Columbia Military Academy. There's where O.E. Philpot threw the block that sprung him loose. We won 7-0, because Johnny Ingram [son of Col. Dan T. Ingram] scooped a pass out of the hands of CMA's big end, Bob Burford, in the end zone.

"That sideline mark? That's where Coach Stroud Gwynn used to pace and worry. His team could be ahead 25 in the fourth quarter, but he would imagine the opponent scoring four TDs in the last four minutes.

"Here's where Dick Inman threw a block that opened the lane for Billy Ford to run 79 yards for a touchdown against McCallie in 1949. Heights won that one 27-7.

"Now it's Homecoming 1961, and we're playing CMA in a tight one. There's the one-yard line where Jimmy Gamble plunged over for the tying touchdown. We won 7-6.

"Let's go back to 1957. There's Bobo Bradshaw recovering three fumbles in the Homecoming game against McCallie, a really powerful team. It's just before halftime and McCallie is on our two-yard line with first down. Lined up for Heights on defense are Gardner Smith, Bobo, Curry Vaughan, John Giangiacomo, Lowell Smith and Mark Thompson. Now it's second and two, then third and two, then fourth and two. Then it's Heights' ball, and there's the one-yard line where our fullback

Claude Maynard plunged for the only touchdown.

"In 1953, Georgia Military Academy [GMA] scored with a screen pass on the games' first play. Harold Greer, our captain, is on the ground somewhat addled from a blow to the head. Coach Gwynn asks him a simple question to determine how addled he really is: 'What do you know, Harold?' Responded Harold, 'I know we're going to win this damn football game.' We did, 40-12.

US Army Brig. Gen. Robert R. Neyland, winner of seven Southeastern Conference and four national championships as University of Tennessee football coach, congratulates his son, Lewis, on being named Heights 1951-52 "Outstanding Athlete."

"It's 1964, we're undefeated, and we're playing Baylor in the season's final game. It's scoreless, and Bobby Gwynn [son of Coach Gwynn] and Jimmy Adkins, our receivers, are racing down the field. Pinckney Guerard spots Adkins and completes a 24-yard touchdown pass. Later in the end zone, Adkins intercepted a game-saving pass. We won 6-0.

"Imagine it's Halloween 1951. We're not a strong team, and we're playing GMA, one of the best prep teams in the south. There are the Rosenbaum twins and Lewis Neyland [son of Tennessee Coach Robert Neyland] and Hamlet Halbert and there's Bobby Glover sprinting in for his second touchdown in a 13-6 upset."

I guess I made my point with her. Maybe I over-made it. She's never mentioned monotony again.

Future attorney, future monk 'match' wits
• *May, 2006*

Hugh Green is a successful Lebanon attorney, a force in the community, and one of five brothers who graduated from Castle Heights.

Randy Weinberg is a Baylor School alumnus, a magna cum laude graduate of Princeton University, a Rhodes Scholar, and became for more than a decade a monk. Question: So, how did the lives of Hugh Green and Randy Weinberg intersect?

Answer: On wrestling mats when they years ago were prep athletes competing in the old Mid-South Conference.

Baylor dominated conference wrestling. Coached by Luke Worsham, recently inducted into the Tennessee Sports Hall of Fame, Baylor had a run of championships probably un-

Hugh Green as '69 senior.

equaled in any Tennessee conference. Baylor was Mid-South wrestling champions 14 times and runners-up five. Randy Weinberg, who won the championship in his class five times, may have been the greatest wrestler the old conference ever produced. Randy wrestled as an eighth grader and four years in high school, and in addition to conference accomplishments won the National Prep tournament.

According to an article in *Sun Magazine*, published in Chapel Hill, NC, "[Weinberg] went on to wrestle at Princeton, where he was injured his freshman year and had to have four shoulder screws. With his wrestling career over, he initially planned to become a doctor, but after graduating in 1974 with honors, Weinberg won a Rhodes Scholarship to Oxford. He was writing his master's thesis on mysticism/science/art in the works of Aldous Huxley when he developed an interest in Buddhism. He became captivated by the quest for enlightenment ...became a monk and eventually returned to England to help establish a monastery."

Attorney Green, circa 1990s.

Hugh Green, a highly skilled wrestler, had the misfortune to be in the same weight division with Weinberg. So, how did Hugh manage to win the title during Randy's dominating years?

Here is Hugh's story:

"I was able to win my junior year [1968] because Randy dropped a weight class just for the Mid-South tournament, held one week right after our close match in Heights' gym. It was not unusual for wrestlers to deliberately lose weight and fall into a lower weight class.

"I have not spoken with him since he beat me in the '69 tournament. I was in no mood to talk. I wanted to be a two-time champion, and I wanted it bad. He prevented me from reaching my goal, and we went our separate ways. I suppose we both learned from those matches, but I liked the lessons he learned a lot better than the ones I learned.

"Years later, I heard he became a monk. That made me feel better, because wrestling at the championship level requires a lot of discipline; I told myself I never had a prayer of beating someone who had the discipline and fortitude to become a monk."

There were three Weinberg brothers at Baylor. Each was a conference wrestling champion, and each was valedictorian of his senior class.

"Randy's brother, Sandy, became a United States attorney, and while in that position prosecuted Marc Rich, the billionaire arms dealer pardoned by President Bill Clinton at the end of his administration, creating an uproar," Hugh said.

"Randy may have been the most accomplished person to graduate from Baylor, where he was not only valedictorian and champion wrestler, but editor of his school newspaper and an accomplished musician. He certainly was the most unusual and talented individual I ever had the pleasure of coming up against."

Weinberg, now known as Kittisaro, left the order in 1991 and eventually married a former Buddhist nun. They organized Dharmagiri, a Buddhist hermitage in rural South Africa where they work on the AIDS crisis and other humanitarian causes.. The remainder of the year, he teaches/preaches throughout this country and Europe.

The former monk and wrestler recently returned to Baylor, and made a talk in which he referred to his match with Hugh Green [but mentioned no names] in the Castle Heights gymnasium that prompted his decision to drop to a lower weight class for the 1968 tournament -- and paved the way for Hugh's march to the championship.

o o o

Luke Worsham's Baylor teams were so dominant and confident that they won by lop-sided scores in most of their dual matches. This prompted Coach Worsham, in the spirit of good sportsmanship, to offer a wrestling clinic for the losing team. At Heights, following a match, each of Baylor's winners would instruct his losing opponent, often offering valuable pointers.

o o o

Hugh Green also remembers an awkward young athlete from Baylor who, during a track meet, hit Heights Coach Stroud Gwynn in the face with a discus.

"He got to spinning around, and lost his bearings," Hugh said. "I thought he had killed Coach Gwynn, but Coach was just bruised."

This young athlete became a legend in football, played for Coach Bear Bryant at Alabama, and later was an all-pro lineman 10 times for the New England Patriots, where he played 13 seasons.

"From what I have read about him, he always gave more credit to Coach Worsham than to Coach Bryant" Hugh said. "I read he is returning to Baylor to coach."

His name: John Hannah.

• After graduating Cum Honore at Heights, Green attended Vanderbilt before transferring to University of Tennessee-Martin in order to wrestle. Earned BS in 1973, MS from Memphis State in 1975, and JD from UT [Knoxville] 1978. Opened firm in Lebanon in 1984, serving as trial attorney; appointed to Tennessee Post-Conviction Defender Committee, served as hearing committee member for Tennessee Board of Professional Responsibility, and was Tennessee Trial Lawyers Association board member. His peers in 1997 selected him to the American Board of Trial Advocates. Continues to live in Lebanon with wife, daughter.

• Four other Green brothers -- all five the sons of Dr. and Mrs. Hugh Edward Green Sr., of Carthage, Tenn. -- also were members of the Academy wrestling team:

James. N. Green '64 – BS from Tennessee Tech, 1968; MBA University of Tennessee, 1969. Official with Commerce Union Bank in early '70's, then owner of international timber export business until 2001. One of 1974 organizers of CHMA Foundation [and Board of Trustees member] to buy Academy from Macfadden Foundation. Currently resides in Santa Rosa Beach, Fla., and has three children, nine grandchildren.

Johnny Green '72 – Attended Middle Tennessee State University, worked with James in export business, and was a banker at time of his death from car accident in 1981.

Joe Green '77 – Attended Tennessee Tech University, engaged in farming and business. Resides with wife in Smith County, Tenn., and they have nine children, six grandchildren.

Jack Green '79 -- Cum Honore Heights grad. BS, Tennessee Tech, 1983. Worked as *Nashville Banner* correspondent before receiving JD from Memphis State, 1986. Judicial Selection Commission for State of Tennessee, 2002-09; with Shelby County Public Defender's Office, Memphis, Tenn., since 1988, and currently supervising attorney.

Historic Mid-South Conference produced many outstanding athletes

 In most of his columns about Castle Heights Military Academy athletes and coaches, and even in some written to cover other topics, JB Leftwich referenced the Academy's participation in the Mid-South Athletic Association [M-SAA] -- sometimes referred to in media coverage as the Mid-South Conference.

Research on the Association and its member schools did not result in a worthwhile or definitive history. Through contact with **John McCall** [former student, athlete, 1961 grad and teacher at longtime M-SAA member and power McCallie School [Chattanooga, Tenn.] - now serving as McCallie School Archivist/Historian] and **B. B. Branton** of <u>Chattanoogan.com</u>, we have compiled a general history of a sports organization of which Castle Heights was a proud and strong member for more than 35 years.

o o o

According to McCall: "McCallie's participation in the M-SAA began in 1933, and that is the year I believe the league was founded. Prior, some of our school's teams participated in the Tennessee Interscholastic Athletic Association. As a 1955-61 student at McCallie, I was active on the wrestling and cross-country teams, and have a clear memory of running in 1961 against Ricky Rogers at Heights. During those years, our best competition after Baylor [another Chattanooga prep school] within the Mid-South came from Castle Heights and St. Andrews [now St. Andrews-Sewanee], but by 1970 the league had come to be dominated by Baylor and McCallie."

McCall said with disbanding of the M-SAA at the end of the 1969-70 school year, most of the schools joined the Tennessee Secondary School Athletic Association, thus ending post-graduates eligibility [graduates of high schools who wanted additional academic and athletic training prior to college].

In addition to McCallie, Baylor and Heights, McCall and Branton indicate these were M-SAA teams for all or part of the league's existence [with some schools not competing in all sports]:

Battle Ground Academy
Franklin, Tenn., established 1889. Still operating 2014.

* Columbia Military Academy
Columbia, Tenn., 1905-1978.
[Reorganized 1979 as Columbia Academy, Christian day school.]

Darlington School
Rome, Ga., established 1905, became coeducational 1973.
^ *Will Muschamp* [football], University of Florida head football coach.

Father Ryan
Nashville, Tenn., established 1925; continues as large high school.

Georgia Military Academy
College Park, Ga., founded in 1900. Became co-educational in 1964, renamed Woodward Academy 1966, boarding discontinued 1993. Now pre-k – 12, and largest independent private school in continental U.S.
^ *Robert Woodruff*, former president Coca-Cola; *Sterling Holloway*, actor; *Phil Gramm*, former U.S. Senator.

Marion Military Institute
Marion, Ala., established 1842; now offers two- and four-year college degrees, with special one-year service academies prep for high school graduates.

Montgomery Bell Academy
Nashville, Tenn., established 1867 as grammar and high school.

Notre Dame Academy
Chattanooga, Tenn., established 1876 with grades nine-12; became coeducational in 1898 as Notre Dame School, and inter-parochial in 1954 as Notre Dame High School.

Riverside Military Academy
Gainesville, Ga., established 1907, grades 7-12, remains male only. For about 40 years starting in 1930, RMA maintained second campus in Hollywood, Fla., with cadets splitting school year. Endowment reached $120 million.
^ *Tommy Prothro* [football], UCLA and Oregon State head coach; *Mickey Mantle Jr.* [baseball]; *Red Sanders*, college football coach.

St. Andrews
* Sewanee Military Academy
Two schools linked by location [Sewanee, Tenn.] and founding entity - Episcopal Church. *Sewanee Academy* founded in 1867 as junior department of University of the South, and became Sewanee Military Academy in 1909. Military program dropped in 1971, and SMA returned to Sewanee Academy. *St. Andrews* established in 1905 on same campus, as was third school -- *St. Mary's School for Girls*, operated from 1896-1968. St. Andrews and SMA became co-educational in 1969, and schools merged in 1981 to become present

St. Andrew's-Sewanee School with boarding and day students grades six-12.
^ *Bill Harlow* [wrestling], NCAA title 1966, World Silver Medal early '70s; *Kix Brooks*, country music

* Tennessee Military Institute
Sweetwater, Tenn., established 1888, closed 1988.

Webb School
Founded 1955 in Knoxville to become third Webb family school -- first in Bell Buckle, Tenn.; second in Claremont, Ca. Webb of Knoxville became co-ed 1968, added middle school 1974, and 1998 expanded to K-12.
^ *Bill Haslam* [football, basketball, track, baseball], Governor of Tennessee; *Chad Pennington* [football, baseball, basketball], NFL career with New York Jets, Miami Dolphins.

Baylor notables according to Branton include *John Hannah* [football, wrestling], Pro Football Hall of Fame; *Hugh Beaumont* [football, baseball], played Ward Cleaver on "Leave It To Beaver." Branton reports **McCallie** graduated *Carroll Campbell* [swimming], Governor of South Carolina; *Bill Brock* [soccer], U.S. Senator; broadcast mogul *Ted Turner*, plus a former MIT president.

CMA, SMA, TMI and CHMA no longer exist.

A football team to remember

• *October, 1994*

In a recent letter to one of my former *Cavalier* editors, I discussed the Academy Homecoming this weekend and mentioned the Class of 1944, who will be here for its 50th reunion.

"What makes this reunion especially interesting is the Mid-South Conference champion football team of 1943. Most of them were members of the '44 class," I wrote. Then I added: "I can name every starter on that team -- 12 of them, in fact, since an early season broken leg took fullback Jimmy Elrod out of action for the rest of the season."

This team above all others, including great ones, sticks in my mind. Rex Twist and Russell Gardner at ends, Bob Page and David Bailey at tackles, Billy Burnett and Don Tanner at guards, Bascom Cooksey Jr. at center, and Pat Parker, Bobby Stewart, Bone Rogers and Jack Spence in the backfield.

The 1943 team was a surprise. Nobody expected the quality of play that developed and carried the team to an undefeated, once-tied season. The 1942 squad, on which most of the '43 team played, was so-so. But in 1943, the team came together, and much of the success is due to the inspiration and skill of Pat Parker.

Nobody would consider an all-time Castle Heights team without Parker, chosen the most valuable player in the Mid-South Conference.

This entrance by a late '60s CHMA Tigers squad was typical of the cadet corps excitement, support of Academy football teams throughout the school's history.

In the fading era of triple threat tailbacks, he stands tall. He also was a demon on defense. He was nationally recruited.

In the third game of that season, Heights played Montgomery Bell Academy of Nashville, a school with a proud football heritage. In the first half played on the Heights field, Pat dashed 28 yards for one touchdown and 48 yards for another. At the beginning of the second half, Coach Stroud Gwynn sent Charles "Cajun" Cook to replace Parker. Cook ripped off three touchdowns on runs of 49, 70 and 56 yards.

When the game was over, ecstatic cadets rushed for the Heights bench to ride Pat and Cajun on their shoulders. Pat had disappeared. With the game headed toward a 53-0 rout, he slipped away, gone to the dressing room and thence to his room to study.

Pat's exploits that unforgettable season began in a 13-13 tie. He executed a 60-yard touchdown run, then later intercepted a pass and ran 63 yards to set up a TD by Bobby Stewart, an all-star player himself.

Heights moved with ease past Tennessee Military Institute 42-12, Tullahoma High School 39-6, and in the season finale beat Morgan School 47-0. The real test was supposed to come against McCallie, but Heights, led again by Parker, won 19-0 in a game which the late sportswriter Art Shemwell '45, said could have gone either way.

The rest of the season was expected to be relatively easy for Heights, but the Tigers almost stumbled against Columbia Military Academy, a surprisingly tough foe that year. Heights finally mounted a 61-yard scoring drive with Pat plunging over for the game's lone score.

But this was not a one-man team. Bobby Stewart, who called the plays, was stellar at wingback. Bone Rogers was a bone-crushing blocking back. All-Mid-South tackle Bob Page led an inspired interior line. Center Bascom Cooksey, untried and a doubtful starter at the first of the season, made second team All-Mid-South -- along with Billy Burnett, Stewart and Don Tanner. Rex Twist, who did not play football as a junior, was an all-conference end. Indeed, there were no weak spots on a team that played both offense and defense.

Three of the players, along with Coach Gwynn and Assistant Coach Lindsey Donnell, are deceased. Pat was killed on Okinawa, Tanner suffered a fatal heart attack, and Jim Elrod was killed in a hunting accident.

Last week, I was chatting with alumnus Judge Ernest Pellegrin '48, who remembers 1943 vividly. Said he: "I still can name every starter."

"Gardner and Twist at ends, Page and Bailey at tackles, Burnett and Tanner . . ."

Coach Lucas and the '54 Tigers

• *April, 1991*

In all of his many years at Castle Heights, where Ralph Lucas won more Mid-South basketball championships than any other coach, he never chewed out an official. He sat calmly on the bench and coached. Even when his teams were behind late in the game, he never appeared worried.

I think his teams were inspired by his behavior and won games as a consequence.

Perhaps his most remarkable coaching achievement was in 1954, when his star players -- mostly post graduates -- dropped out of school at the end of the first semester [and end of the football season], leaving inexperienced personnel. His team dropped from a projected winner to a conference patsy.

Baylor, one of the best teams of the era, beat Heights by more than 20 points in the last game of the regular season.

In the Mid-South tournament, played in the home gym of archrival Columbia Military Academy, Heights drew as an open-

Tigers teams coached by Col. Ralph Lucas won 10 Mid-South championships during the league's four decades of existence.

Whether as coach, teacher or Academy superintendent, Colonel Lucas made time to listen to and advise cadets seeking counsel -- here in the Lucas' apartment in Bullard.

After winning Mid-South basketball championships in 1954, 1955 and 1958, this 1961 Tigers team was the school's last conference champion and that of Coach Ralph Lucas, who stepped down in the mid-'60s to devote full time to his Academy administrative duties.

ing round opponent Georgia Military Academy, an unknown quantity which had not participated in season play. Heights came from behind to win 50-49.

In the semifinal game, Heights met undefeated Baylor -- at that time "the University of Nevada-Las Vegas" of the conference -- the product of an excellent athletics program. In much the same fashion that Duke beat UNLV for a national championship, Heights pulled a monumental upset with a 54-50 victory.

The Heights decision over Baylor supposedly eliminated the last major obstacle in McCallie's march to the title. True to form, McCallie surged to a huge first quarter lead while Ralph Lucas serenely viewed the title game looking like a detached spectator.

Late in the first quarter, two busloads of Heights cadets arrived to wage a cheering battle with the CMA cadets, who supported McCallie.

Heights won the cheering contest -- and the basketball game by a margin of two, winning the conference championship on a combined spread of only seven points.

This is one of my fondest memories in 40 years of Castle Heights sports.

Catching up with a Heights legend
• *November, 1996*

Charles Izaguirre, aka Carlos Izaguirre but more popularly known as "Izzy," is a Castle Heights legend of mythical proportions. Or perhaps a myth of legendary proportions.

'Twas in the early 1930s when a young boy from a foreign country arrived alone at the Lebanon railroad depot and began to walk toward his destination. His father, a Honduran diplomat to this country, had placed him on a train and told the conductor to see that the boy made the proper connections.

Walking alone and just age nine, he was offered a ride in a one-horse wagon driven by an employee of Castle Heights Military Academy. Maybe this ride was providential, since Castle Heights was the destination of Izzy -- then known as Carlos -- who

Charles Izaguirre as '41 CHMA senior.

was destined to grow up on the school campus. Perhaps it also was destiny that placed him in the care of Academy junior school house-mothers who nurtured him, loved him and taught him life's values.

By his senior year of 1940-41, there was hardly a soul in these parts who had not heard of the athletic exploits of Izzy and his legendary cohorts -- John North, Hugo Heidenreich, Ray Enders, Tex Robertson, John Sellers, William "Big Daddy" Griffin and others.

"Castle Heights won the Mid-South basketball championship three of the four years I was in school," Izzy recalls.

But he does not tout that he was the pulse of the remarkable groups who wrote their names in the record books. In fact, it was Izzy who set the tone for the entire cadet corps. Probably no more modest athlete ever influenced a student body more than Izaguirre at Castle Heights. His modesty spilled over, and his talented teammates were not moved to swelling their heads and thumping their chests because Izzy didn't let his honors go to his head.

His upper class years became glory years at the Academy. He and his teammates marched triumphantly to the conference championship in football – three times. During the winter months,

Pentagon employee Izaguirre, circa 1990s.

143

Dominating and winning the Baylor Relays, and four individual event trophies, and earning its first Mid-South Conference championship, the 1941 Tigers track team featured a number of quality athletes -- including Charles "Izzy" Izaguirre [third left, first row].

they won the basketball championship, and in the spring, the track championship.

The stories grew and multiplied about the native Indian youth from Central America. Izzy, with his high cheekbones, swarthy complexion and perfect posture, had the looks and the skills that made him the "Jim Thorpe of Castle Heights."

Soon, newspapers were touting the athletic derring-do of this Native American. Apparently, nobody asked Izzy about his ethnic origin.

"Is it true you are an American Indian," I asked the now 70-year-old former star last month when he appeared on campus along with his former teammate, Hugo Heidenreich Jr., for Homecoming '96.

Not so, he said.

"Paul Redick made up that story," said Izzy. "I am no more Indian than you are. Actually, I am Basque, Spanish and Italian."

Paul Redick, story-teller nonpareil now of Franklin, Tenn., was a Castle Heights Junior School instructor during Izzy's tenure on the Hilltop. His story telling skills, like Izzy's athletic exploits, became part of the legend of Castle Heights. It wasn't that Paul was falsifying, he was simply embellishing. He probably had no idea his embellishment would live throughout most of the remainder of the century.

Modest and with no trace of vanity, Izzy was intensely competitive. Because he ran and competed with such grace and ease, some fans did not recognize the fire that propelled him. Izzy's unselfishness and modesty are part of the legend.

One of the great stories which still occasionally surfaces centers on Izzy's performance in the 1941 Mid-South track meet held at the University of the South in Sewanee, Tenn. Leading in the 440-yard event, Izzy glanced back over his shoulder and saw Raymond Enders, his teammate, hot on his heels and well ahead of the Georgia Military Academy runner who was highly favored to win the race. According to legend, Izzy slowed ever so slightly and let his teammate win the race.

"Well, did you?" I asked.

"Pure myth," said Izzy. "Another one of Paul Redick's stories."

Izzy was in the javelin competition when the call came for the 440-yard run. He set aside the javelin, planning to resume competition later, to enter the 440.

"But I wasn't feeling right. Something was wrong. I just didn't have my usual kick. I knew Enders was pressing me, but he won the race on his own. No intentional help from me."

Izzy went on to play on Vanderbilt's wartime informal football team. After the war, he earned his degree at the University of Maryland.

Though not a citizen at the beginning of World War II, causing U. S. Navy officials some consternation, Izzy served meritoriously and subsequently was awarded for his 40 years of Pentagon service.

• After his 1941 Heights graduation, Izaguirre first went to Cumberland then enrolled at Vanderbilt University. Eager to be a part of World War II, he enlisted in the Army at Florida's Camp Blanding as a Signal Corps Sergeant. During training, Izaguirre's father requested his son be discharged for non-citizenship. At Izaguirre's urging, Blanding officers and Judge Advocate General attorneys administered his citizenship oath. Discharged in 1945, he, his sister and mother briefly lived in Mexico before Izaguirre returned to the U.S. and entered the University of Maryland -- where he received a B.S. in business administration. Izaguirre worked for the Naval Air Systems Command in the Pentagon for more than 40 years, retiring in 1985. He received four citations from Chief of Naval Operations for distinguished service during the Vietnam war. He and his wife, Jo, married in 1954, and had four children, two grandsons. Izaguirre died in 2007, at 84, and is buried at Arlington National Cemetery.

• Among **"Guestbook"** entries posted by Kala Funeral Home of Edgewater, Md., in connection with Izaguirre's 2007 services:
"Izzy was poetry, a symphony in motion. He was in his late teens, I in my early 20s, when we both served on the staff of Camp Hy-Lake, a boys summer camp near Quebeck, Tenn. He was in his prime and probably the best athlete I ever knew. And he was a role model for the campers -- a study in grace and graciousness, a model of manhood every father hoped his son would become.
- JB Leftwich, Lebanon, Tenn.

"Izzy came to my hometown when he was 8, to attend Castle Heights Military Academy, and stayed until he graduated in 1941. He is remembered as one, if not the best athlete who ever attended the Academy. I feel fortunate to have known him then and now. You could not have wanted a more wonderful friend."
- Jessie Ruth Hall, Lebanon, Tenn.,
    She is the widow of Izaguirre CHMA teammate James Henry Hall. Hall, originally from Canada, died during World War II [and is listed on the Heights War Memorial] as a member of the Canadian Air Force.

Halloween, snow and great football
• *October, 2002*

As I write this, there are 11 days left in October, the month of changing colors. But so far there has been little change in foliage. Trees remain green, grass is growing, some summer vegetables are still on the farmers market.

O. E. Philpot Jr. as 1951-52 CHMA post-graduate.

My day lilies are totally disoriented. They are green and growing. They look like they were in the middle of spring.

One pair of birds is confused. They are building a nest in our carport. Planning a fall family, maybe?

Twice in my lifetime, at this point in October, we were 10 days away from a snow.

A half century ago, the Castle Heights football team played a game in the snow here. On Halloween. 'Twas a good omen. We beat a previously undefeated team which was expected to crush us.

Actually, it was 51 years ago when the 1951 team defeated Georgia Military Academy 13-6 to the surprise of the cadet corps and the delight of Coach Stroud Gwynn, one of prep football's all-time great coaches.

The coaches' game plan was a major factor in the victory, but the leadership of O. E. Philpot Jr., who later was elected to the Castle Heights Football Hall of Fame, was just as important.

O. E. was a post-graduate. He was an outstanding center-linebacker. Most of the other players were inexperienced overachievers. O. E. convinced his teammates they could win. And they did. Thus the big victory was on Halloween in the snow.

The Castle Heights class of 1952 met October 12 for its 50th reunion. Included were players from the 1951 team, including receiver Bill Bandy, linemen Hamlet Halbert and Harry Leggett, and undersize tailback Forest Atkins -- who in the '51 season scored the winning touchdown against Columbia Military Academy.

During my four decades at Castle Heights, a half dozen football teams etched places in my memory. The 1951 team is one of them.

Loneliness on mat haunts CHMA wrestler

• *August, 2009*

Alan Sillitoe's "The Loneliness of the Long Distance Runner," among other reminders, calls attention to the reality that not all sports focus on teams or on teammates as supporting players.

Butch Russo -- one of a platoon of great Castle Heights wrestlers that included Buzzy Fryer, Paul von Weigandt, Paul Ulbrich, Curtis

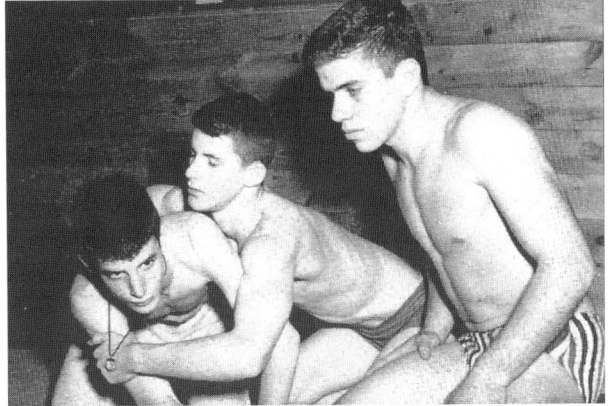

Butch Russo [right] oversees, as 1958-59 captain, Academy wrestling teammates' practice session.

Shelton, Carey Bob Bussey, Gus Smith, Tommy Lowe, Danny Evins and other Mid-South Conference champions -- recently wrote a short essay that caught the essence of "aloneness" of a participant on a mat with only his skills and willpower in support.

A quarterback relies on an offensive line, a pitcher has an outfield and an infield, and a basketball ace looks to four teammates for support. A wrestler relies on himself.

Wrote Butch:

"No one had his back while on the mat. He was alone.

"The wrestlers were acutely aware of their circumstances – two opponents on the mat before partisan spectators.

"One would triumph, the other lose. A win or a loss would reflect in the team's standing. But that is where team concept ended.

"Other than being pushed by his coaches and teammates to greater exertion, no one could help him. This was his moment, his opportunity to win or his battle to lose.

"It was a lesson in self-reliance."

Butch learned rapidly in wrestling. He lost one match, later avenged his loss, and won three matches in the 1959 Mid-South tournament en route to the 167-pound championship. He also was 1958 Mid-South champ in his class.

He wrestled one year at the University of Missouri, where he had to prove himself each week by wrestling the Missouri state high school champion in order to participate in the upcoming collegiate meet.

Academically, Butch was not doing as well. He was enjoying college life and abandoning study habits instilled in him at Castle Heights.

He transferred to Louisiana State University, earned a degree in microbiology while improving his grade point average but not enough for acceptance into medical school.

He applied, and was accepted, to pharmacy school, improved his grade averages, reapplied to medical school, was accepted, and today is Dr. Lawrence Russo.

Heights Homecoming 2002 and Butch Russo '59 [left] joins longtime CHMA faculty member Capt. Bobby Todd to reminisce about Mid-South wrestling and athletics.

Butch was a slow starter in academics. In his first two years of high school, he earned four credits prompting his father to consider trade school for his son.

Complicating matters, he suffered from an attention disorder, and "reading any book for 10 minutes was like sitting in a pile of ants," he said.

A friend was planning to attend Heights, and this set Butch to thinking a change of scenery might lead to a change in academic performance. Selling his dad on the idea challenged Butch's salesmanship skills.

"Dad had a hard decision to make," Butch recalls. "He had to weigh the cost of sending me to Heights against putting up with me at home. Fortunately, he concluded the tuition cost was a good investment."

This scene played more than half a century ago. His arduous journey through college and medical school is due in large measure to the lessons he learned at Castle Heights, forgot in early college years, and recalled in pharmacy and medical schools.

"I would have been another average student and below average achiever, had it not been for the lessons taught to me by dedicated and knowledgeable men who saw something besides a mischievous and too-energetic trouble-making youth. They saw something to salvage, and taught their lessons well," he said.

Although a champion on the wrestling mat, Butch did not fare well playing football at Heights.

"I was a 'call-back,' one of the regular students Coach Stroud Gwynn would call back to participate on the varsity. Unfortunately, I tore a cartilage in my left knee and elected not to have surgery. For that reason, I could no longer participate in football. The knee has bothered me for years," he said.

He underwent arthroscopic surgery Wednesday.

Among his greatest memories are his years at Castle Heights and his experiences pitting his skills against the wiles of outstanding wrestlers from Baylor and McCallie schools.

As cadet Master Sergeant, Butch Russo assisted his platoon with correct arms procedures.

And among the values he learned on the mat was a discipline that ushered him through academic challenges in the years that followed.

• Earned pharmacy degree in 1967, and graduated from LSU in 1970 with medical degree. Interned San Joaquin General Hospital, Stockton, Ca.; studied at Alton Oschner Hospital, New Orleans, as orthopedic surgeon, practicing 1975-87 in Morgan City, La. Moved to New Orleans area in 1987, practicing until 1998 retirement. He and his wife, Clara, have been married more than 50 years, and retired in Kingwood, Texas, in 2000. They have three children -- Alexandra, Lawrence Jr. , and Christopher -- and six grandchildren, one great-grandchild.

Maybe the greatest Tigers football team?

• *February, 1997*

The 1953 Castle Heights football team probably was the best and most talented aggregation of players during my association with the school -- a tenure which began in 1941 and spanned more than 40 years.

In my opinion, it was the best team the great football coach, Stroud Gwynn, put together in his 25 years as head of the program. I think the 1953 team was better than Coach Gwynn's Mid-South Conference champions of 1948 and 1964 [a team ranked the number one prep school in the nation]. It perhaps has an edge on the 1962 champions, who also were talent laden.

And because of the depth of 1953 talent, this team was probably superior overall to the 1943 champions, led by legendary tailback Pat Parker, which lacked depth.

Harold Greer '54, member CHMA Football Hall of Fame and named All-Mid-South Conference guard from 1953 Academy football team.

Earl Cato, the scintillating wingback on the singlewing team, sparkled among a galaxy of stars who went 9-0 for the season, scoring 273 points while yielding 63.

Earl was one of the most dazzling prep school halfbacks I ever saw. Fans came to expect him to burst loose for a long touchdown run. They rarely were disappointed -- 43 yards against Tennessee Tech freshmen, 80 yards against Notre Dame of Chattanooga, 90 against Columbia Military Academy, 78 against Darlington, 85 against Georgia Military Academy, 55 and 75 against Riverside, 65 and 55 against Sewanee.

Cato, however, was only one among many exciting players on the 1953 team.

Frank Clayton, a gifted tailback who, as was expected of tailbacks in the singlewing system, could run, pass and punt. He was a fine breakaway runner.

Larry Wray, one of the best offensive ends -- also a great defensive player -- during my stay at Heights.

In a system that relied on power plays, Clayton threw seven touchdown passes to Wray to set a modern Heights record. [Little is known of the early teams' statistics.]

Cato and Wray were named co-captains of the all-conference team.

There were other great ones: Bobby Burkhart, the blocking back who masterminded strategy on the field; Billy Walker, a plunging full-back; Jack Jennings, who in any other year would have been the star of the team.

And in the line: Rodney Thomas, center-linebacker; interior linemen Jack Warwick [later a Tennessee Tech star]; Frank Walker, and Watt Williams Jr. From tackle to tackle, these linemen may have been the best assembly in my time.

But the best of the team, in my opinion, was an undersized guard named Harold Dean Greer, pound for pound perhaps the greatest linemen in Heights history. I have never known a more motivated and dedicated football player than Harold, who not only made the all-conference team but also the All-Southern team.

He was the leader, the rallier, the soul of the team. In tough situations, the team turned to Harold Greer. Example: Riverside took an early 7-0 lead and looked unstoppable. A hard blow left Harold addled. Coach Gwynn asked him: "Do you know where you are?" His response: "No, but I know we're gonna win this game." Outcome: Heights, 41-13.

There were notable substitutes who were to emerge in the next season, including Bobby Lannom, Carey Thompson and Clyde Ward, all of Lebanon, and Butch Jordan. Two other Lebanon cadets on the squad were David Overstreet and John Freeman.

It should be mentioned here that another Heights alumnus made a contribution to the team. Joe Gwynn Atkinson '38, one of the great coaches of all time at Lebanon High School, started Greer and Watt Williams, who played as post-graduates at Heights, on their careers.

Death has taken a toll on this team. Harold Greer, Watt Williams, Rodney Thomas and Clyde Ward, a Vietnam War casualty, are gone.

'Dark Horse' Baxter Seminary surprises Tigers
• *February, 1988*

In l936, Castle Heights had one of its best basketball teams, but the cadets lost twice to Baxter Seminary -- founded in 1910, in Baxter, Tenn., by the Central Tennessee Conference of the Methodist Episcopal Church and its Board of Education -- a little school about which most of the Heights team knew little.

The star of the Baxter team was Johnny Thomas, whose nickname at the time was "Abe" because his schoolmates thought he resembled Abraham Lincoln. Johnny was a little more than six-three, and probably the most talented of a gifted team. He was the first high school player I know about in this area who developed a one-hand shot, a maneuver which would have benched him on many teams but which met with the approval of Coach Doc Prickett -- because, you see, Johnny was an accurate shooter.

Castle Heights was the only Mid-South Conference team Baxter (my alma mater) played during the regular season. The two teams met in home-and-home games, and Baxter won them both, much to the surprise of the cadets. Some way, Baxter managed to raise enough money to send its team to the Mid-South tournament, held that year in Nashville. There was a full l6-team bracket which meant that the Baxter team, which had not stayed overnight for any of its games before, spent several nights in Nashville.

It was pretty heady stuff for the players. Although nobody gave Baxter much of a chance to advance, the little school won its first round game, then its second, earning for itself the label of "dark horse." Then Johnny led the team to the finals where it again met Castle Heights. The old "it's hard to beat a team three times in a season" theory worked. The Cinderellas from Baxter went home with the runners-up trophy.

Stardom never affected Johnny Thomas; he remained one of the most popular students. He graduated, went to work for DuPont in Old Hickory where he continued to play basketball; remained on his job after DuPont sold his division to the Olin company, rose to manufacturing superintendent, and later helped start plants in Indiana and North Carolina.

Johnny and I were friends at Baxter Seminary, but not truly close. After I graduated in 1937, we lost track of each other until about three years ago. At an auction in Gladeville, we introduced ourselves to each other, at first not recognizing the other as a former schoolmate.

"Johnny," I said. "When we were in school, you were seven feet tall. Now we are eye-to-eye."

Of course, he wasn't a seven-footer, but he was so much taller than the rest of us that he seemed that big.

"I'm not as tall as I was in school. Actually, I'm two inches shorter." He explained.

Just a few years ago, he developed a back ailment which was diagnosed as tuberculosis of the spine. Then came surgery, resulting in a shorter spine, a long recovery and some doubt on the part of the physicians that he would ever walk again.

First he crawled, then he pulled himself to a standing position, and finally he walked. Although his basketball days are over, he is still in pursuit of the ball -- this time, a golf ball, which he hits long and accurately. The last time we played, he was two over par. He now lives in Mt. Juliet, and our paths intersect frequently. A friendship that lapsed for almost half of a century is on track again.

Two of Castle Heights most notable athletes earned U.S. Olympic medals -- Pete Rademacher '48 [left] in 1956, and William "Bill" Dudley III '47 in 1948. [Rademacher accomplishments page 50.]. Dudley was 1947 U.S. Junior 200-yard champion, and competed on USA 4X100-meter relay unit at the London games. He attended Tulane University, and was swim team captain while winning SEC and AAU titles. He earned a Tulane mechanical engineering degree in 1953, and founded Dudley Engineering in 1965. He died in 1978, at 47. Rademacher continues as a Heights National Alumni Association director.

DEAN OF TENNESSEE'S PREP SCHOOL COACHES

CASTLE HEIGHTS'
STROUD GWYNN

34-YEAR HEAD COACHING RECORD: 184-99-25 .640 at WATERTOWN, GALLATIN and CASTLE HEIGHTS ...

COACHED ALL-AMERICANS BOBBY MAJORS AND JOHN OGLES AT HEIGHTS AND HAD 135 MORE SIGNED TO GRANTS-IN-AID

HIS TEAMS WON 7 MID-SOUTH OR MIDSTATE CHAMPIONSHIPS

Inducted 1985 into Tennessee Sports Hall of Fame.

154

Coach Gwynn remembered
for more than coaching prowess

• *November, 1987*

On a plaque at the edge of what still remains as the Castle Heights football field, near the 50-yard line, there is an inscription that reads: "In recognition of his unswerving dedication to sports, his school, and the cadet corps."

As part of the 1971 CHMA "70th Anniversary" Homecoming celebration, Coach Stroud Gwynn was honored with a personal plaque for his Academy and athletic accomplishments by a Macfadden Foundation official.

With these words and with appropriate ceremony, the field was named in October, 1979, in honor of Lt. Col. Stroud Gwynn, one of the most successful football coaches in the Academy's as well as the state's history.

During a 25-year period beginning with the 1947 season, Stroud Gwynn's teams posted a 184-99-25 record, were three times undefeated, won five Mid-South championships, produced two All-Americas, and sent a small army of players to college on scholarships.

Stroud died about five weeks ago at 76, leaving behind a legacy of achievement in athletics which was recognized and highlighted when he was elected in 1985 to the Tennessee Sports Hall of Fame.

Distinguished as he was in coaching, the dimensions of this man were not measured with the yardstick of athletics. His achievement in athletics is more a manifestation of his dedication to principle than a monument to his life.

And so the focus of this column is not on his well known sports record, but on Stroud Gwynn the man, my close friend for more than four decades.

Because of this closeness, it is difficult to crystallize thoughts about him. Emotions are too strong, memories too poignant for objectivity.

I tried to think of a fictional character as an analogy. Is there a character in fiction so punctual that when he says 9:15 he doesn't mean 9:16 or perhaps 9:30 ? So meticulously honest that he listed fractions of miles on an expense account? Who never worried about what he said because

155

he always told the truth?

There is no analogy. Stroud Gwynn was unique.

He was the ultimate pragmatist. What you saw is what you got. He was without guile or pretense. He rarely praised and never berated his players. He simply told them they had played a good game, if indeed they had played a good game.

He was never abusive or profane. His swear-word was "Sam Hill" -- "What the Sam Hill do you think you're doing?," "Sam Hill, you were supposed to block that man." Frequently he spoke of his players as little "Pee-Willies." Some of his little Pee Willies weighed 270 pounds and made all-conference.

He was a successful recruiter. He never painted glowing pictures; he told his prospects, many of them high school stars, life

Stroud Gwynn ended his 40-plus-year CHMA career as Lieutenant Colonel and Athletic Director, having spent a decade traveling on his own visiting alumni to raise funds to keep Heights open.

at Heights would be without frills, academics would come first, and they would be at the bottom of the military organization. We marveled at his recruiting success.

He professed to be a pessimist, but deep down he always thought he could win. He was systematic and organized, but he had a sense of humor, and he could laugh at himself. He tackled problems head-on, and he, as much as any other, was responsible for the Academy's remaining viable during the last 12 years of its life.

He was a fund-raiser for the school, but observed few of the professional fund-raiser's hypes. He simply glued his ear to the telephone,

He never embellished. Professional fund-raisers cringed at his technique because he told it as it was. And he got the money. Many alumni gave as much because of Stroud Gwynn as because of Castle Heights.

As the plaque states, he was dedicated to his school. But those of us who were his close friends knew a more intrinsic reason for his success in raising money, recruiting students, and winning games. He knew a trade secret.

Integrity.

○

• Stroud Gwynn played football and baseball at Lebanon High School, then played football and earned his AB at Maryville College. He coached at Watertown, Tenn., one season, then at Gallatin High School for eight years [including two Mid-State titles] starting in 1935. He joined CHMA in 1944, teaching chemistry and becoming head football coach for 25 years starting in 1947. He had four undefeated teams in his total career, and five Mid-South Conference championships at Heights. He and his wife, Rebecca, had one son -- Robert "Bobby" Stroud Gwynn played football under his father's tutelage, graduating as Heights' valedictorian in 1964. He returned for a post-graduate year 1964-65, and earned a football scholarship to Georgia Tech. He is in the Heights Football Hall of Fame. [*Yearbook Dedication, page 301*]

Sept. 30, 1987 / Letter to Alumni:
"It is with great sadness and personal sorrow I write to inform you of the passing of Stroud Gwynn...For many of us, Stroud was Mr. Castle Heights; for the past year [since the Academy closed in 1986] he has been the only full-time representative of the Alumni Association, and was a key factor in our success...We owe him the highest accolades...On a personal note, I have never known a man of greater honesty and personal integrity. It has been an inspiration to work with him. We who are left must be certain the work to which Stroud devoted himself is continued with the same energy and attention. His memory will guide and inspire us..."
-- Horace V. Whitten '59
1987 Heights Alumni Association President

• **March, 1988 / Castle Heights Alumni News:**
"I am sure most of you now know of the passing of Stroud Gwynn last September. He will be sadly missed. It was through Stroud's love and dedication to Castle Heights and the Alumni Association that we can enjoy our success...Stroud was a key factor in reorganization of the Heights Alumni Association from a social group that met at Homecoming events to a body responsible for its own business and financial affairs. He negotiated with the Landmark Corporation for lease of the [Col. Dan T.] Ingram House on Hill Street for use as our Alumni House and office, and [with help of others] secured all of the memorabilia gathered by the Heights Foundation Board before the auction was held for campus property...He then began traveling for the Association, visiting with alumni all over the country, asking for money. It was always a thrill to visit with him after his trips, to hear him talk about the way you would extend a warm welcome in your home or office and spend time reminiscing about old friends and days you spent on The Hilltop. Your encouragement along with financial support ensured that Castle Heights was still alive in the hearts and minds of her alumni. With Stroud gone, it is up to us to continue where he left off. We will endure."
--Frank Hartley '64
1988 Alumni Association President

In the beginning, there were sports...

By Col. Dan T. Ingram, Superintendent
Excerpt from "Diary of Our Own 'Mr. Chips'" / *October, 1963*
Written for Alumni Newsletter

Dan T. Ingram as 1922 Heights coach, commandant in 1929.

Where the gymnasium now stands, a small apple orchard sloped down to the campus' edge. I thought it beautiful, and knew I was going to like it -- and I have for 42 years.

School began the next day [September, 1921], and I discovered I was assistant football coach under Tic Luna, the tactical officer of Company B [Reserve officers taught military tactics and drill in those days], head track coach and instructor in general science and U.S. History.

Our chief athletic rival in the '20s was Morgan Prep, run by the father of our present beloved Maj. R. Kenneth Morgan. They were terrific in football and from the start of this and every later season until they closed [in 1950], our ambition was "Beat Morgan." We had to wait until 1924 to do it, 6-0, and this was a memorable day to me because the corps and half of Lebanon went to Petersburg, Tenn., to the game on a special train and we celebrated with songs and yells all the way back.

Also that same year, a game with the Georgia Tech freshmen was scheduled with us in Atlanta. It was supposed to be a breather for the Tech frosh; it did not count on our schedule. There were no eligibility rules between us, and Tic, wishing to save a varsity back for a regular game, asked me to play. I was feeling sharp though it had been four years since I played on the Flying Squadron at VMI. I made the mistake of getting the ball on the first kickoff. It was short and rolled several yards, giving those 11 maniacs time to get to me. (The only time I ever felt worse after a game was the year the faculty played the alumni in a very uncharitable charity game on the Heights field, at Thanksgiving, and held them to a single touchdown. I think Finney Hamilton and Joe Graves both hit me at the same time in that one.)

In 1925...my track team won the Vanderbilt Invitation meet. In January '29, I became Commandant and stopped coaching. I had enjoyed the eight years of assisting with football and occasionally baseball. Two of our football boys made All-America during this time, Buster Perry '24 at West Point, and "Gump" Araial '27 at Auburn. In baseball I had twice put on the Tiger uniform to pitch against the college teams of Birmingham Southern and Howard (we won 'em), and every spring I had pitched for the faculty in the hard-fought faculty versus varsity games. Yet I believe I got more pleasure from track. We were lucky and went five or six years without losing a dual meet, and occasionally won the Invitations. It was a lot of fun…

[The purchase of Heights in 1929 by Bernarr Macfadden resulted in three major innovations]…the first, which soon was copied by our rivals, was instituting an athletic program in which every boy could take part. These were then called the minor sports, because football, baseball, basketball and track were then the majors; the minors included golf, tennis, judo, soccer, boxing, wrestling, swimming, softball and fencing. To do this, he bought the Mitchell Estate that surrounded the campus [and] included the handsome mansion…increasing our campus to 200 acres. Each cadet not participating in a varsity sport was required to enter the intra-mural program…

Sons playing on teams coached by their fathers often are thought to be "under stress." How about attending CHMA where your dad is commandant -- as did Dan T. Ingram Jr. '47 (left), and John Ingram '52. The Ingram's daughter, Alice, nicknamed "Boots," was early '40s Lebanon High graduate. Dan was elected Senior Class president; John was Cum Honore, Senior Class president, and on the boxing, tennis, football and basketball teams.

It has been my simple belief that although life is admittedly hard at times, if the game is played fairly, it can be honorably won or lost…Play hard, but fair, and no matter the score, you can live proudly with yourself. I live proudly, here.

The Virginian's Alma Mater Featured in Pat's New Movie

By Robert Stanley

Virginia Military Institute, pretty girls, color, and music, highlight one of the holiday seasons best movies, "Mardi Gras," starting tomorrow at the Capitol.

Lt. Col. D. T. Ingram's alma mater is the scene for this military school holiday starring a list of teen-age favorites. Headlined by Pat Boone, who finally kisses a girl, the flick smoothly moves Gary Crosby, Tommy Sands, Christine Carere, and Sheree North from the hills of Virginia to the pomp and ceremony of the annual New Orleans festivities.

Exchange Excerpts

Students Put Finishing Touch on Electric-Chair

By Clarke Waggoner

Students at White Station high school, Memphis, are putting finishing touches on their electric chair.

The students have no intentions of really using it on any teachers, as the chair is to be entered in an upcoming science fair there.

Other projects include an x-ray machine and a one-octave piano.

for its fifth annual Roman banquet to be held in March.

At Tri Memphis, Oakley d called the term mat musicians. He next the studer

Profile

'Big Jess' Sites CHMA Greats

By Bob Cleveland

He smokes a pipe, he's quiet, he's friendly — his name, "Big

with some of the cadets.

"I like the game and some of the boys here are pretty good. There's always someone who wants to learn a trick shot or how to play the game," he said.

He went on to say that his best opponent through the years has been Maj. C. V. Baker, Heights mathematics instructor.

After watching most of the athletic events (especially football) during the past two and one-half decades, Jess has, of course, singled out some of his favorites.

"Well, let me see here — Way back, there was that Parker boy (Pat Parker, '44), Good shifty runner, he was. Then there was that fast Cato fella (Earl Cato, '53), and

was pretty good at just about anything."

Jess also mentioned others of who the editors had no immediate recollection.

Head Custodian

SPORT-SIDE

By Julian Stallard

So near . . . yet so far

This adage has been repeated many times—perhaps a few too many—but it applied very well to a situation occuring on the hilltop this winter. If you glanced at the box score (in the last issue of The Cavalier) of the McCallie or Baylor basketball games, you might have noticed one of two things. In the McCallie game Josh Nunn exploded with a 34 point outburst and Dave Nitschke followed up with 33 points in the Baylor game.

For several days after each game cadets were how close these two fine performers just missed the 36 points. However, as well as they played, for as they put out, all was for nothing. For nothing in the s

On The Hilltop

All Was Fine Till Day He Lost a Rifle

By Hank Thorn

David Hall, the red-headed townboy, has trouble keeping up with things. At first his locker was small and no one even in the hall he had lost anything. A until the day the trouble pened: He lost his rifle!

It seems that Hall w ing stack-arms, and got weapon back. At least story he tells. After an ing search on the dril decided to take the Army. Off he went Castle Heights Military Academy. School found the "mishap" to the morale, discipline, precision, and proficiency. Sugg be dropped."

Even the might of ever ready to help, was Today, the mystery rema is it?

Pessimistic View But It Could Happen Here

"Attention: to whom it may concern. Official report of Third army inspectors Roberts and Durrant concerning Honor School status of Castle Heights Military Academy. School found

Although this is a highly pessimistic look a Third army headquarters in Atlanta, it is ar possible and probable without the effort and co cadet corps.

Pledge Question Arises

Council Studies Clubs' 'Hazing' Procedures

To shine, or not to shine; that is the question.

Service club pledge lists and a 2-week initiation period set aside for the mild "hazing" of the pledges has been a long established tradition at Heights, at least for the old members of the organizations.

Recently, however, controversy has arisen over just how much these pledges should be made to do. Club presidents have agreed

"This question is now only a topic for discussion, but it is hoped that agreements can be reached and that a set of standards can soon be drawn up," Maj. L. K. Bradley, faculty advisor for the Round Table council, stated.

Co-ordinates Activities

The Round Table council is the student council of the Hilltop, and is responsible for co-ordinating activities of the clubs. The topic has been discussed in the council meetings but nothing definite has

3 Mid-South Tourneys Scheduled This Month

Castle Heights will be represented at the end of the month in Mid-South tournaments by three teams — championship defender and first and second runners-up in their respective sports.

Chattanooga will host two tournaments: wrestling at Baylor, Feb. 21 - 22, and basketball at McCallie, Feb. 26 - 27 - 28. The swimming tourney will be held at the Vanderbilt university pool in Nashville.

St. Andrew's also edged Heights (69) last year with 77 points.

* * *

Swimmers Carry Burden

The elimination of Georgia Military academy from M-S swimming competition has shifted coach Ro t that bert Hosier's team to the number ed for one spot.

GMA, M-S title-holder, withdrew e said. from the meet at Vanderbilt in chosen

In It's 15th Year

Succession of 'A' Sabre CH Tradition Since '44

By Gary Coe

One of the foremost of Heights many traditions, the handing down of the Company A sabre from each commanding officer to his successor, is in its 15th year.

This tradition began in 1944, the year Fred Kremer, son of Mrs. Jeanette Kremer, was killed. To commemorate his death, his sabre

was given to the senior officer of Company A to be passed to other Company A commanders in sequence.

Graduated in 1939

Kremer graduated from Heights in 1939 an commander of "A", vice president of the Heights "Y", and a member of the honor council, among other honors.

John Castro, a senior from Cincinnati, is now the commander of ompany A. John, very active in hool affairs, is president of the ational Honor Society, a member the swimming team, and last vice president of the Heights

Upon his gra ited States ed entered Wi

On The Hilltop

Bright Circle Poses Puzzle For Painters

Heights after-taps brush-wielders have this week been put into the "spotlight" with the addition of the 15 circle-surrounding flourescent beams.

The old "tradition" of painting the cannon has become somewhat of a trial as the flustered cadet will now have to brave not only the possibility of 25 demerits, but also the brilliance of the towering menaces.

All is not lost, however. It seems that some amateur Rembrandts have already planned to paint those now-green light poles with striking red and white stripes.

Cadets last week scurried to their

Selection of College Poses Major Problem

By David Hall

One of the most important decisions facing a high school student concerning his education is: "What college will I attend and what will I choose as my major when I get there?"

Maj. L. K. Bradley, Heights headmaster, and Dr. Ernest Stock-ton, president of Cumberland uni

shouldn't try to attend a schoo knows he isn't prepared for," st Major Bradley. "A field of st should not be selected as a m if the student feels he is not p quately prepared for it or that interests lie elsewhere."

"Too many boys worry about being able to make their ch early," he continued.

"It a student is not decided, might begin with a liberal course, as the subjects gathe there can be integrated into ot areas whenever a person sees he said.

Latin Quarter

Club Propone Arreglar el Corral de CH

Por Orlando Segarra

En la última edición de éste p iodico hicimos constar que en edición daríamos mas detalles so diferentes cambios, concernient actividades del Club, que se llevadós a cabo antes de que curso escolar finalizáse.

Dichos cambios no serán re ñados, por lo tanto, todo pu calificaráse cómo una falsa alarm El Club Latino empezára a tra

In It's 29th Year

Circle Hallowed Ground In Sight of Old Cadets

By Hank Thorn

One of the first things that a freshman learns is the freshman rule concerning the "circle," located in front of Main g.

The second thing that quite a the new men do is promptly rd a tradition that was almost 30 years ago, with the help of Mrs. Mildred Armlate wife of the academy nt.

Men May Enter

The main idea of the circle is tly old men are permitted to ly walk on the "hallowed ground" and the benefits. This year, how-more than ever, new cadets llegn to respect or honor the cadet at Heights learns is the and old men are doing to dissuade them.

me time, the Circle was only panse of gravel in the general ance of a circle. In 1930, Mrs. rong designed the present-ival and planted the hedge hich still remains. The trimming the freshmen were also to effect at this time.

Recalled to Duty

cannon, was placed in the Cir

For several years, the cannon been given a very distinct r military appearance by bold m bers of the cadet corps — aided brush and paint. So far this y however, little attention has b paid the olive drab artillery pi much to the delight of the scl painters.

The Cavalier

Saturday, February 28, 1959   P

● All-American, NSPA
● All-Tennessee, THSPA

Exchange Excerpt

Howe Cadets Giv Extended Vacation For Good Conduc

By Bill Harwell

Cadets at Howe Military have earned an extra day on Spring vacation, B. B. Bouton demy superintendent, rece

SPORT-SIDE

by bradley

Newt Henley, World leader in wrestling! That's what the Heightsand best supporters in the gym thought last Saturday afternoon . . . ough Newt did his part to convince them.

In just six minutes, the 117-class redhead decisioned a Mid-eduled South championship wrestler, gave the team a triumphant air, and in early blew to smithereens the theory that "high school athletics is an unrewarding imposition on academics".

The (small) crowd went wild, but Newt kept cool until he finallyta High won a 5-2 decision over McCallie's Martin Spangler. Spangler, present the c 108 champ, had beaten the Heights alternate captain four times—ilor Circ once in an earlier meet at Chattanooga this season.   complete

The buzzer sounded . . . a headguard flew to the rafters . . . t Newt turned redder, yelling "I did it, I did it!" . . . and Maj. J. B. rough r Heights may not have a world champion, but don't try telling e instr Newt Henley.

* * * *

Revision of History

A threat to the highest individual scoring in the Mid-South basketball circle has been posed by St. Andrew's, and demonstrated against Heights.

Gary Hassman, a Saint who helped jail Heights 50-47 two weeks ago, heaped up 35 of his team's winning 50, missing the 1952 record of a Notre Dame cager by two goals.

Fred Farley's high of 38 points was fashioned against Heights

Chapter Five

Guest Columnists

"I find interesting characters or lessons that resonate
with people, and sometimes I write about them
in a novel, in nonfiction, in the sports pages, and
sometimes in a column...But at the core I always
ask myself, 'Is there a story here? Is this something
people want to read?'"

-Mitch Albom, Novelist / Sports Journalist

"As much as the Pulitzer is the hallmark of
journalism, I think what I love the most is when
somebody says they took my column and it's in
their wallet. I have had people open their wallet
and show me a corner of a column."

-Regina Brett, Author / Pulitzer Prize Finalist

THE DRILL:
Periodically, usually around the Christmas holidays, JB
Leftwich would take a break from his weekly column.
He would ask former cadets, and sometimes other faculty, to fill in -- knowing his readers were going to
continue getting a quality product, plus the advantage
of new perspective from a variety of professionals
who all had one thing in common: their graduation
from and/or continuing love of Castle Heights Military
Academy. Those included are representative, and all
were written with concern that they would meet JB's
expectations.

Overleaf Photo:
Excellent writing by his staffs, whether in news stories
or columns, was a main JB objective.

Photo Credit:
Collected from issues of *Cavalier*

Sounds of Macfadden Gym echo

Guest Columnist: *Charles W. Ward '42*

• *Published November, 1992*

JBL Preface: The Castle Heights buildings -- Armstrong, Ingram, Chapel, Main, Tower – now commune in silent melancholy around The Circle, harboring memories of days long gone when hundreds of gray-clad cadets romped through their halls. Just below The Circle, the gymnasium faintly echoes the excitement of games and matches and big band music. But wait, let Chuck Ward '42 tell you about it...

C. W. 'Chuck' Ward as '42 senior, noted architect.

No one has ever mistaken our Gym for an architectural gem... In fact, I've looked through every book in my architectural library... Unless I've overlooked it somewhere, there isn't one single illustration in any of them of our beloved Bernarr Macfadden Gymnasium.

And that's a shame, for many of the good times in our young lives were enjoyed there.

We can remember those great basketball teams that called this home. The Tigers were Mid-South Champions... always. Many a time I sat in the balcony to watch Johnny North and Ray Kirkpatrick and Carlos "Izzy" Izaguirre and George Palmer and Tommy Moore cavort around the hardwood in their Maroon and Gold satin underwear. Then there were Raymond Enders and Buddy Boyer and Roger "Bones" Hamilton and Pete Diffenbaugh and Si Ragsdale and Jimmy Elrod and so many others.

There was even one memorable game when, cheered on by Chick Muller, we really ran up the score... 29-18 against Nashville's

Wrestling matches were a Macfadden Gym staple.

163

Montgomery Bell Academy.

When Capt. Tony Flores, coach of wrestling, left for Fort Benning, outside Columbus, Ga., cadet Raymond Hughes took over the team -- which held its matches in the gym -- and led Bill "Spider" Roberts, Bill Ross, Carmine Caputo, Les Brauer and Bill Sleyster to yet more victories.

The gym was not all sports, though. In the southeast corner of the basement, Capt. Ralph Lucas taught typing. Next door, Capt. Bill Blades tried to impress on Marshall Treppendahl and me the vital force that physics could play in our lives -- Trep got it, but I never understood how it was supposed to work. Capt. M. H. Stopinski tried to unravel the mysteries of algebra for Bill Hall and Eddie Brown, and Capt. Phil Partridge explained ancient history over and over to Jack McCarthy, Henry Rigby and me. They were all good guys and great teachers. If we'd paid any attention, we might have learned even more.

Balcony seating was crammed for Tigers basketball.

And forget the dances. Things were different then... you actually put your right arm around your girl, which was nice in itself, but the best part was in snuggling up close to perfume and to a gardenia corsage and to a usually responsive and often surprisingly well-filled strapless formal. Even better was when your date was Jessie Ruth Williams.

Francis Craig and Charlie Nagy played real music for us. [Craig was a songwriter and Nashville dance band leader who in 1922, as an undergrad at Vanderbilt University, wrote "Dynamite" *[now VU's official fight song]*. He also wrote and recorded "Near You," which was 1947's top hit.

What a concept: up-close, personal dancing.

Nagy was a gifted musician who played drums for U.S. army bands in WWII.] Their music had a beat you could dance to... a melody you could hum... and lyrics you could understand. And they tried hard to swing those

164

tunes we loved, like Tommy Dorsey's "Opus One," Charlie Barnet's "Cherokee," Glenn Miller's "In the Mood," and Artie Shaw's "Begin the Beguine."

Even though Heights' faculty officers were supposed to watch our every move, some few

Yearly social highlight: Formal graduation dance in gym.

didn't take their chaperoning seriously and just about every cadet and his date (except me, I guess) usually found a way sometime during the evening to do some world class smooching. Even I remember one memorable evening. There was this blind date from Ward-Belmont School for Women [which in 1951 became the coed Belmont College] in Nashville... an exceptionally knowledgeable girl...

So while Fletcher "Fletch" Harris and a goodly share of the other accomplished hell-raisers lived in The Tower... and John Boyd Scott and the really sophisticated cadets holed up in the top floor of The Chapel, just a whole lot of what we remember as the good times happened just north of the football field in that hallowed spot we called "The Gym."

Author Update:
• Charles W. "Chuck" Ward was associate editor of CHMA's first yearbook [originally named The Hill Top before being changed to *The Adjutant* at suggestion of Commandant D.T. Ingram] and was JB Leftwich's first editor of *The Cavalier* [*next page*]. Ward was on the Academy boxing team, president of Heights-Y, charter member of Order of DeMolay and Red Key Honor Society, debate team captain, earned rank of Second Lieutenant, and was corps adjutant. He and the Leftwiches became good friends through the years, and in 2014 he still was corresponding with Jo Doris.

JB's First: Ward sets benchmark

JB Leftwich mentored more than 60 cadets serving as editors of *The Cavalier* and *The Adjutant*, in addition to teaching mathematics to more than 1,000 students, during his 38 years on the Castle Heights faculty. Here is the fascinating story of his first *Cavalier* editor -- a fitting pacesetter for the "JB Legacy."

> *"I am delighted to be of any help possible in honoring the memory and heritage of my wonderful friend and mentor and inspiration during my teenage years at CHMA [1938-42]. Although we were only intimate friends in 1941-42 when he was faculty sponsor of* The Cavalier *and I was his first editor, we renewed our friendship during my first return to* The Hilltop *in 1985, and remained close until his recent demise. He was a true and wonderful friend..."*
> Charles W. Ward, Tulsa Okla. / April 2014

o o o

Platoon Leader Ward landed at Utah Beach 24 months after Heights graduation

December 7, 1941, and Charles "Chuck" Ward is a 17-year-old Castle Heights Military Academy cadet. His father -- who traveled the world overseeing oil fields -- and his mother are in South America, where they are forced to remain until the end of the war. After graduation from Heights, Ward briefly attends University of Oklahoma, and at 18 [December, 1942] enlists and enters Officer Candidate School, Fort Benning, Ga.

December, 1943, Ward -- a newly commissioned infantry lieutenant and platoon leader -- is in Northern Ireland training with "Red Diamond" [the 5th Infantry Division] for the coming invasion and liberation of Europe. D-Day plus three, Ward's platoon lands at Utah Beach and advances south to the city of Angers. The Fifth Division is reassigned to Gen. George S. Patton, and fights in Metz and the Battle of the Bulge, cracks the Siegfried Line, crosses the Rhine opening a path to Frankfurt, participates in the German surrender in the Ruhr, and ends in Czechoslovakia which is to be occupied by Soviet troops.

Ward is discharged on Dec. 24, 1945, and returns to the University of Oklahoma to complete a degree in architecture. After three years in the Army -- and approximately 40 months after editing his last *Cavalier* and leaving The Hilltop -- he had risen to the rank of captain and commanded over 100 men; won a Silver Star [presented by General Patton personally], Bronze Star [with "V" for valor], Purple Heart, Combat Infantryman Badge, and the French Croix de Guerre, Presidential Unit Citation.

Ward's career and accomplishments following his OU graduation in 1950 are no less extraordinary. He began his career working for architect Leo A. Daly in Omaha, Neb., and began his practice with Tulsa architects Leon Senter and Donald McCormick. He began his own firm in 1958. Among Ward's notable architectural projects in Tulsa are the Tulsa Central Library, Public Schools Education Center, Rudisill Regional Library, Southminster Presbyterian Church, Tyler Memorial Chapel, Civic Center Plaza, Police Detention Center, two major YMCA centers, the Parkland Plaza Office Building, and the Allie Beth Martin Regional Library. His Rosenburg Library is in Galveston, Texas.

Ward also oversaw completion of the master plan for the Oklahoma State Library in Oklahoma City, Texas Maritime Museum in Galveston, Texas, and multiple offices, distribution centers and manufacturing facilities in Texas and Oklahoma.

In 2007, he was one of seven OU graduates earning the Regents' Alumni Award honoring their dedication and service to the university.
In 2010, the Tulsa Foundation for Architecture recognized Ward for his contributions, hosting a reception in the architect's preserved historic former home -- a mid-century Ward design known as "Comma House," where he and his wife, Shirley, started living in 1963. [He moved to a retirement facility in 2006 after her passing.]

The Oklahoma Arts Council in 2012 honored Ward with the Governor's Arts Award for his impact on communities and education through the arts. His professional and civic affiliations are numerous, and he has provided academic service to Tulsa Community College and to the universities of Tulsa and Oklahoma. Phi Delta Theta Fraternity hon-

Ward's illustrative skills were honored by Oklahoma Arts Council and University of Oklahoma

ored him with its Distinguished Achievement Award.

His love for OU [where his wife and their two sons also graduated] is exemplified in two unique endeavors:

■ In 1984, he created his *Fearsome Football Forecast* newsletter including a depth chart, pre-season predictions and witty commentary. He mailed it annually to more than 100 OU "fanatics." Trips to Norman for home games were a family affair until around 1999. He fondly remembers when Bud Wilkinson was a new coach, and recalls legendary players Tommy McDonald, Darryl Royal and Junior Thomas.

■ Ward taught himself to sketch during his college years, and began sending out intricate pen or pencil drawings of OU campus buildings on the covers of his *Football Forecasts*. And for more than 20 years, he created original Christmas cards from his drawings of the world's great cathedrals.

Ward considers raising granddaughter Elizabeth [and her brother, Charles IV], starting in the 90s with he and his wife in their late 60s, perhaps his greatest accomplishment.

In spite of such an outstanding career and personal and family life, however, Ward's greatest achievement may be something he never thought twice about and never mentions in interviews. In 1991, with both Ward and wife Shirley nearing 70, they took in two orphaned grandchildren -- 11 and 15 -- and began child rearing all over again. The Ward's oldest son, Charles III, died in 1991, after his wife had died of cancer in 1989.

"I wish I could say we thought it all out back then, but we didn't," the elder Ward said. "It [raising the grandchildren in a tight-knit family of overachievers] was something that had to be done, so we did it."

Granddaughter Elizabeth and her brother, Charles IV, both eventually graduated from OU with bachelor's and law degrees -- "It gave me an excuse to go see more Sooner football games," Grandfather Ward said. She is, at 34, an attorney with Tulsa Samson Energy, and her brother an editor of the Juneau, Alaska, *Empire*.

"Of all the wonderful things he is known for, most people don't know what a fantastic dad and granddad he is," Elizabeth said.

The Wards have two other grandchildren -- by son Leslie and wife, Mary -- who grew up in Hawaii. Granddaughter Patti is a writer for the BBC in London, and Joey is a pediatrician in Honolulu.

Heights' Christmas electrically charged

Guest Columnist: *Capt. Gene E. Hale, Faculty*

• *Published December, 2003*

Capt. Gene Hale was beloved instructor, Headmaster during his 28-year Heights career

No two weeks in the school year were more electrically charged or brimming with anticipation than the fortnight in December that led to Christmas break at Castle Heights.

Maintaining a focus on academics posed a challenge even for the most studious. Even the highest ranking cadet officers strained to retain focus during drill. Athletics events served to relieve tension, but the approaching Christmas vacation lurked also in the backs of athletes' minds.

These days were exhilarating, even for the faculty that subdued their own anticipation in order to execute lesson plans and to maintain a reasonable resemblance of military discipline.

I came to the Academy in 1958, beginning an odyssey which lasted until the fine old school closed in 1986. My wife, Elizabeth, and I, with one child and another on the way, moved into faculty quarters in Bullard Hall to begin our tenure.

Teaching at Castle Heights was not as much a job as it was a way of life, and an experience based in trust. Testifying to this was the informal contract, not even a written document, which bound me to the Academy.

In the same vein, a tacit understanding between cadet and instructor was as much a factor in discipline as the Book of Regulations, which prescribed and detailed behavior.

Rules were a little less rigorous during the days of early December, a period of festivity I remember with nostalgia and fondness. This was an interval accented with merriment and zest as cadets envisioned a holiday from uniforms, drill, classes, athletics and inspections.

I remember how much had to be done before Christmas leave. There were airline tickets to be purchased, transportation to be arranged, and trinkets to be purchased for girl friend and family. Divisions were decorated to compete for a prize. Maj. John L. Sweatt -- perceived to be as taciturn as befits a biology teacher and head of the Science Department -- led the singing of Christmas carols. Festive meals were prepared.

But all was not Camelot in these electrifying days before Christmas break. A sizable number of cadets who lived in Latin American coun-

Heights division Christmas parties were natural kick-offs to the upcoming holidays respite. JB Leftwich made the rounds of the celebrations to record the merrymaking pictorially. Three common elements in most JBL Christmas party photos, thanks to cadet initiatives: *1] Cigars.* Though unable to smoke them inside, many cadets felt these a perfect prop. *2] Senior class rings.* Delivery to seniors usually came just before Christmas break, and cadets wanted to show them off. *3] The "we're Number One" salute.* Not always easy to spot, these usually were displayed subtly -- and in some cases, ingeniously.

tries, and others from more distant parts of the U.S., remained on campus while fellow cadets rushed to their home surroundings.

Perhaps most anxious were those cadets whose activities during fall term had led them to the commandant's office where judgments were made and demerits were assigned.

If a cadet had outstanding demerits when vacation began, he was assigned to the "Bullring," where he walked one hour for each demerit, and where the supervising faculty officer -- his break from the school routine also delayed -- was as unhappy as the culprits.

In the spirit of the season, the walkers sang - not Christmas carols, but school pep songs such as "Hail!, Castle Heights!" -- though it always sounded somewhat like a misspelling of "Hail" led off the song.

Highlighting the joyful, high spirited days leading to the break from classes were the division Christmas parties. Each floor of a barracks [dormitory] was designated a division, run by cadet officers and supervised by a faculty officer -- who lived in quarters on that division and who, especially if married, often furnished party refreshments. One year, I provided barbecue, which the cadets seemed to enjoy until I told them they were eating goat.

During the division parties, rules and regulations were relaxed and general merry-making was in order.

Even today as holiday seasons approach, the joy and excitement generated by cadets before Christmas break comes into focus, bringing back fond memories and treasured bonds.

The charged atmosphere, the pent up energy of young males about to be freed from a restrictive environment, the comradeship among the cadets that also embraced faculty officers - all were manifest in these golden days.

For the cadets from foreign lands stuck on campus during the vacation period, life was not entirely dreary. Their fellow cadets who lived in Lebanon [the "day boys"] and their teachers often invited them to Christmas dinner.

Castle Heights was a way of life. Though not perfect, Heights had heart, a component which may become endangered in our times.

Author Update:
• BA, English, Martin College; MA, Education, Middle Tennessee State University. Joined Heights faculty 1958. Taught history, economics, English; served as Assistant Headmaster and Headmaster. Subsequently taught at Mt. Juliet Christian Academy until retirement. Married to Elizabeth Jane Robinson, Lebanon native, for 38 years until her death in 1994. Three children -- David, Heights '74; Michael '79; Amy Beth, 1984-86, graduated from Friendship Christian School after CHMA closing -- three grandchildren, one great-grandson. Amy Beth Hale has served on the Board of Directors of the National Heights Alumni Association since 1987. [*Yearbook Dedication, page 301*]

Risky move saved discipline

Guest Columnist: Cavalier Editor *LeRoy Dowdy III '62*

• *Published November, 1961*

JBL Preface: *In connection with 1961 Heights Homecoming, Dr. Laban Lacy Rice -- at that time the sole remaining survivor of the original Academy founders -- spoke to alumni at a dinner at the Lebanon Golf and Country Club. This is the* Cavalier *article.*

William L. Dowdy III as '62 senior, universities professor.

Had it not been for a severe disciplinary measure by Heights' founders in the Academy's early years, CHMA might not occupy its present important position in the field of secondary education.

This viewpoint was offered by Dr. Laban Lacy Rice, who with two other men established the school in 1902. He said the three founders [Rice, O. N. Smith, I. W. P. Buchanan] found it necessary to dismiss more than 50 students.

Dr. Rice, speaking at a Castle Heights alumni dinner, said it was customary each spring for small traveling shows to exhibit in Lebanon. "All had certain features objectionable to many citizens, but one in particular had a reputation so unsavory" the school management decided against granting a holiday so students could attend.

"We were challenged to make a severe decision when 52 boys broke campus in defiance. Even the merchants protested our decision to dismiss the boys," Dr. Rice said. "The students reasoned we could not afford to dismiss so many at one time. They acted brazenly, and at close of day sauntered back in a jaunty mood. My reasoning was we were a young school and that we would be headed in the wrong direction if we allowed them to put it over on us."

Dr. Rice said the dismissed students left the Hilltop singing the school song, and only one of the parents protested the dismissals. He said the boys showed no resentment. Seniors were allowed to return to take exams and graduate. [The incident occurred six weeks before end of school year.] Underclassmen were allowed to return the following fall.

The 91-year-old retired educator, who also served as chancellor and

Dr. L.L Rice [center], CHMA co-founder, was 1961 Homecoming guest. Joining him were Col. H. L. Armstrong [right] and John Fite Robertson, Heights class of 1911. Robertson by then was prominent Sarasota, Fla., attorney who had --- in June, 1920 -- married Martha Lynne Buchanan, daughter of Academy co-founder I. W. P. and Willie Elkin Buchanan and also a Heights grad (1916). The Robertsons had two sons, one of them John Fite Robertson Jr., a 1940 CHMA graduate killed in World War II.

president of Lebanon's Cumberland University, expressed "humility in being a pioneer, under Divine instrumentality, in laying the foundation that was to rise to an institution of wide respect and recognition."

"The first year we operated in Main, which served as dining room, kitchen, engineering department, study hall, infirmary, headmaster's office and recitation area. All phases of activity were conducted in that one building," Dr. Rice recalled.

He commended his co-founders for their part in establishing the school -- Smith for instituting a morale that was continued through the years, and Buchanan with the most important role: Heights business management.

"I. W. P. Buchanan was more responsible than any other mortal for the founding of Castle Heights. He engineered the deal that secured the Hilltop. He consulted with the architects," Dr. Rice said.

He also commended Heights President Col. H. L. Armstrong for his more than 30 years of leadership.

Dr. Rice said his 20 years at Castle Heights were "the busiest and dizziest of my life." And in a more somber note: "I am the sole remaining founder. I am the sere and yellowed leaf, dangling on the treetop, knowing winds of winter must shake it loose and it will fall to the ground."

Author Update:
• BA, Duke University; MA, PhD, Tulane University. US Navy service included four years active duty, more than 12 as Naval Reserve Intelligence Officer, retiring as Commander. Academic career stints at USAF Air War College, Dalhousie University, US Army War College, Boston University, Mount Saint Mary's College, Acadia University, England's Lancaster University, Johns Hopkins School of Advanced International Studies. Research/teaching in more than 60 countries; retired 2012 as Professor of Political Science, Alabama State University. Extensive publishing career, including co-editing two books -- *Pulling Back from Nuclear Brink: Reducing and Countering Nuclear Threats* and *The Indian Ocean: Perspectives on a Strategic Arena*. As member of London's International Institute for Strategic Studies and International Studies Association, lectured at schools/academies of Navy, Marines, Air Force and armed forces of foreign countries. He and wife, Maria Teresa Paone of Italy and New Orleans, have one son, Morgan. Continues research / writing in retirement in Montgomery, Ala.

'What counts is making honest living'

Guest Columnist: Cavalier Editor *Joseph Lipscomb Jr. '66*

• *Published June, 1966*

JBL Preface: *Columbus S. Chambers retired June 1, after 15 years in the Castle Heights maintenance department.* Cavalier *editor Joe Lipscomb wrote the following for the April issue of the CHMA newspaper.*

Joseph Lipscomb Jr., the only 3-year Cavalier editor, as '66 senior. Highly decorated with multiple academic and military honors.

His name is Shorty -- Columbus S. "Shorty" Chambers -- but even if his fellow maintenance men know his actual given name, they don't ever use it.

For one thing, he's been Shorty too long (for 15 years he has fired boilers and cut grass at Castle Heights).

And for another, he's short (5 ft., 2 in.).

Any afternoon one can find him in a place that doesn't seem much of a reward for 65 years of honest living -- the boiler room under the Academy Junior School administration building. The room has two chairs, an old bed, a wall calendar and a boiler. It's dark. But even without a fireplace, it can be a cozy place on a cool spring day.

Shorty treasures that old seat in the corner, especially this year -- which is his last.

"Now I may be retirement age, but I'm in perfect health, and only Uncle Sam is making me quit work."

You notice something special when he says "work" -- the "w" and "k" came out a little emphatic.

"It's funny, but I never get tired of riding the mower and shoveling coal. A man's got to make an honest living the best he can. Making an honest living is what counts.

"Some of these younger fellows just look at that old dollar mark when they choose a calling, but personally I know that when you're happy with your work, the money doesn't really matter."

While he was talking, I was reminded that even in today's economy custodians don't flourish, and that he was one of those rare people actually living a favorite dictum of back-porch philosophy.

He probably was steeped in back-porch witticisms as most folk from Smith County, Tenn., are. When Shorty was a boy, there were only nine grades in the local school, and "after the county gave me all the education it could, I farmed."

"I'd still be farming today if my daughter had not suggested hiring me to Mrs. Wallace Foreman [Academy dietitian]."

Shorty leaned back in his leaning chair, and he saw me noticing a pocket knife bulging from his traditional "train engineer" outfit.

"Yes, I've had a lot of knives - more than 500 - in my time. I take a cheap one and trade for a better and a better and a better one, until I get a good blade. Some of my fellow traders are Colonels around here -- [Leonard] Bradley, [Lindsay] Donnell

Dr. Joseph Lipscomb, Emory University.

and [JB] Leftwich. I guess when the government retires me, knife trading will be an even more important part of me."

He said that "boys up here haven't changed a bit in my 15 years; the school really isn't much different either, and it has been good to me."

You wonder whether Shorty really had been transformed much either; but laws are laws, and this summer will be the last one that he vies with his favorite peevish lawn mower.

Next fall when frost signals winter, somebody else will sit in the leaning chair, but chances are the replacement won't look like an engineer or trade knives.

And he may be a good boiler man, but he won't be a Shorty Chambers.

But don't feel sorry for Shorty - just have pity on those new suckers in Lebanon who'll try to beat him in a knife trade.

Author Update:
• Worked part-time at *Nashville Tennessean* while earning BA, Vanderbilt University. PhD, Economics, University of North Carolina. Joined Duke University 1975 in Sanford School of Public Policy and Department of Community + Family Medicine. Named Chief, Outcomes Research Branch, National Cancer Institute 1999, publishing extensively about and working on measures of cancer care quality, health economics, measurement of cancer costs, quality-of-care evaluations and related topics. One of three editors of 2005 book, *Outcomes Assessment in Cancer: Measures, Methods, Applications*, and sole editor of *Physician Staffing for the VA*. Joined Emory University 2004 as Professor of Health Policy & Management and Georgia Cancer Coalition Distinguished Scholar at the Rollins School of Public Health. Married Vanderbilt graduate Carolyn Egger of Kingsport, Tenn., in 1971, and they have one son, Bennett. Carolyn worked in medical library positions, and was named Fellow in the U. S. Medical Library Association in 2014.

• Joseph's brother, Bailey, is a 1968 CHMA grad. Earned pharmacy and doctoral degrees in pharmacy and medicinal chemistry, University of Tennessee. Recently retired from Medtronic, international leader in medical device technology. Bailey and wife Laura Lee live in Munford, Tenn. They have a son, Bailey, and daughter, Mary Baxter "Sunny" Biden.

To swing or not, just flip a coin

Guest Columnist: *Leonard K. Bradley Jr. '58*
• *Published July, 1999*

**L. K. Bradley Jr. as '58 senior,
Vanderbilt professor.**

"So, Bradley, you can't tell me what it means to be a swinger of birches?"

Paul Wooten, holding forth in his basement classroom in the Castle Heights Military Academy gym, had just lit into another student who obviously had not read his Robert Frost. That's OK by me, usually, but this time, c'est moi.

"Well, even if you can't read, I would have thought a boy growing up around Lebanon at least would have been a swinger of hickories."

PW punctuated his sermon with a mighty flip of "the coin," which bounced off the concrete walls of the classroom.

All eyes were on the coin. Would he catch it? Could he bank it from one wall to the other?

Aside from being a fair -- or, rather, a pretty efficient -- disciplinarian, PW was known widely as the best American literature teacher on a campus full of good teachers. He also had a great smile, but you just didn't see it in the classroom. In fact, if you were a student at Castle Heights, my recollection is that you hardly ever saw it at all.

This classroom stuff was just too serious for that. To say nothing of being sternly rebuked by PW in his role as assistant commandant. In fact, in his classes, if you didn't keep your eye on the coin, you'd better keep it on the ball.

And the ball, to PW, was "what IT means." And IT could be anything -- that search for truth, that search for meaning, that dread dead-end pursuit of adolescence which has no answer.

The trick is, you see, that adolescents don't know that these questions have no answers. Adults do, we learn later, but adolescents don't.

That tricky PW. He could have been president. Asking us those questions which had no answers. Of course, it never occurred to us students that he might be asking because he didn't know. He just covered himself by saying something lame, like "my answer won't work for you -

176

you have to find it in yourself."

Yeah, sure. And I'm just wondering, sitting in English class, whether I can have the car Friday night. Then I'll swing, PW.

But, that coin. Bounced off a thousand walls a million times over PW's years at Heights. A silver dollar with edges so rounded by hitting the walls and the floor in that classroom that it no longer had the milled edge. Just worn down over the years like the resistance of so many Heights cadets in English class.

Of all the teachers at Heights, PW was the only one who had such a clear trademark as that coin. Others had idiosyncrasies, quirks of behavior or language, but nothing they could carry around in their pockets.

But that was in 1956 or so. Much later, maybe about the mid-80s, I was sitting in a Lebanon funeral home visiting I-can't-remember-who [or, whom, as PW would say]. And sitting next to PW, as a matter of fact.

"So, what happened," I say, "to that silver dollar?"

He pulls it out, flips it a couple of times and puts it back into his pocket.

A week later, I get a very small package in the mail. It's "the coin." No note, no nothing. Just the coin.

So, to any other adolescents hereabout who suffered under the ponderous questions and stares of Paul Wooten, punctuated by a flippant flip of the coin, I'm serving notice that you'd better watch out.

The coin is still in service.

Author Update:
• Sergeant, U.S. Army 1960-63. Earned two degrees at University of Tennessee, 1963-68, while working as Copy Editor for *Knoxville News-Sentinel*. Began 28-year career for Tennessee State Government in 1968, serving as Policy Advisor for three governors, Vice Chancellor of State University and Community College System, Deputy Commissioner of Department of Human Services, and Research Director for Comptroller of the Treasury. Member of Political Science faculty at Tusculum College 1996-2001, and Public Policy professor at Vanderbilt University 2001-2010. He and former wife Sue Walls Bradley have two children, four grandchildren.

'Integral part of something extraordinary...'

Guest Columnist: *Frank Clayton '54*

• *Published November, 2006*

**Frank Clayton '54,
All Mid-South**

Upon my arrival at Castle Heights in early August, 1953, I wasn't impressed, and after two weeks of two-a-day football practices, I was even more disillusioned.

But after becoming acquainted with my teammates, Coach Stroud Gwynn, and the "teacher with the camera," Maj. JB Leftwich, conditions started to become more tenable.

I soon developed a rapport with my teammates and respect for Castle Heights that has endured for more than 50 years.

As the football team began to shape up under Coach Gwynn's methodical, patient and skillful coaching, my perception was that I was an integral part of something with the potential of becoming extraordinary.

I was among some of the most talented football players ever assembled at CHMA. I genuinely felt very appreciative and fortunate, indeed.

Earl Cato of Hartsville, Tenn., one of the finest athletes and runners I had ever seen, had an uncanny sense of timing and talent to break away, becoming famous for long scoring runs. Earl would position himself to be on a dead run and at full speed within a few seconds of receiving a punt or kickoff.

Harold Greer of Lebanon was one of the most tenacious, agile and hard hitting guards I ever played with. On defense, he "out-quicked" blockers despite being double-teamed on almost every play. He moved at maximum efficiency, unmindful of probable injury. In the Georgia Military Academy game, Harold received a kick to the head. Cut and with blood running into his eyes, he reluctantly left the game – only to be patched up and return to action almost immediately.

Many of us were post-graduates [attending Heights after graduating from high school], including Larry Wray who had played for Nashville Isaac Litton. He was no stranger to me, since my Oak Ridge High School team played Litton and sustained its only loss. Not only a stellar receiver, he was a potent force on defense at either end or in the backfield. Because of his speed, agility and quickness, he was a vital force on offensive plays.

The other end was Humphrey Folk, one of the few veterans on a

The 1953 CHMA football team, 9-0-0, won the Mid-South Conference champion-ship, with three of its players now in Castle Heights Football Hall of Fame -- Earl Cato, Frank Clayton, Harold Greer. The Tigers also won the 1957 and 1964 Mid-South title. First championship was in 1939, with repeats in 1943, 1948.

squad of mostly new cadets. An underclassman, he was a good receiver and a stellar defensive player.

Left tackle Frank Walker was our largest player -- 6-foot-2 and 220 pounds, big for the '50s. He was a three-sport athlete at Haleyville, Ala., High School the year before. An appendectomy after our third game sidelined him for three games and probably kept him off the All-Mid-South team, but he earned a scholarship to the University of Alabama.

Center Rodney Thomas, also of Hartsville, was the anchor of a ter-rific line. Snapping the ball to a tailback or a fullback in the single-wing offense requires concentration and skill, but Rodney was adept at this task. In addition, he was a bone-crushing linebacker and one of the Ti-gers' "48 minutes" players.

Jack Warwick at left guard made up for lack of size with unusual strength, speed and determination. He was one of the more cerebral players with a thorough understanding of the game. After graduating from Heights, he played at Tennessee Tech in Cookeville.

Watt Williams of Lebanon was our right tackle. He was unusual in size for that position, weighing only 170 pounds at 6-foot-3, and not the typical Mid-South Conference interior lineman. He was solid as a rock, and delivered the sharpest blows our opponents would experience.

Billy Williams, the fullback, had the rock solid strength to grind out tough short yardage and enough speed to be a breakaway threat. Our team seldom punted, but when we kicked, Billy averaged more than 40 yards per punt.

Our blocking back was Bobby Burkhart, another undersized "Phenom" no more than 5-foot-8 and 160 pounds. Bobby played with heart and determination, and was an unerring blocker. He was a good pass receiver, and in the single-wing formation if given the opportunity, a competent runner.

This is an overview of the football team some believe was the Academy's best. I am one of those who think so, but I may be prejudiced. I was among those who played for this 1953 Mid-South Conference championship team.

o o o

JBL Note: Some believe Frank Clayton may have been the equal of any single-wing tailback in Castle Heights history. He was a dynamic runner and an adroit passer who excited the cadet corps and a host of fans. Clayton made the all-conference team, and the '53 squad was undefeated while playing some of the toughest secondary school teams in Tennessee and Georgia -- out-scoring their opponents 273-63.

Four of the starters are known to be deceased: Rodney Thomas, Watt Williams Jr., Humphrey Folk and team leader and captain Harold Greer.

Selecting a best team in the history of a school is tricky. But old-timers who watched Heights' football teams during its last half-century always mention the teams of 1943 and 1953.

Author Update:
Attended Memphis State University, graduated from Florida State University with engineering degree. Played on 1956 FSU football team with Lee Corso. Worked for Pratt-Whitney, Union Carbide, Chrysler Space Division [at Redstone Arsenal and Cape Kennedy] and with Martin-Marietta, where he retired in 1992 in Oak Ridge, Tenn. He and his wife, Carolyn, were married more than 40 years, and have two children, four grandchildren.

Anticipation surged as Christmas neared

Guest Columnist: *Philip S. Huguenin '59*
• *Published December, 2005*

Stan Huguenin as '59 senior, with wife Pat for 50th in 2011.

It first really hit around Thanksgiving. Sure, Heights cadets thought about Christmas periodically throughout each fall, but turkey time was when it became THE focal point.

And the point was simple: Freedom. We were getting to leave Heights for up to a month to be with family and friends at one of the most important, joyous times of the year.

The Christmas leave also was meaningful as our first real break from the military/academic regimen starting late summer. It allowed a month-long reprieve from worrying about January's first-term final exams, and deep down we knew it was all "downhill" once we returned in the new year. (Downhill because laws of nature seem to dictate time flies faster January-May than August-December.)

The entire mood of the cadet corps and faculty changed during days leading to holiday vacation. There was less stress, fewer problems, excited anticipation, more smiles, reduced tension, and petty conflicts dissolved between roommates/dorm mates/teammates. And there were the division Christmas parties.

Even now, it's amazing to recall 600-700 males (this was before Castle Heights went co-ed) and 40-50 faculty members almost overnight turning friendly toward all and becoming quite socially and seasonally aware. Names were drawn for gift-giving [primarily "gag" items] and cadets chipped in for presents for the single or married faculty advisor presiding over each floor/barracks. The parties were held on the midweek night before the day of departure, and food and beverage (nothing alcoholic, of course) and loud music -- maybe Chuck Berry singing "Run, Rudolph, Run;" the Drifters' "White Christmas;" Elvis and "Merry Christmas, Baby" -- were highlights of the up-to-four-hour celebrations. One personal treasure is an aging black and white photo [*next page*] of the 1958 Tower barracks Yule fest. Jeans [dungarees] were pants-of-choice along with tee shirts, sweatshirts, Eisenhower jackets, athletic

Tower's usual "eclectic" mix of cadet roommates helped ensure the typical CHMA dorm Christmas party in 1958. Barracks faculty officer Capt. Howell Pearre [taught English, guided the National Forensic League chapter] is upper left [with glasses, under drum cymbal]. A spring reward was being among the six or seven Pearre selected to watch the Academy Awards in his first-floor apartment, well-past curfew and lights-out. [Note: Only a cigar appears to be missing from the usual three dorm party icons (*page 170*)].

letter sweaters, button-down madras shirts. Streamers hang from the ceiling, every single cadet is smiling or laughing, and the seniors are easy to spot because they're the ones making sure the camera catches their raised hands sporting just-issued senior rings. As they say, a "picture is worth a thousand words" -- and this photo and those like it of all Heights' Yule parties [*page 170*] ooze the carefree happiness and devil-may-care attitude of hundreds of guys home-bound.

Other important elements of the Heights' Christmas leave:

■ Concerns and worry about gifts for those back home were non-existent. What greater present for parents than just to have their sons home for the holidays -- and ready, like it or not, to be shown off at the shopping center, the drug store, at church services. (As one got closer to graduation and his final Heights Christmas, however, it was not unusual for cadets to realize a full-color portrait in uniform -- in a formal setting in Seats Studio in downtown Lebanon -- was the perfect parents' gift. With a smaller copy for any girl friend[s].)

■ For cadets living outside Tennessee, was it going to be a "train or plane" Christmas? You eagerly awaited word from home about travel arrangements, hoping for an airline ticket because you would be "free" that much quicker. Or, if you lived not that far away, you could go Greyhound or Trailways. And then you made plans -- usually joining a group to rent a cab --to get to the Nashville airport or railroad station.

Once home, a cadet became the single focus of family and friends rather than a last name and rank standing at attention among hundreds like him. He was – if lucky -- enveloped in love, respect, admiration. Though perhaps posturing at Heights as independent, idealistic and maybe even a tad cynical and above it all, the cadet at home at Christmas welcomed -- admitting it or not -- the familiarity, warmth, safety and security of his friends and family, this special time of year.

Many Heightsmen now look back on this annual Yule ritual and understand the strange, unique relationship between the spirit and meaning of their Heights barracks celebrations and those encompassing the traditions, joys and love of their families' personal Christmases.

Author Update:
• BA, Liberal Arts; BS, Journalism, University of Florida; graduate work University of South Carolina. [In college, edited first yearbook, newspaper at Manatee Community College, Bradenton Fla.; managing editor, *Orange + White*, University of Tennessee; editor UF's *Orange Peel* humor magazine, writer for *The Alligator* daily. In 1970s, founded/edited statewide *Florida Campus* magazine as sideline venture.] Reporter/columnist for *Sarasota Herald-Tribune*, followed by executive positions at two Chambers of Commerce before directing marketing/corporate communications for more than 30 years at three electric utilities. He and wife, Pat Alley Huguenin, married more than 50 years, with three children, five grandchildren.

The famous, feared 'Freshman Dip'

Guest Columnist: *John H. Spurlock '58*

• *Published November, 2006*

John Spurlock as '58 senior, '90s university professor.

Word was out among the Castle Heights cadet corps in May, 1958, that four football players -- all of them post-graduates -- were determined not to be thrown into the Heights swimming pool, the traditional end-of-school-year ritual signifying first-year Academy cadets' acceptance as "old cadets."

Nine of us seniors were equally determined the unwilling converts would be "baptized," despite their boasting they would engage in fight or flight, using any means necessary to avoid being dipped.

At the end of a Sunday meal on that gorgeous late May day, Col. D. T. Ingram, Academy commandant, gave the highly-anticipated-but-never-sure-when signal: "Gentlemen, Freshman Dip!"

The mess hall exploded into a revolving color wheel of Sunday parade regalia being thrown aside - gray blouses, ties and hats discarded, waiters and trays knocked over. Some freshmen offered little resistance, others were tackled as the four football players ran over would-be captors and out the mess hall doors with nine of us in hot pursuit.

With the four horsemen and the nine pursuers now running in stark white Sunday parade shirts and trousers, the cross-country chase began -- past the Academy president's home, down across the school golf course, in the direction of Town Creek, toward the Lebanon Country Club we sped. The gap between pursuers and pursued was about 200 yards as all parties jumped into and splashed across the brackish gray-green waters of the creek.

About one mile farther into the race, we nine were severely upbraided by a lady for running through her field at twilight and scaring her horses, now running about wildly. We apologized before leaving, not pausing to tell her about the four horsemen who had preceded us.

Approximately one mile beyond the Lebanon Country Club, we nine realized the chase was hopeless. Two of our number -- Battalion Commander Myron McClellan and Adjutant Robin Berrington -- decided on a change in plans and had us march in single file beside the road back to Heights. When cars approached, we would place our hands with fingers intertwined atop our heads like German war prisoners as McClellan told motorists we had escaped from Heights and he was taking us back.

At dusky dark, our squad paused on the road in front of the Lebanon Country Club. In line with the new plans, eight of us gave our watches and wallets to one in our group who subsequently would rejoin us.

A May formal dance was in progress on the Club terrace with gentlemen and ladies formally dressed in pastel-colored tuxes and gowns. We crawled toward them in line like an unseen infantry squad, pausing in the darkness just beyond the shimmering pool.

At the command, "Now!," we were all up and running toward the pool, giving our Rebel yells, ladies screaming as eight of us jumped in. Swimming to the far end, Berrington accidentally hit me in the right eye, and then we all began our desperate run to Heights.

Filled with fear but hope of avoiding the commandant and slipping unobserved up to my room, I walked through the front doors of Main Hall with a black eye, my white shirt and trousers a greenish-gray dirty mess, water squishing from my filthy dress shoes. Unfortunately, Colonel Ingram came down the hallway, clipboard in left hand. Face to face we stopped and exchanged salutes.

"Ouu-e-e-e, Bouy! [his Southern pronunciation of "boy"], where in the hell have you been?" he demanded.

"Sir, a group of us chased four football players across country to beyond the Lebanon Country Club, but we couldn't catch 'em!"

"Well, Bouy, you look awful! Get on up to your room, take a shower and get cleaned up!"

Squishing up the front stairs of Main, I realized and was truly thankful that I had just received a reprieve from "God."

Author Update:
BA, West Virginia University; MA, Ph.D. University of Louisville. Professor 38 years at Western Kentucky University, member WKU Graduate Faculty 20 years [specializing in American and Kentucky literature, linguistics]. At 2005 retirement, named Emeritus Professor of English by WKU Board of Regents. Authored *He Sings for Us: Sociolinguistic Analysis of Appalachian Subculture and of Jesse Stuart as Major American Author* in 1980. Member Jesse Stuart Foundation Board of Directors, editorial staff 20 years. Co-editor, contributor to *History of Lewisburg and North Logan County, Kentucky* in 1999. Married 52 years to Elizabeth Sue Williams; daughter Christy is WKU associate professor, granddaughter is college freshman.

Heights' 'brothers' reunite during WWII

Guest Columnist: *William D. Goodner '64*

• *Published December, 2004*

Bill Goodner as '64 senior, 2010 in Tokyo with wife, Sherre.

This is about two Castle Heights cadets who grew up in the same family, went to the Academy together, were separated by the events of World War II, and reunited in the middle of the collapse of Nazi Germany.

Coles and J.D. Goodner Jr. grew up in Alexandria, Tenn., during the 1920s and 1930s. J.D. was born in 1922, at about the same time his grandfather -- who had remarried late in life -- had another son, Coles. Even though one was an "uncle" and the other a "nephew," they grew up almost as brothers. When time came for high school, the decision was made that they would attend Heights.

Both became class leaders -- Coles elected vice president of the senior class, and J.D. secretary/treasurer. Coles excelled in basketball, while J.D. excelled in dating the local "Ice Cream Queen," Mary Elizabeth [Liz] Scheuerman of Lebanon's Perfection Dairy family.

Following 1941 graduation from Heights, both went to Vanderbilt University to continue their educations. Immediately after Pearl Harbor, however, Coles and J.D. and all of their Delta Kappa Epsilon fraternity brothers joined the Army. Coles became a pilot and J.D. was an infantry lieutenant.

J.D. was assigned to the 45th Infantry Division ["Thunderbirds"] of Oklahoma. After 18 months of

Coles [left] and J.D. Goodner, CHMA seniors in winter, 1940.

training, he became part of Gen. George S. Patton's invasion force into Sicily in July of 1943, where he participated in the "Battle of Bloody Ridge." In September, J.D. was under fire again during the invasion of Salerno on the Italian peninsula. (Years later he would tell his children that this was where he pulled out the picture of Mary Elizabeth that he carried through the war, and "kissed her good bye.")

Meanwhile, Coles completed training to fly the Boeing B-17 Flying Fortress, and was deployed to England in September, 1943, as part of the 8th Air Force. On October 14th, he piloted his craft in the infamous Schweinfurt raid, the mission -- later referred to as "Black Thursday" [60 B-17s were lost, 12 crashed in England, and 650 airmen went missing] -- against the main ball bearing plant that supplied most of the German war effort. After dropping his bombs, Coles put his Fortress into a nose dive toward the ground – trying to convince German pilots that his plane was hit. However, the ruse did not work.

When Coles pulled up, five German Messerschmitt fighters were on his tail. Bomber gunners shot down four of the five before running out of ammunition. The remaining fighter pilot proceeded to knock out all but one of the bomber's engines, and Coles had to put the plane down in a potato patch in France. (Members of the crew credited Coles with saving their lives through his skill in safely landing the plane.)

German troops soon captured the crew and moved them east into Germany. Coles was subsequently transported to Stalag Luft III, a Luftwaffe-run prisoner-of-war camp [depicted in the 1963 movie, "The Great Escape"] that housed captured air force servicemen. It was

May, 1945, after reunion in Nazi Germany, J. D. [left] and Coles Goodner.

near the town of Sagan, 100 miles southeast of Berlin.

J.D., unaware of his uncle's fate, continued in the Italian Campaign -- participating in the Anzio invasion and the campaign to take Rome. He was wounded twice during this period, and earned a Bronze Star for valor in combat. Through letters from home, J.D. was made aware that Coles was missing and did not know whether his uncle had survived. Early in 1944, the War Department informed the family that it knew Coles was a POW, but not where. In August of 1944, J.D. participated in his fourth invasion landing on the coast of Southern France.

Throughout the remaining months of 1944 and early 1945, many letters crossed the Atlantic between J.D., Liz and other family members expressing concern over Coles' fate. Since communications were difficult, much uncertainty existed. However, a single bazaar event in early 1945 confirmed that Coles was still alive.

In an attempt to obtain food for himself and some of his fellow prisoners, Coles wrote a check on a scrap of cardboard for $100 to buy a "box of food" from someone providing supplies to his camp. This improvised check made its way back to the bank in Alexandria, Tenn. Coles' father was called to examine the document, commented that he recognized the handwriting, and guaranteed the check would be honored. He was thankful to know Coles was still alive at that time.

About the time the cardboard check was being written, the Germans – fearing repatriated prisoners would rejoin the final battles to defeat Germany -- began moving POWs in Poland and Eastern Germany back into Western Germany. Coles' camp was force-marched west in January of 1945.

Relatives Meet As One Liberated

Capt. J. D. Goodner, Jr.   Lt. Coles Goodner

A family reunion was held recently in Germany when two Tennesseans, an uncle and his nephew, both 22 years old, and former Vanderbilt students, met two days after the uncle, 1st Lt. Coles Goodner, a prisoner of war of Germany since October 12, 1943, had been freed by American forces from Stalag VII-A near Moosburg. The

Nashville Tennessean reports on Goodners' reunion.

In April of 1945, the 45th Division moved into Germany. As the Allies overtook POW camps, J.D. would check prisoner lists to see if his uncle's name appeared. Finally, as the 45th moved into the very large Stalag VIIA at Mooseburg near Munich [130,000 Allied prisoners], J.D.'s persistence paid off. He found Coles' name on a roster, and was able to locate his "much thinner" uncle.

The reunion is captured on an 8mm movie frame shot that day, an image treasured by the family over the years. As the story goes, J.D. inquired, "Who's in charge here?" Following a pause of confusion during the chaos, J.D. declared himself to be in charge and announced that Coles was coming with him. He took Coles back to his unit, outfitted him with fresh uniforms, and made sure Coles got plenty to eat the next couple of weeks. Coles was sent home in May, 1945; J.D. in July.

J.D. and Liz married in August, 1945, with Coles serving as best man and Martha McAdoo of Lebanon as maid of honor. The newlyweds subsequently moved to Lebanon, started a family [five children -- three sons who went to CHMA and two daughters], and J.D. was involved in business and sales in and around Lebanon until his death in 1994. Liz

J. D. Goodner, wife Liz, son Rod Goodner '83 attended 1985 Heights Homecoming.

died in 2002. Coles and Martha married in September, 1945, moved to Jupiter Fla, and opened a small department store that grew into a successful business while they raised two children -- the son also going to Heights. Coles died in 2002, three days after Liz. Martha continues to live in Jupiter.

Author Update:
• William D. Goodner is a Lebanon native, one of five children of J.D. and Liz Goodner, and a grand-nephew of Coles Goodner. Earned BS, MS in electrical engineering from Georgia Tech; spent 10 years in government service in Intelligence Community followed by 30 years in private industry, primarily with SPARTA Inc. [products and services to Defense/Intelligence/Homeland Security sectors of federal government]. Married 44 years to Sherre Gray, sister of 1966 Heights grad Tere Gray, and they have three daughters, four grandchildren.

•Coles' son that went to Heights:
Mac Goodner '67; he and wife Judy live in Jupiter, Fla.

•J.D.'s CHMA sons:
William, column author, living with wife Shere in Huntsville, Ala.; John F. "Jack" Goodner '72, with wife Debbie in Lebanon, Tenn.; and James "Rod" Goodner '83, with wife Beth, also in Lebanon.

Lebanon from the clouds

Guest Columnist: *Maj. Paul T. Wooten, Faculty*
• *Published May, 1986 [originally written 1965]*

Maj. Paul T. Wooten, circa 1960s.

Back when I was a young man, nobody ever called me magnificent - but I did have a flying machine. Oh, it wasn't mine, it belonged to the airport manager and he was afraid I'd break it, but I thought it was mine - and almost every morning before breakfast I would climb over the airport fence, heave and tug at the hanger door until it finally slid back, and drag my flying machine out into the bright day that I always felt would probably be my last.

Magnificent or not, more than one young man is needed to wake up an airplane. There was only one of me. The disorganized business that began at this point with oil gauge, gas gauge, prop, wheel chocks, switches, spars and nerves was unbelievable then and of no interest to anyone now, except maybe to the Civil Aeronautics Administration and there's no need to upset them. But I did get the thing started, usually, and with me in it, usually, before it had gone too far to catch.

So, the other day when somebody asked if I would like to go up and fly around a little, I became a voluble veteran who quickly changed into a very quiet novice - because things just simply aren't the same.

Lebanon has a good airport now. Dull. But good. The paved, light-bordered runway has nothing on it but infinity. There used to be weeds. Rabbits. Sometimes cows. Today there is nothing to "watch out don't hit."

Another aircraft coming in is no longer a delightful surprise. The pilot and airport manager will have been yelling back and forth ever since the plane left Bowling Green. There is a whole mess of "Zebra Ten, this is Lebanon Unicom over and out and roger and one Aeronca on the downwind leg," and I can't listen fast enough for half of it.

On those bright, long-ago mornings, a pilot flying his plane off a Lebanon runway into the north wind or the south wind or the west wind could look down and see fields that would do for an emergency landing, and goats and fences that wouldn't - and over to one side or back behind him would be Memorial Hall Tower and the Public Square and Town Creek and all. Now, though, the pilot finds that he is climbing right out of the middle of a city, and if he has to land in a hurry it's going to be on somebody's split-level mortgage.

Some of the old landmarks are still down there. The Tower, of course, and the Square with General Hatton's monument - but the General's a little harder to find than he used to be. Maybe most of the old landmarks are still down there - but the differences catch the eye, and the old is all but lost in the new.

I had known, of course, that the town is larger now; but I hadn't known how much larger until I saw it again from the air. Prettier, too. From the air. If there had been as much to see two dozen years ago as there is today, a young man in his flying machine might never have come down.

These days, though, the young man doesn't have much time to look. The airplane is full of dials and lights and pointers that once weren't there to worry him. A surprising number of other airplanes clutter up the old wide reaches of quiet sky. The radio squawks and squawks and rasps and squawks.

They don't even call the throttle a ramble-handle any more.

Author Update:
• Graduate of Cumberland University; MA, Middle Tennessee State University. At Heights [Junior and Senior schools] 1932-66, with exception of 1942-45 as World War II Lieutenant, Chemical Warfare Service. Chairman of CHMA English Department, and served as assisting and Acting Commandant. English Department Chair, Nashville's Father Ryan High School, 1966-78. He and his wife, Lillian Crowder Wooten -- both deceased [Paul in 1986, she in 2005] -- had one daughter Merritt [also deceased] and a granddaughter. For more than 10 years, Wooten wrote columns for Lebanon publications, and his poetry was published in multiple national publications [including *Saturday Evening Post, Field and Stream* and *Jack + Jill*]. Paul was nephew of Col. H.L. Armstrong's first wife, Mildred.

You can go home again

Guest Columnist: *Terry G. Hawkins '70*

• *Published in 2006*

**Terry Hawkins as '70 senior,
2005 newspaper publisher.**

How does a potential disaster evolve into a summer reunion among folks who have not seen each other in more than three decades? With some good timing and a realization that we all are getting older, and that sometimes it's simply time to do something rather than just talk about it.

After a night of particularly heavy rains a couple of weeks ago, an early bird employee of the weekly newspaper I publish in Southeast Arkansas woke me.

The back of the shop "has water," she said; water that had soaked the carpets, doused envelopes of photos and generally caused a mess -- although the computers had been spared.

I hurried to the office and, after assessing the damage and helping spread out hundreds of photos to dry, it was casually mentioned that the office next to mine -- used only for storage -- also was wet. There were soaked boxes filled with records and receipts, containers of stuff used parade floats in years gone by, some empty boxes. No big loss.

Then I realized water had invaded a huge box with photos and negatives from years of events such as the Dumas, Ark., "Ding Dong Days" festivals and Dumas High School Bobcat football games.

Not a lot was ruined, and many were photos I would never need again anyway. But I hate to waste photos, especially now that -- like most newspapers -- we are virtually all digital and rarely have "real" ones we can use and later give to folks as keepsakes.

One of the last boxes I opened turned out to be from my house, filled with old books, among them my Castle Heights *Adjutant* yearbooks from 1967-70. They were damp, but after the better part of a weekend under the big blowers brought in by local carpet cleaners, all four made it through with nothing worse than crinkled pages.

As I leafed through them, senior cards fell out, carrying names I barely remembered -- especially those I had collected from the older cadets when I was a freshman and sophomore. I'd made a point to keep

192

them, though for the life of me I can't think why.

I have not been much of an alumnus; I never attended a reunion before or after Heights closed, and the only former CHMA cadets I have seen since visiting classmate Joe Alsup in Nashville [too many years ago to remember] are Gerald Wayne Loyd and Harold Farmer, and that's because they live here in Dumas.

But I have always been very glad I went to Heights, even as unhappy as I was as a ninth grader from the southernmost corner of Arkansas suddenly transplanted to Middle Tennessee.

Two of the first people I became friends with were Joe Alsup and another "town boy," Jack Leftwich. We were on the Tiger swimming team under Col. Bob Hosier's direction, and were still close when we graduated in 1970.

Many of those memories remain firmly lodged in our heads, but the photos and words in those yearbooks tell stories all their own. So my first thought when I opened the box was that I might have lost that little part of my past, one I really wanted to hold onto.

I do stay in touch with Joe and Jack by e-mail, but we haven't been in contact very often. I occasionally send Joe something I know will elicit a response and always gig him on his birthday, and I communicated fairly often with Jack when his son was in Iraq. And they both tell me a little now and then about their families and the guys [and gals] in our group at Heights 36 years ago.

I sent Joe and Jack each a report of the water damage -- and my little trip down memory lane -- and we exchanged a few e-mails over the next few days. It wasn't long before a "maybe" trip to Nashville at the end of June to visit Joe, in from Oregon, evolved into "Let's do it!" that will -- unless plans change -- include a gathering of old friends, bringing together people I have not laid eyes on in more than 35 years.

Odd. Who'd have figured a little - okay, a lot of - water running down a wall would open up such a flood of memories, most of them pretty good? Apparently one can go "home" again, even if it's to a place that was home for only four years better than a third of a century ago.

And I'm ready; it's been far too long.

Author Update:
• BA, University of Arkansas-Monticello. Newspaper experience with multiple papers in Arkansas, including more than 30 years with *Dumas Clarion* of which he is now publisher and managing editor. *Clarion* and Hawkins have won more than 250 Arkansas Press Association awards [including one for above column]. Director of Dumas Chamber of Commerce; past chairman, Main Street Dumas. Successfully fought leukemia, recovering after chemotherapy and bone marrow transplant from brother, Phil, who also attended Heights.

Lebanon, Tokyo surprisingly 'similar'

Guest Columnist: *Robin Berrington '58*

• *Published in December, 2008*

Robin Berrington as '58 senior, 1990s American Embassy in Japan.

Tokyo, Japan [11.25.08]: "Change" has been one of the political buzzwords in 2008 in the U.S., but here in Japan it applies to more than politics.

I am standing in front of Tokyo's newest attraction: Mid-Town Tokyo, a major urban development project. Its centerpiece is a multi-storied Ritz Carlton Hotel surrounded by sleek buildings with shops and restaurants. It has transformed its neighborhood. But why am I writing about Tokyo in *The Lebanon Democrat*? Recent trips to Lebanon and then Tokyo -- places that, although far apart on the globe, were crucial to my early personal and educational life -- vividly illustrate how much change has altered things.

In mid-October I returned to Lebanon for the 50th reunion of my class of 1958 at Castle Heights. When I turned off I-40, I was astonished at the sprawl of hotels and fast-food spots identical to the entry into almost any town in America today. In a word, this was not the South Cumberland Street I fondly remembered. Along West Main I spotted a few old, familiar sights -- the movie theater near the public square, the spire of Cumberland University, and a motel my parents used to favor -- but when I turned right on to Castle Heights Avenue, such landmarks became scarce. Except for the Mitchell House [now a Cracker Barrel property] and the old Main [beautifully restored as Lebanon City Hall], it was hard to find many remnants of the old Heights campus.

And when I stood on The Hilltop and gazed out behind the old campus, what once had been a panorama of unspoiled fields was now a vast housing development with dozens of homes.

Saddest of all, however, was the public square of Lebanon. It now boasts so many antique shops that the Wilson County webpage proclaims Lebanon "the Antique City of the South." Perhaps. But along with the empty shop fronts, they make the public square just a shadow of the dynamic place I remembered. Elderly tourists are the only ones likely to wander this area now, not the young people or families heading in and out of the movie or patronizing one of the mom and pop stores that used to line the Square. One wonders what General Hatton [commemorative statue] thinks of this change in the "downtown" Lebanon he has surveyed for decades.

And the connection to Tokyo? After Heights, I studied Japanese in college, and eventually spent almost 20 years of my Foreign Service career at the American Embassy in Japan. Since my retirement in 1999, I have managed to get back to Tokyo more than I have Lebanon, but coming so soon after my Lebanon visit, I realized my reaction to the Tokyo of 2008 was little different from my reaction to the Lebanon of 2008. Urban development schemes like Mid-Town Tokyo have made the city look more like any other modern, international metropolis -- tall buildings, noisy streets, and stores with names like The Gap or Benetton.

They also have wiped out the wonderful old parts of Tokyo that gave the city unique character. For a foreigner, it's just like another Los Angeles or Singapore with every convenience you would expect to find. Tokyo may be 1,000 times larger in population and area than Lebanon, but with every new Marriott or Outback Steakhouse -- and you can find them both in middle Tennessee as well as in Japan's capital -- a little bit of the original soul that identified these communities is gone.

And that's what puzzles me. Both Japan and Tennessee took pride in those special traits that set them apart. What happened to that pride? Why have they allowed themselves to morph into that dull uniformity of modern consumerism?

But change is inevitable. One can vainly protest it, or one can look for positive elements and celebrate those. And that is what I choose to do. Change can mean life-style benefits for many people. New real estate may lack the charm of the old, but it is probably more convenient and healthier to live and work in. Collecting antiques can lead to an appreciation of tradition and heritage. Large urban renewal efforts stimulate economic benefits for the greater community. And if change makes more people happy and content, as long as the negatives do not outweigh the common good, then why denigrate the result?

Although I may lament disappearance of the old, I still have memories to treasure. The new Lebanon and Tokyo of 2008 may no longer be quite my style, but I can accept the pleasures they give newer generations. I just wish there were more of a graceful compromise allowing both old and new to coexist.

Author Update:
• BA, Wesleyan University; MA, Harvard University. Peace Corps volunteer, Thailand, 1963-65. Worked for U.S. Information Agency [with service in Washington, DC] and U.S. Information Services [overseas duty, primarily in Tokyo [18 years], with assignments in England and Ireland] more than 30 years -- 1967-1999. Subsequently Deputy Director, President's Committee on the Arts + Humanities in the Clinton administration. Retired in Washington, active in volunteer programs involving Japan, music and the theater.

Macfadden's physical culture laboratory

Guest Columnist: *B. Edward McClellan '58*

• *Published April, 2008*

Edward McClellan as '58 senior, Indiana University professor.

Mark Adams, health editor of *GQ* magazine, has written a fascinating new biography of Bernarr Macfadden, a man whose influence reached all the way from the publishing houses of New York City to Castle Heights Military Academy, which he owned for many years.

"Mr. America" -- subtitled How Muscular Millionaire Bernarr Macfadden Transformed the Nation Through Sex, Salad, and the Ultimate Starvation Diet -- is published by Harper-Collins.

Macfadden -- who presided over a publishing empire that included such magazines as *True Crime* and *True Romance* and the newspaper, *The New York Evening Graphic* -- was best known for his commitment to physical culture, a sometime bizarre combination of nutrition and exercise. He also was a pioneer in the world of "yellow journalism," filling his publications with gossip columns by Walter Winchell and illustrations that bordered on pornography.

An early advocate of weight-lifting, Macfadden devoted years to cultivating his physique and sponsoring contests rewarding other body builders, including the famous Charles Atlas, whom he discovered. In pursuit of fitness, Macfadden often walked 25 miles to work, sometimes in bare feet.

Macfadden also was one of the

Macfadden Publications, started in 1918, became one of largest magazine publishers of 20th Century.

major food faddists of the twentieth century. He favored vegetarian diets [raw if possible] and unpasteurized milk along with long periods of fasting. A critic of scientific medicine, he believed diet, exercise and cold baths could prevent or cure virtually any disease.

On one occasion, Macfadden tried to treat one of his children suffering with convulsions by dipping her in hot water, a supposed cure that killed the child. Unruffled by the event, he blamed his wife for the death; she had not made the child tough enough. To relieve his wife's grief over the death, he suggested she walk the 200 miles between Athol, Mass., and New York City in snow and cold (when she agreed to have another child, he bought a train ticket for her).

To mark his 70th birthday, Bernarr Macfadden was featured in triptych in *Physical Culture* magazine.

Macfadden was a well-known womanizer. He was married four times, and was the father of a number of legitimate and illegitimate children.

Politics was never a central interest for Macfadden, but he briefly entertained a run for the presidency in 1936 on the Republican ticket, then later ran unsuccessfully for a senate seat in Florida as a Democrat.

Macfadden purchased Castle Heights in 1928. He saw the military Academy as a laboratory for his ideas about physical culture. On one occasion, he ordered employee Ed Sullivan [later a major figure in television] to prove the superiority of Castle Heights boys by matching its football team against the best that New York had to offer. The Heights team delivered the desired whipping, beating St. Johns Preparatory School 26-0 in a game played at Ebbets Field.

Adams does not write in any great detail about Macfadden's relationship to Heights, though he does mention the little known fact that Macfadden brought Italian Fascist cadets to the Academy for a short period of training in 1931. Macfadden was a great admirer of Mussolini and of Germany and Japan until it became clear they posed a significant threat

Appointed by President Herbert Hoover to study child health and welfare in Europe, Bernarr Macfadden was impessed with Benito Mussolini's Academy of Physical Education. Macfadden paid for a delegation of Academy youth to tour the U.S., and it arrived at CHMA in June, 1931. Col. H. L. Armstrong made Heights available for three months, and the youth were introduced to baseball, and received instruction in wrestling, swimming, football, fencing and boxing.

to the United States.

"Mr. America" is an exceptionally well-written and well-documented biography. Adams manages to capture both the character and influence of his colorful subject. He also is able to draw direct lines between Macfadden and contemporary food and exercise programs. He even sees Macfadden's publications as a forerunner of today's reality TV shows.

Anyone fascinated by American popular culture in the twentieth century could hardly find a better introduction than this delightful biography. Former Heights cadets will discover the reason they were not allowed to season their food with black pepper. [Macfadden frowned on spices]. They may also feel a sense of relief that Macfadden was not more directly involved in the Academy management. Wise leadership seems to have successfully insulated the institution from the worst of Macfadden's prescriptions, for which generations of faculty and cadets can be grateful.

Author Update:
• BA, MA, Wesleyan University; PhD, History, Northwestern University. Ohio State University faculty 1966-70; professor Indiana University 1970-2003. Served as editor, *History of Education Quarterly* and of *Journal of American History*. Authored <u>Moral Education in America: Schooling and the Shaping of Character, 1607-Present</u> in 1999. He and his wife, Mary, married more than 45 years, have two sons, one grandson. Retired as Professor Emeritus of Education and American Studies at IU. Brothers Myron (1958) and Alan (1962) also attended Heights.

Heights collection of autumn memories

Guest Columnist: *James R. Jewell Jr. '62*

• *Published November, 2009*

James R. Jewell Jr. as '62 senior, US Navy officer.

SAN DIEGO – The *Lebanon Democrat* I received last week had one of my Castle Heights heroes on the front page.

John Sweatt, son of Maj. John L. Sweatt Sr. of biology fame in the basement of the old gym, stood on the left of the photograph on page one. (Recalling Major Sweatt's "great frog dissection" still makes me smile.) John was a member of the 1959 class, and he took me under his wing when he was a 1959-60 post-graduate and I was a tiny sophomore blimp on the radar of Coach Stroud Gwynn's Tigers football team.

The other photos in the paper and on a social section of the paper's website showed "old folks frolicking" at Heights Homecoming with their classmates of 50 years ago. To me, John does not look any older than he did in August, 1959, when we began our two-a-days pre-season practice. I had not yet accepted I was not going to be the six foot, 180-pound second coming of Doak Walker, the SMU Heisman Trophy winner and NFL star for the Detroit Lions. I was 5-foot-6 and 128 pounds of not real bright. The 128 has morphed into something more substantial. The 5-foot-6 has become permanent.

After morning practices – where I would lose 10 pounds of water weight – John gathered the "town boys" and headed to Johnson's Dairy, where we each bought a half-gallon of orange drink and gulped down before returning to the Hilltop. Through that season, John took care of me. He, Earl Major and I all ended up with Naval careers, but I will never forget him watching out for the tiny sophomore.

The photo also evoked memories of Castle Heights autumns.

The sounds came first, when I was young growing up in Lebanon. On Sundays, the CHMA band's marching songs for the afternoon parade wafted down Castle Heights Avenue to our yard where I played in Middle Tennessee foliage at its finest. Later, there was my daily walk through the Academy arched gate up the narrow drive through the overhanging trees in their brilliant browns, yellows, oranges and reds.

Somewhere in my piles of Heights photographs, there is one of Sharry Baird Hagar who was on the 1961 Homecoming court and my date for the weekend [*see right*]. She and other court members are near the football field with aster bouquets – known as a talisman of love and a symbol of patience -- pinned on their jackets. Young women seemed to be prettier in the fall.

Castle Heights 1961 Homecoming remembered by Jim Jewell '62 was as action packed as those of recent vintage reported by JB Leftwich. [The Tigers beat a favored McCallie 7-6.] Sharry Baird [left], Queen Celeste Norris and Suzanne Landis formed the Homecoming Court, and CHMA co-founder Dr. L.L. Rice was featured speaker [*page 172*].

Pleasant memories: Castle Heights football in the splendor of fall, maroon and old gold football uniforms blending with the harvest colors, military march music matching the mood. John Phillips Souza would have loved autumn Saturdays at Castle Heights.

Assistant coaches Jimmy Allen (not just a coach but a good friend), Frank North and David Robison were all one could hope for as a high school player. Maj. Robert Hosier -- he and his wife two of the nicest people I knew in Lebanon -- had one of the greatest accents ever, though Col. Dan Ingram's Virginia accent remains my favorite of all time. Headmaster Col. Leonard Bradley -- always in control, gracious, concerned about every student.

The gate is gone along with those glorious trees. The road is a thoroughfare, not an entrance to a way of life, also long gone. The gridiron is now Stroud Gwynn Field, but more of a track for exercisers, youth soccer and festivals.

Those autumns were an amalgamation of folks. The Heights football team consisted of "town-boy" cadets Jim Gamble, Mike Gannaway, Earl Major, Jimmy Hatcher, Bill King and me; on-campus cadets Jimmy Nunn, Day Johnston, Ronnie Ewton, Buzzy Fryer, Dan Pritchett, Desmond Coffee, Ronnie Naar, Hugh McCoy and Tommy Higgs; and local post-graduates such as John Sweatt, Ed Lasater, Larry Bucy, Gordon Skeen, Jimmy Byrd and Kenny Berry. And the "PGs" from out of town such as Snookie Hughes, Happy Harper, Joe Chambers, Rusty Hodges, Delton Truitt, Bate Hobbs, Jim Pfeiffer, Kirk Mills, John Taylor, Doug McAfee and Glenn Hickey.

And thinking of Jimmy Hatcher...it was in August, 1962, he invited me and Capt. Burke Herron to join him for a week in Daytona Beach. We took off in Burke's 1960 Ford Falcon, staying at the Frontier Motel.

We bought a supply of shrimp, hot dogs and cereal, and hit the beach. Jimmy and I chased waves and girls, Burke basked, and we hooked up with some Auburn University football players waiting for pre-season training to play touch football twice a day. The motel jukebox played Ray Charles, and at night a full moon gleamed.

But it is a Brigadoon, a place I cannot go again unless I wake up in the middle of a hundred-year sleep.

As I looked at the front-page photo, I wondered if John had a sense at Homecoming of returning to Valhalla. He has gone on to success as an important cog with Cisco Systems, an American multinational corporation that designs, manufactures and sells networking equipment. He married one of Lebanon's true beauties and an intellect to boot in Suzanne Mitchell Sweatt. I suspect Castle Heights autumn is even more poignant for him. He was steeped in it.

When I saw that photograph, I remembered those halcyon days, which don't seem to exist with their innocence any more in today's commercialized, homogenized world, and how John made them so much better for me a half century ago.

Author Update:
• BA, Middle Tennessee State University; graduate study Texas A+M University. Began 21-year career with US Navy in 1968, attaining rank of Commander and serving on six ships -- including USS Yosemite as executive officer over 900-personnel organization. Awarded Navy Commendation Medal for superior performance. Tour duty included serving as Associate Professor, NROTC, Texas A&M. From 1985 to his 1989 retirement, he was Leadership & Management Education Program Director, Naval Amphibious School, overseeing 40-member personnel department. He lives with his wife, Maureen, in San Diego, where he is Director of Programs for Pacific Tugboat Services. He is author of *A Pocket of Resistance: Selected Poems*, and writes a weekly column for *The Lebanon Democrat*.

Lebanon full of surprises, temptations

Guest Columnist: *Rodger Tarr '59*
• *Published December, 2009*

Rodger Tarr as '59 senior,
Illinois State University professor.

Fifty years ago, I graduated from Castle Heights. Graduation Day was an idyllic moment with the sun showering beams of light over Lebanon. Proud parents watched as we marched proudly in full dress uniform and polished brass into Macfadden Auditorium -- and then braved stifling heat [no AC in those days] -- to receive our diplomas. Afterwards, lingering hugs and shameless tears of goodbye were endured by all.

We of the Class of '59 not only were leaving our beloved Heights, we were leaving Lebanon, the city that welcomed and nurtured us as we began the climb toward manhood. Lebanon, in so many ways, served as a protective mother in absentia. Now we were leaving her, for many of us forever. Parting, as Shakespeare counseled, is, indeed, sweet sorrow.

Returning to Lebanon brings back a flood of memories. I recall vividly walking down her tree-lined boulevard of stately homes from campus to the Square. I grew up in rural Florida, where rattlesnakes, gators and panther were an expectation, not a surprise. To me, Lebanon was a wonder, especially the activities surrounding the square on a busy Saturday afternoon. I recall as if it were yesterday the farmers, some fiddling and most chewing, selling their fresh meat on the southwest corner. That astonished me, since I had never witnessed such, even in my rural Florida.

Lebanon also was full of surprises and temptations. The stores on and near The Square gobbled up hard-earned dimes.

Movies at the Capitol, closed in 1980, were cadet favorites. It was renovated and reopened 2013 for special events -- such as the CHMA 2013 Homecoming dinner.

202

Historic downtown Lebanon Square in 1960s with statue of Gen. Robert H. Hatton, born in Ohio and resolute the Union should not dissolve into civil war. When the Southern states seceded, Hatton -- a Cumberland University grad and Lebanon attorney -- cast his lot with the Confederacy. Earlier he served in Tennessee General Assembly, lost a race for governor, and was elected to U.S. House in 1859. Brigadier General Hatton, 35, was killed in 1862 commanding the Tennessee brigade in the Battle of Seven Pines.

That movie theater, south of the square, was our den of iniquity -- where we learned much more than we needed to know about "the darker side of love." However, the fresh air of Lebanon seemed always to revive our common senses. My roommate, Alger "Country" Watkins [I nicknamed him "Country" because he was from East Tennessee—he liked that], and I and our best friends John Smithson and Archie West spent endless hours walking the streets, so enthralled that on occasion we barely made it back to campus before curfew.

Mind you, Alger and John were true country boys, and soon they had me mastering the art of chewing tobacco -- starting out on "loose," then progressing to "plug," and finally to "twist." It was a sign of passage to be able to chew the vaunted Wilson County twist. The Lebanon shopkeepers -- especially those at the little market, approximately halfway from the campus to the square on the left -- were astonished at our capacities, and said so in that incomparable Tennessee twinkle and lilt I came to admire and finally to love.

And who can forget The Lighthouse, across from campus on the road to the ever-beckoning Nashville, a city out-of-bounds to us, hence a mecca of imagined sin and teenage dreams. Every Saturday morning after room inspection, we gathered at The Lighthouse to imbibe the best

"Modern day" [i.e., 1950-60] photographs of Lebanon's Lighthouse Diner could not be found, but this 1940s view -- reportedly with then-owners Curtis and J. O. Williams -- was provided by Historic Lebanon. Within walking distance of CHMA, the Lighthouse featured hamburgers, fries, shakes and a "six-for-25 cents" jukebox. Not-approved late-night runs by cadets for food were risked, and faculty officers serving weekend OC [Officer-in-Charge] duty regularly checked the Lighthouse for absent-without-official-leave [AWOL] cadets. A Shell station, rental car agency and chiropractor's office followed at the diner location.

-- ever creamy milk shakes and piping hot fries. We stuffed our quarters (six songs!) into the jukebox and listened to the plaintive anthems of Don and Phil, Patsy, Mother Maybelle, and Hank and Johnny. Few protested that music, which for us at least was a mandate, not a choice.

My most overwhelming memory of Lebanon was the day I cried, unabashedly, for the first time in public. It was in the Capitol Theater. We had gone to see Ernest Hemingway's "A Farewell to Arms," starring ruggedly handsome Rock Hudson and the stunningly beautiful Jennifer Jones. The novel and the movie are the equal of any Shakespearean tragedy. The scene of Jones dying in the arms of Hudson in a hospital in war-torn Italy was and still is too much to bear. Tears and sobs were palpable throughout the theater. The warm sun that greeted us upon departure brought little solace.

Reluctantly, I now must bid you fine citizens of Lebanon, past and present, adieu. But not before assuring you that if it were not for Lebanon, the lives of the cadets who passed through Castle Heights would have been markedly different. Yes, Lebanon meant that much to us, of this I bear witness. Thanks so much for welcoming and caring for us. The indelible history of our long grey line and the city is inextricably linked. To paraphrase the immortal bard, so long as there are words to write and eyes to see, Lebanon will perish never.

One Lebanon landmark in place in 1902 when Castle Heights School opened was this entrance arch. The middle segment was for wagons and buggies, the two sides for pedestrians. It stood until the late '50s, when West Main was changed from two to four lanes. The mid-'90s illustration is by Chuck Ward '42, JB's first *Cavalier* editor (page 166). Ward is a noted Tulsa, Okla., architect, and was honored by his alma mater -- the University of Oklahoma -- and the Oklahoma Arts Council for his artistic talent (including illustrations of many OU buildings and great cathedrals of the world).

Author Update:
• BA, Florida Southern College; MA, Kent State University; PhD., University of South Carolina. Distinguished Professor Emeritus and Professor of English Emeritus, Illinois State University, and editor of a number of books on Thomas Carlyle and Marjorie Kinnan Rawlings. During his faculty career, he received a National Endowment for the Humanities Research Fellowship, was a Fulbright Senior Research Scholar in Great Britain, and a Post-Doctoral Research Fellow at the University of Edinburgh. He and his wife, Carol, also an ISU Emeritus Professor of English, have been married more than 30 years and have one son.

Remembering the wrestling restauranteur

Guest Columnist: *B. B. Branton*

• *Published January, 2012 / Chattanoogan.com*

Cracker Barrel Restaurant founder Danny Evins taught former Tyner Academy [Chattanooga, Tenn.] grad Jim Inglis -- a 1967-68 CHMA post-graduate -- some important life lessons in the winter of 1968.

High on the list – besides a good single leg takedown – was "be careful who you play poker with."

Evins, who died this past Saturday [January 14, 2012] at the age of 76, was a volunteer head wrestling coach at Castle Heights Military Academy in 1967 and 1968, and only a couple of years away from making his fortune in the now famous down-home restaurant chain whose headquarters are located near the old Castle Heights property.

"Instead of your usual school bus for road trips to McCallie, Baylor, Sewanee Military Academy or Columbia Military Academy for matches, Danny had this customized Big Orange Trailways bus completely furnished [kitchenette, beds], along with a driver," said Chattanooga native Inglis. He is a retired teacher from East Ridge Middle School and a member of the 2008 inaugural Hall of Fame class at Tyner.

"That was pretty sharp way to travel for a bunch of teenagers. Danny did everything first class."

During those trips, Evins – a former Mid-South Conference wrestler at Heights in the early 1950s – would play poker with the wrestlers for small stakes [a dime or 25 cents] and win every hand on every trip.

"On our last trip of the season, he showed us how he won. He turned every card face down and could correctly identify each one," Inglis stated.

Jim Inglis as 1967-68 CHMA post-grad.

"I marked the deck," Danny said with a smile. "Boys, the lesson to learn – be careful who you play cards with."

Evins, who earned all Mid-South honors in wrestling in 1952 and 1953, went from slick poker player to savvy businessman almost overnight as Cracker Barrel has grown from one store in Lebabnon in 1969 to more than 600 restaurants in 42 states.

"He was a good coach and worked us hard," said Inglis, who also lettered in football for Heights on its 7-0-2 team in the fall of 1967, and later was the head wrestling coach at Riverside High School [Decaturville, Tenn.] in the 1970s.

"My first thought when my Dad dropped me off at Heights in September of 1967, was 'What did I do to deserve this [dorm student at a military school],'" Inglis recalled.

"But looking back, it was a great time for me as that year of prep school experience would prove beneficial in college, both academically and athletically," stated Inglis, who would earn All-Ohio Valley Conference honors as a senior [1971] in football at Middle Tennessee State University.

"The teachers and coaches made you feel at home."

While Inglis attended CHMA that one season, Hugh Green was a four-time Mid-South medalist at Castle Heights [1966-69], including 1968 115-pound champion.

"Danny was a very good wrestler in the early '50s and really helped us for a couple of years in the late '60's. His motivational speeches before a match were a little unortho-

Danny Evins '53 [center, last row] was volunteer CHMA wrestling coach in the late '60s, prior to serving 1974-86 as Heights Foundation officer trying to keep the Academy open while at same time serving as CEO, Cracker Barrel Restaurants.

dox as his pep talk for me before my 1968 finals match was 'just don't get pinned,'" said Green, who went on to wrestle at UT-Martin, with a laugh.

Author Update:
• 1969 graduate of McCallie, University of Mississippi 1974. Former Sports Information Director of Sewanee, University of the South, and two other colleges. Previously Information Director, Athletes in Action, and member Board of Directors, Tennessee Wrestling Hall of Fame. Writes for *Chattanooga.com*, organized in 1999 as one of the first full-service web-only daily newspapers.

Chapter Six

Homecomings

"To look backward for a while is to refresh the eye, to restore it, and to render it the more fit for its prime function of looking forward."

-Margaret Fairless Barber

THE DRILL:

Homecoming at Heights was always a special time during the Academy's existence, moreso for enrolled cadets and their families -- who used the event to visit their sons [and daughters] midway between late summer starting of classes and upcoming Christmas break. Once CHMA closed, however, Homecoming became a "celebration of what once was," and faithful alums from all over the country began returning to The Hilltop to make sure the "Heights spirit" continues. JB Leftwich -- as did other faculty who attended until they passed -- found the October weekends rejuvenating, as evidenced by the columns he wrote after each celebration.

Overleaf Photo:

Main and The Circle were Homecoming "square one." Evident is yet another Heights tradition: SHEET DECORATIONS - the hanging of multi-colored sheets from barracks windows urging Tigers teams to victory.

Photo Credit: JB Leftwich

Henry, Chuck, 'Cajun' and the '40s boys

• *October, 1985*

They were telling their stories of Castle Heights, these "boys" who were my pupils and friends during the war years, these men in their late 50s and early 60s who returned to campus last weekend.

It was a trip down Memory Lane, adventure into the past, as they recounted their experiences and remembered the times that were and, in some instances, that never were.

I was a kid with them, a 21-year-old beginning a 38-year teaching career in 1941, and at the time more attuned to the cadets than to the faculty and administration. I was Captain Leftwich on campus, saluted and "Sirred," but off campus to the ones who became close friends, I was just plain JB.

They grew up, married, became fathers and grandfathers, retired, and many of them died. They went in large numbers to North Africa, Normandy and the South Pacific, and many were casualties. Their names are on the War Memorial which is the hub of the Lower Circle on the Heights campus.

Last weekend they gathered, and told their war stories and their Castle Heights stories.

There was **Henry Rigby**, battalion commander in 1941-42, during my first year at Castle Heights -- Henry with the piercing gray eyes who could stare a hole through an insubordinate cadet (even through a young faculty officer) and who may have been the best Heights battalion commander I ever knew.

Henry left to become a hero with the infantry, was severely wounded in Normandy, still nurses the pains of five bullet wounds. His wife is writing a book about his experiences.

Said Henry of the current cadets: "They need to dress it up a bit. They could look sharper." Henry did not remember he said the same thing about the cadets under his command 44 years ago, but he knows when a cadet should dress it up.

There was **Charles "Cajun" Cook**, a senior in 1942 but at Heights as a post-graduate until called to service late in 1943.

"The other boys kept telling me about the picture show and Shannon's Drug Store [then the cadet gathering place] but I didn't know anything about them during my early years because I was always on the `bullring' on town-leave days," Cook remembered.

"One day **Thane Hooker**, the battalion commander, was talking to a bunch of us on the `bullring,' and he said, 'One of you could be battalion commander, if you would set your head to do it,' and he took off his saber chain and pitched it to me.

"That set me to thinking and I made up my mind to become battalion commander. I still have that chain."

In the fall of 1943, Cajun (he's Charley now, but we couldn't think of him as Charley), came back for his Heights PG year and was battalion commander until the draft board issued an ultimatum and he enlisted in the Navy, but not before having his day as a football hero.

Thane Hooker as '40 post-graduate.

There was **Charles "Chuck" Ward**, editor of *The Cavalier* and my good friend. We had not seen each other since he graduated in 1942. Chuck listed his address then as Cartagena, Colombia, South America. His father was in the oil business, so Chuck knew far-away-places.

"Until I came to Castle Heights, I had attended one-teacher schools, small schools for United States citizens in foreign countries. Heights almost overwhelmed me. I'd never seen a school so big," Chuck recalled.

There were others here on this memorable weekend . . . **Chick Muller** and **Raymond Hughes** and **Art Shemwell** and **Bill Moore** and **Ed Brown** and **David Mancosh** and **Robert Spann** and **James J. "Jay-Boy" Sanders** and **Kenneth Atchley** and **Dan Andrews** and **Joe Basore** and . . .

Thane Hooker, who tossed the saber chain to Cajun Cook, did not attend. He survived the Bataan Death March, but later died in U.S. attack on a Japanese ship on which he was being transported as a prisoner of war.

• This was the largest Homecoming celebration while CHMA was operating. Twenty-eight Homecoming weekends have been organized since 1986, and attendance averages 350 yearly.

Nostalgic journey for the Class of '43

• *October, 1993*

Their hair is thinner and their waists are thicker, but this wonderful gang of free spirits who are the Castle Heights Military Academy Class of 1943 in many aspects are the same kids whose senior pictures appeared on their name tags during their 50th reunion this weekend.

They gathered on the campus with the same zest that marked their years as cadets, albeit many of them graduated from Castle Heights right into the Armed Forces, some to fight fierce battles, suffer wounds and some to die in combat.

There was a rumor circulating during the weekend that some of the '43ers for old times sake had painted the cannon -- which, incidentally, is layered with coats of paint applied by generations of cadets. The rumor was false. The cannon was painted, but a much younger graduate was the perpetrator.

The 86 members of the Class of '43 came to the Academy 50 years ago from all over the country. Why did so many come such a long distance to go to military school?

Herb Schuler, Woodbury, N. J., simply picked Heights from a magazine advertisement. In those days, most of the leading military schools advertised in *National Geographic, Good Housekeeping, Boys' Life* and other publications.

"I liked what the ad said, so I wrote for a catalog and ended up at Castle Heights," he said.

Paul Kyyhkynen, now a retired trial lawyer living in South St. Paul, Minn., was another who came a long distance to attend Heights. How did a Minnesotan with a strange sounding name come to be a cadet at CHMA?

"Well, because Dad said he didn't like the gang I was running with. He said pick out a school, you're going to a military academy. So I got the catalogs, and chose

Advertisement used by CHMA in '70s in national publications, many directed to mothers.

Heights."

Then there was **James J. "Jay-Boy" Sanders** -- who only had to travel 30 miles from Nashville -- a top cadet, and as a senior, battalion commander. Jay-Boy's experience in World War II is another column.

And **Robert G. Spann** of Waverly, Tenn., whose nickname is too politically incorrect to mention.

The **Means** twins, **John**, now of Washington, D. C., and **Dick**, now of Annapolis, Md., grew up on the corner of West Main and Castle Heights Avenue. They were identical then, but not now. Dick, aka "Oscar," has a beard.

"Didn't you used to be twins?" a classmate asked

.   Tennesseans **Bobby Stewart** [wingback], Gallatin; **Lacy Fields** [end], Clarksville; and **Billy Burnett** [guard], Milan -- members of the undefeated, once tied, Mid-South champion Heights football team of 1943 -- recalled teammate **Pat Parker**, one of the Academy's greatest athletes, who was killed in World War II. Bobby pitched a no-hit game while on the Heights baseball team.

Former Cadet **Bob Granacher**, Atlantic Beach, Fla., was largely responsible for gathering 23 of the 1943 classmates for this Golden Anniversary celebration. Bob says his wife **Mary Lou**'s unrelenting determination to track down class members was a major factor in the success.

More than 200 total alumni, the largest number ever, gathered on the campus. The big turnout to a large measure was due to the efforts of **Rob Hosier** '63, president of the Alumni Association, who has made Castle Heights a principal interest. And not to be overlooked are Rob's wife, **Susan**, and his parents, **Col. Robert** and **Frances Patton Hosier**. It's a family hobby, and hobbies require work.

Among the group were quite a few members of the Class of 1963, observing the 30th anniversary of their graduation.

The old boys -- and a few girls -- gathered around the War Memorial to pay tribute to the casualties, many of whom were members of the classes of the early '40s. They were distressed to hear the War Memorial -- and Smith Chapel and Ingram Barracks and the Armory -- may be razed if Castle Heights Avenue is extended as planned to the new U.S. 70 Bypass highway.

It was an interesting day for Colonel Hosier and for **Col. Leonard Bradley** and for me, probably the only survivors of the 1942-43 CHMA faculty.

My son, **Jack Leftwich** '70, observed: "Dad, I can almost guess the year the alumni graduated by the way they address you. The '40s call you 'Captain,' the '50s 'Major,' and the '60s 'Colonel.'"

True. And the '70s call me JB.

Hosiers important part of Heights' past, future

In virtually every column JB Leftwich wrote about Castle Heights' Homecomings since 1987, he references the work of Rob and Susan Hosier -- and rightfully so.

Prior to the closing of CHMA in 1986, a volunteer Alumni Association Board of Directors comprised of graduated cadets -- who elected one of their own to serve as annual Association president -- oversaw operation and fundraising of the alumni group. It was the strong, vital effort of Lt. Col. Stroud Gwynn in 1986-87 to keep the Association afloat and ensure its independence after the Academy's closing.

Hosier '63, now a retired high school history teacher in nearby Gallatin, Tenn., began serving as Association president in 1988. "Heights is my hobby. I really don't have any other additional outside interests, and the Alumni Association is very important to me," Rob said.

While Rob serves as president of the Castle Heights National Alumni Association [HNAA], it continues to operate with a 25-member volunteer Board of Directors. His wife, Susan, agreed in 1988 to keep the alumni database updated, serve as bookkeeper, prepare annual required financial statements for multiple governmental entities, edit a newsletter, and coordinate/schedule each year all Homecoming activities.

As JB notes in one of his columns about that year's weekend Homecoming festivities, "and it is all possible because Rob stepped forward -- along with Susan -- to take responsibility for alumni activities and, in effect, perpetuate the life and 'existence' of his alma mater."

And, most important, it's been a "family affair."

One longtime member of the CHMA faculty, joining in 1939, was Col. Robert Hosier. He earned his BS and MS degrees from VPI [now Virginia Tech], taught history and economics, and subsequently headed the Social Science Department before retiring in 1973. For more than 25 years, he was Heights swimming coach, leading his teams to nine Mid-South Conference championships during three decades. He and his wife, Fran-

Col. Robert and Frances Hosier

ces, were married more than 56 years, and had two sons, Rob and Richard, and two grandchildren. [*Yearbook Dedication, page 299*]

• Rob '63 [BS, Austin Peay State University; MAT, Middle Tennessee State University] and his wife, Susan, have one son, Brian.

• Richard '66 [BS, Tennessee Technological University] and his wife, Lois Ann, have a daughter, Ginger. Richard also has served on the HNAA Board of Directors many years.

From a 2002 JBL column:
Frances Patton Hosier, 88, who died recently, was a pianist, a faithful member of the Baptist Church, a teacher and a sparkling conversationalist. But her identity assumed another dimension in her latter years when she, her son, Rob, and her daughter-in-law, Susan, more than any other force preserved the CHMA Alumni Association. She was one of the icons of the Academy and her death removes a rich resource of Castle Heights lore

Lieutenant Colonel Robert B. Hosier

The City of Lebanon proudly names this aquatics complex in honor of Lieutenant Colonel Robert B. Hosier. It was the request of Jimmy Floyd to recognize the accomplishments of Colonel Hosier. Colonel Hosier served as an instructor in military studies and social studies at Castle Heights Military Academy for many years. He also served as a swimming coach for much of that time, and was a member of both the Castle Heights Military Academy Sports Hall of Fame and the Tennessee Swimming Hall of Fame. Colonel Hosier taught hundreds of young people to enjoy aquatic competition, swimming and diving. "Colonel Hosier meant a great deal to me and all the other cadets. His influence went beyond that of instructor and coach. He was good for us in every way." -Jimmy Floyd, 1998

Col. Robert Hosier began his outstanding career in mid-1942, taking over the swim team from then-coach Capt. Vern Crissey, called to active duty. During three decades, Hosier's squads captured the most championships of any Heights athletic team. His overall dual meet record was 155-66-3, with 10 undefeated seasons and nine of CHMA's 12 Mid-South titles. Fifteen Heights swimmers and three relay teams made All-America [top 10 among U.S. prep schools]. Most prominent Tigers swimmer was Bill Dudley '47, member of the 1948 U.S. Olympic Team.

Weekend to remember for many Heights alums

• October, 1995

October's first weekend was one to remember with weather only a Superior Being could design and deliver for Castle Heights alumni, and for members of Lebanon's First United Methodist Church.

Ah, what a day was Saturday at Heights, where alumni in record numbers returned for two class reunions and for a general gathering which reached numerical heights under the dedicated direction of alumni president Rob Hosier and his wife, Susan.

'Twas the 50th anniversary of the Class of 1945, many of whose members went directly into the armed forces to participate in the ending of World War II.

How well they turned out and what wonderful citizens they are. At their dinner Friday night there were five physicians -- **Joe Bethany Jr.** of Eutaw, Ala.; **Sam Carney** of Madison; **Douglas Ey** of Huntington, West Va.; **Charles Gill** of Nashville; **George Pakis** of Jackson, Tenn. And two Florida dentists, **Dick Brooks** of Punta Gorda, and **Jim Nagelson** of Winter Park, both basketball players at Heights.

Successful '45ers in other professions included **Dan Andrews** of Dickson, Tenn., bank president; **Joe Neff Basore** of Bella Vista, Ark., land developer in at least two states; **Donald Jones** of Murray, Ky., educator, and on and on.

The Class of 1970 also gathered in force. They, too, have made and are making their marks in the professions, in commerce, in industry and in the military.

Members of early '40s classes had their own dinner meeting. Among them **Bascom Cooksey** of Lebanon; the irrepressible **Means** twins, **Dick** and **John**, formerly of Lebanon; **William L. Moore**, Caldwell, Idaho; **Joel Morris**, Nashville; **Henry Rigby**, Medina, Pa., 1941-42 battalion commander; **James J. "Jayboy" Sanders**, Nashville, 1942-43 battalion commander; **Woody Sisk**, Hot Springs, Ark; **Marshall Treppendahl**, Woodville, Miss., and my old friends, **Bobby Spann** of Waverly, Tenn., and **Chuck Ward** of Tulsa, Okla.

John [or is it Dick] Means as '43 senior

There were four widows at the early '40s dinner: **Liz Goodner** and **Jessie Ruth Hall**, both of Lebanon; **Jean Smith**, Nashville; and **Mary Fisher Wright**, Mississippi.

Lebanon attorney **Hugh Green** '69 and **Larry Russo** '59 walked up to me at the same time. A coincidence -- each was a Mid-South champion wrestler.

Olympic heavyweight champion **Pete Rademacher** '48 and **Tom Elliott** '47, neighbors in Ohio, seldom miss an annual meeting. Also regulars: **Bob Lundquist** of Stockbridge, Ga.; **Judge Ernest Pellegrin** of Gallatin; **Ted Lavit** of Lebanon, Ky.; **John Scott** of Nashville, and the three **McBride** brothers of Murray, Utah.

Every Sunday, cadets in full dress lined up near The Circle -- based on religious affiliation -- and marched in formation to the closest appropriate church.

As for the First United Methodist Church, a Castle Heights story emerged as the new Family Life Center was dedicated. Bishop Robert H. Spain, a featured speaker at the morning service, recalled three decades ago when he was pastor and the church was located on East Main Street.

"Castle Heights was at its peak in those years, and the cadets marched in formation to the church of their choice," he said.

"Since we were on East Main, more than a mile from the Heights campus, several Methodist cadets signed up as Presbyterians because the Presbyterian Church on West Main was the closest to the campus, so they had a shorter distance to march.

"So, the First Methodists moved from East Main to West Main, and closer to the campus than the Presbyterians. As a result, Methodist attendance picked up."

•Technically, closest to campus was the Episcopal Church mission, headquartered in a large old house almost directly across West Main. The number of Episcopalian cadets in the 1950-60s was small, but they were more than diligent in their attendance, perhaps because Commandant Col. D. T. Ingram and his wife also were members. Maj. Laurence Dillon, CHMA band director, did most of the mission's altar area carpentry.

Times that were and perhaps never were
• *October, 1996*

From nearby and faraway they came to recapture times that were and, perhaps, some that never were, and to visit what remains of the once proud prep school known as Castle Heights Military Academy.

They viewed the gutted Main Building, being restored by the City of Lebanon, some recalling their rooms on Fourth Main, an aerie guarded by squeaky steps that protected its residents from surprise inspections by either cadet or faculty officers.

They wandered around first floor Main, once the home of the cadet guard house, the administration offices, the post office, and apartments which served as quarters of three headmasters -- Colonels Dan Kendall, Ernest Stockton and Leonard Bradley. And they spotted the office of the fabled Col. D. T. Ingram, a little man with clipped mustache and a Virginia accent who meted out justice fairly but firmly.

They tried to spot the sites of Tower, Halls, Ingram, Gym and Chapel, which -- unlike Main, to be the future home of Lebanon municipal offices -- fell to the wrecking ball. But they focused largely on bygone days, the friends they made during their years on The Hilltop and the great teachers from whom they learned not only English, science and history, but values and principles.

Col. Ernest Stockton [right, with Col. H. L. Armstrong] was 1957-58 Headmaster and vice president before being named 18th president of Cumberland University [1958-1982].

Saturday was one of those days that only God can make -- clear blue skies and crisp autumn temperature. October at its best, and a day alumni added to a collection of days they treasure.

On Friday, alumni were ringing in the event in grand style at the Executive Inn, where the Class of 1946 held its Golden Anniversary celebration, and at the Lebanon Country Club where the Class of 1956 and the classes of the early '40s gathered.

These reunions didn't just happen. **Tom Page** of the football playing Page brothers spearheaded the drive to get his fellow '46 cadets together. It was an eventful week for Tom, who the day before had to put his brother, **Bob**, in a Nashville nursing home. All Mid-South tackle on the champion team of 1943 and one of the finest physical specimens ever to play on a Heights team, Bob has Parkinson's disease.

While the '46ers were whooping it up, across town the Class of 1956 was similarly engaged. So, why did the '56ers jump the gun and gather for a 40th reunion instead of waiting until 2006 for their 50th?

"Didn't want to take a chance on missing it," said **John Thompson**, now of Plano, Texas, who engineered the gathering. John, as have others in his age bracket, overcame a heart condition.

Thompson was valedictorian and 1955-56 battalion commander of the corps. From Heights to the University of Tennessee to study mathematics and eventually computer science. He now admits an addiction to computers. Distributed at the class reunion were clear, legible copies of *The Cavalier* which John scanned into his computer and which **Bill Shipley** had printed.

Reunions are annual affairs for the classes of the early '40s, but absent for the first time were **Oscar Atchley** and **Ottis Viall**, who died since the last reunion.

Strangely, now that the Academy exists only in our minds and dreams, Homecoming crowds grow with each passing year. But maybe, not so strange after all.

On a lighter vein, Lebanon Mayor Don Fox told the alumni how workers now restoring Main had discovered a cache of *Playboy* magazines hidden in the wall of one barracks room. The mayor asked if anybody wanted to claim them.

The guilty former cadet, if in attendance, remained silent. Probably because he was afraid **Col. Robert Hosier** -- still active in attendance

at Homecomings and one of the very few Heights faculty members from the early '40s still with us -- might put him on military report.

Though Col. Robert Hosier could be strict with his history students and swim team members, his sense of humor and dry wit were well known, as evidenced by this Heights yearbook spoof portraying him as a Homecoming Court member.

Day to remember: 'New' Main, old memories

• *October, 1997*

From as far away as California -- even Hawaii -- they came back to hallowed grounds and many of the buildings that once housed Castle Heights and served as their home for a varying range of years.

They come in increasing numbers, this year more than 350 alumni and wives, seeking to recapture poignant memories, to relive memorable events and to renew old friendships.

Graduates from as early as 1936 [**Jeff Atchley** of Lebanon] and 1937 [**Joe G. Atkinson** also of Lebanon] and 1938 [**Joe Martin** of Lexington, Va.] joined with later alumni for a day deemed perfect for a school homecoming.

It was all possible because one graduate stepped forward to take responsibility for alumni activities and, in effect, perpetuate the life of his alma mater [*page 215*]. And although Castle Heights is producing no new alumni, the annual gatherings of former students will continue at a high level until the life spans of Heightsmen run their course.

Roger Davis
as '57 senior.

The Heights class of 1947, whose 50th anniversary gathering was organized and promoted by **Tom Elliott** of Pinkerton, Ohio, bulged the attendance line. The '57s, who heard the summons of fellow member **Ted Lavit** of Lebanon, Ky., also were generously sprinkled among the ranks in celebration of their 40th anniversary

One of the features for the Class of 1957 gathering came when classmate **Bob Peel** of Plano, Texas, prompted by the most nationally famous member of this class -- **Roger Davis** of Santa Monica, Calf. -- described briefly the eight years he spent as prisoner of war in Vietnam. Peel, who backed off from specific details, received a standing ovation.

Roger's career as an actor flourished in the '60s and '70s when he starred in the TV series *Dark Shadows*, *The Gallent Men* and *Alias Smith and Jones*. He also had star billing in feature

Bob Peel as
'57 senior.

221

Jon Roger Davis of TV's '70s *Alias Smith and Jones* fame was active in all facets of CHMA: swimming, track, cheerleader, *Cavalier*, *Adjutant*, Round Table Council, DeMolay, Heights Christian Fellowship, and multiple National Forensic League state and regional championships.

length movies, and was married at one time to Jaclyn Smith of *Charlie's Angels* fame. [Davis developed land and built luxury homes in southern California until 2010, and also renovated the famous Seelbach Hotel in his hometown of Louisville, Ky.]

Grads from the classes of the early '40s return every year for their own celebration, and this year included **Bascom Cooksey** of Lebanon and **Russell Gardner** of Austell, Ga., linemen for the undefeated Heights Mid-South 1943 Conference champions. And **Charles "Cajun" Cook** '42 of Kirby, Ark., and **Raymond Hughes** '42 of Memphis, along with **Scott [Bashaw] Fordice** '57, also of Memphis, made it back wheelchairs and all.

This year the morale was higher. Instead of viewing sorrowfully a decaying Main Building, the alumni scanned and visited within a sparkling renovation that now serves as Lebanon City Hall.

"But you can count on one thing," said Lebanon Mayor Don Fox, "It remains the Castle Heights Main Building. That will never change."

Indeed, Main never before in my 60 years of knowing it, sparkled with the radiance that now embraces the structure. This was a building that the mayor promised alumni two years ago. He, the City Council and countless supporters lived up to that promise.

Perhaps the emotional high point of the weekend came Saturday afternoon when the new Heights War Memorial of black granite, which now occupies a space on the campus immediately in front of Main/City Hall, was dedicated. A feature was a flyover of four T-34 Navy Trainer airplanes piloted by Deborah Baugh and John Baugh of Lebanon, Tom Patton of Nashville, and Joe Howard of McMinnville, Tenn. This was arranged by **Frank Hartley** '64 of Antioch, Tenn.

In a perfectly timed function, the four airplanes approached from the east, flew over the assembled alumni and into the west with one plane peeling off to the north. Then, they made a second pass flying from the south over Main -- and alarming a flock of pigeons.

Thanks to efforts of Lebanon's then-Mayor Don Fox, the most recognizable symbol of Castle Heights Military Academy—Buchanan Hall / Main Building on which construction began in 1901—was purchased by the city in 1996. In 1998, the preservation/restoration project resulted in a beautiful, modern city hall with character and designation on the National Register of Historic Places.

Breaking the emotional tension, Mayor Fox said of the pigeons: "Those are the Lebanon Air Force."

The original War Memorial was located in front of Macfadden Auditorium and in the path of the new Castle Heights Avenue North.

Homecoming was like a revival. Spirit soared because buildings dear to the hearts of the alumni will continue in service. Said one early '40s graduate: "Castle Heights will never die as long as these buildings exist, and as long as there is a living alumnus."

Restored Main vision of Lebanon mayor

In Spring, 1994, Lebanon Mayor Don Fox was driving east on West Main when he looked left and saw a huge wrecking ball slam into Macfadden Gymnasium, one of the oldest still-standing buildings on the former Castle Heights Military Academy campus.

"We had lost a lot of our heritage," Fox said. "Every time a building like that or a historical landmark goes down, part of Lebanon disappears. To me that's Lebanon going down, not forward."

Thus Fox began his campaign to provide a larger, centralized administration facility for the City of Lebanon -- then with departments in seven locations throughout the area -- while at the same time preserving an historic landmark. In 1996, the city purchased the most recognizable symbol of CHMA -- Main Building / Buchanan Hall -- and its three-acre site. Purchase and restoration costs were held under $2.5 million through management of the city's engineering, public works and building inspection staff. The result is a beautiful, modern city hall with character and designation on the National Register of Historic Places.

"It [old Main] was nationally known for the better part of a half century," said Rob Hosier, president of the Heights National Alumni Association, who considers the Academy as one of Lebanon's first major industries because of the money it brought in.

"At one time during the course of a school year, the two biggest functions in Lebanon were Castle Heights' Homecoming and graduation," Hosier said. "We had scads of people coming and filling hotels/motels, restaurants and buying from retailers. Not to mention nine months of cadet in-town spending."

In 1998, the Rebuild Tennessee Coalition [a chapter of Rebuild America Coalition] presented Mayor Fox and the City of Lebanon an Award of Merit for the preservation / restoration project. That same year, city officials held a "note burning" to mark final payment on the administration building.

Buchanan Hall -- four stories, brick construction, Cookeville sandstone foundation -- was designed by architect Tom Chamberlain, and built in 1902. The city preserved the exact look of original Main, though much of the masonry had to be repaired or replaced; original woodwork, including stair handrails, was saved and restored; new windows, each custom made because of various size openings, were installed; and a new town meeting hall added to the back of the original structure was bricked to match.

"When we initially proposed purchasing and restoring Castle Heights Main, there were rumors of tax increases and years of debt for city taxpayers," Mayor Fox said. "I am proud to prove those dire predictions false. We were able to restore Main to its former glory, and give it back to the people of Lebanon. "

Homecoming warmth prevails

• *October, 2000*

The goddess of weather, in a mood contrasting her happy performances in recent years, failed to smile on the Castle Heights Homecoming last weekend. The fickle fairy spewed forth a witch's brew of gray skies and unseasonable frigid temperatures for the annual event which now draws more attendees than the number who appeared when the Academy was a viable educational institution.

Despite warning by weather mavens of a chilling blast, many of us appeared on the scene poorly prepared for a verification of the dire consequences of a fulfilled forecast. We shivered but refused to yield. The schedule of events flowed unhampered. Mayor Don Fox, city officials and lay volunteers met a challenging schedule to open the new city museum, appropriately located in the basement of the Heights Main Building -- now known as Lebanon City Hall -- just before the visiting Heightsmen and Heightswomen swarmed to The Hilltop.

A nostalgic and appreciative Class of 1950 returned for its 50th anniversary and dinner in an affair to remember, orchestrated by class member **Ed Campbell**, known by his fellow cadets as Campbell, EB.

Of special significance to me was the return of editors of the two cadet publications I sponsored for many years. **Dr. Ed Laughlin** was editor of the school yearbook when he was Cadet Ed Laughlin; both he and I back then pored over copy and galley proofs, correcting errors and toning stories.

The day before the reunion, I once again carefully read senior biographies and viewed senior portraits in *The Adjutant* just to refresh my memory. All of a sudden, the error jumped out at me. Above the picture of **Tommy Lowe**, later to become a highly successful Lebanon businessman, was the caption: Charles P. Lowe. It was a half century too late to change it to Charles T. Lowe. To Tommy's credit, he never complained. At least not to me.

Marshall Cox was editor of *The Cavalier* which won state and national honors. After Heights, he graduated from Vanderbilt and Ohio State College of Law. He became a partner in a prestigious New York law firm. He retired in 1997.

**Marshall Cox
as '50 senior.**

225

There was a pair of Jacks attending the class dinner. **Jack Daniel** and **Jack Higgs** were linemen on Coach Stroud Gwynn's 1949 football team -- undefeated until its last game, losing to archrival Columbia Military Academy. Jack Daniel, at 145 pounds, was starting guard. Jack Higgs was starting tackle. Each later earned doctorates in education.

Dick Inman, CHMA linebacker and center, played at Georgia Tech and coached 16 years at Tech and West Virginia University before turning to manufacturing and later to real estate development. He came to Heights as a young postgraduate and liked it so well he returned for a second postgraduate year.

In the backfield of the 1949 team was **Jimmy Bradshaw**, now Dr. Jim Bradshaw, successful Lebanon physician. Also in the backfield was **Johnny Greer**, a postgraduate at Heights after an outstanding football career at Dickson High School. During warm-up for the opening game with Georgia Military Academy, John and a visiting player collided. John suffered a knee injury which limited his playing time. He could have been the difference between winning the last game of the season as well as a postseason game in Daytona Beach, Fla.

Albert "Skip" Friend, after graduating from Heights, entered Ohio State, did not like college, joined the Marines. Says Skip: "Korea made me wonder if my judgment had been sound." He returned to marry Eve Clemons "who lived long enough to hold all six of our grandchildren."

Skip loved the trains. "I followed those trains for 36 years, working as a road conductor." He turned to gardening, now finds himself talking to the plants and gathering earthworms to go fishing.

And so they go-- doctors, lawyers, engineers, dentists, railroad conductor, teachers, and more. Most of them had successful marriages. Some of them had unsuccessful first marriages, but successful second marriages. Others lost their wives in death.

On this cold day in October, they reconnected, just as other classes before them have done. In their minds, they repositioned the buildings now missing from the campus and recalled their days in Bullard, Tower, Ingram, Halls and Main.

And they remembered another cold day when they formed around The Circle in January weather as fabled Commandant D. T. Ingram molded their discipline.

• Daytona Beach postseason football game was Shrine Club Beach Bowl, Dec. 30, 1949. CHMA lost 20-7 to Bullis Naval Preparatory School, then located in Silver Springs, Md. Attendance was 3,500. Bullis was founded in 1930 as a US Naval Academy prep school, and moved to its current Potomac, Md., site in the '60s.

'Heights Spirit' alive, vibrant as ever

• *October, 2003*

From out west to just off the old campus on Lebanon's Main Street they came in search of times that were and -- their memories colored by fleeting decades and spun by an eager desire to capture the feeling and spirit of a once great institution -- in search of times that never were.

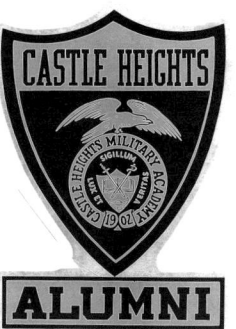

Their stories were enhanced and the drama of faded encounters perhaps a bit expanded as they connected with classmates and schoolmates, many materializing from dim memories into realities as they gathered for another Homecoming at the once great Castle Heights Military Academy.

For the classes who graduated in "3" years -- 1943, 1953, 1963 -- and two later decades, October 10-11 were special dates, the days for class reunions integrated in the larger scope of Homecoming.

The Class of 1963 began a marathon reunion Friday afternoon and was still at it during a breakfast Sunday morning. Said my son, Jim Leftwich: "We just hated to say goodbye."

The special bond that bound them as cadets reasserted itself as they rediscovered their fondness for one another. Even boys (to me, their teacher, they are still boys, including the Class of 1943 even in this year when most of them turn 78) who were not close as cadets found the passing decades had strengthened once casual relationships.

The real and yet mystical element that binds them is alive and as vibrant as ever. It's called Castle Heights Spirit, a living unique force that has to be experienced in order to understand fully.

But those outside the family of cadets and teachers recognize it, even feel it. Mayor Don Fox, who worked untiringly and negotiated a masterful political strategy that culminated in the purchase of Castle Heights Main Building which now houses city offices and city hall, acknowledged he feels the Heights Spirit in his office in Main.

Said the Mayor: "I never attended Castle Heights. I attended Lebanon High School. But I was certainly 'connected' with Heights cadets. A left hook here and a jab there. . ." He was pointing to his chin.

Saturday loomed as a nearly perfect day, a few placid clouds but largely a clear sky with moderate temperature. Alumni President **Rob Hosier** '63 and the Alumni Association Board of Directors exhaled as the day matured into near perfection.

This was the year after what would have been the 100th birthday of Castle Heights. Attendance was a few below the record number who returned to the campus last year. Few noticed the difference.

The Class of 1943 convened 10 years ago for its Golden Anniversary. The nostalgia generated at that meeting never faded. They met again Friday night at the Lebanon Country Club. **James J. "Jay-Boy" Sanders**, 1943 battalion commander, was the force that brought them together.

They were more subdued, these '43 cadets, than they were in their 1993 gathering. They clustered around tables, sipped their wine and told their stories once more. They went home at an early hour, still aglow with their renewed fondness for each other.

One myth was dispelled. Evidently, outsiders can and do feel the Castle Heights Spirit. James A. Crutchfield, speaking to the gathering about his new history book, *Hail!, Castle Heights!*, said he experienced it distinctly as he researched records for the publication.

An event blending humor and solemnity sparked the conclusion of the alumni luncheon. With the mayor officiating, alumnus **Jamie Metzger** '85 and Anita Adams, a former pupil of Rob Hosier's at Gallatin High School, were united in marriage. Without dissent, the alumni approved the union and hoped the Heights Spirit would bless their marriage.

The Academy history is available from the Castle Heights National Alumni Association [www.castleheights.com].

Once again, the alumni returned to an historic tradition and elected a "Sweetheart of the Corps" -- an annual tradition formerly resulting in a full page in each *Adjutant* yearbook -- and this time it was the efficient and endearing Susan Hosier, secretary-general of the alumni association. *[Many yearbook editors asked celebrities to select the "Sweetheart," and among those agreeing were Bob Hope, Steve Allen, Gardner McKay, Robert Cummings and Heights' own Roger Davis '57.]*

It was finally over Saturday night after the final dance and last goodbye at the annual alumni banquet. Their humor is more mature, the emotion is deeper, and the experiences of their days at Castle Heights are embedded crystal clear in their memories.

As they adjourned, the haunting notes of "Taps" played softly but distinctly in their minds, and the Spirit of Castle Height surged through their psyches and energized their souls.

Heights discipline most important dynamic

• *October 2004*

Castle Heights discipline, at once rigid and mystic, perhaps is the one ingredient most remembered and still observed in the lives of its thousands of alumni.

Each year at the Academy's Homecoming on the old school's one-time campus, former cadets will flag former faculty members and recall incidents having to do with disciplinary experiences.

Although often difficult at first, the Heights discipline may have been the most important single dynamic they learned as cadets. In later life, they will tell you, it saved them from embarrassment or a horrendous experience, and, in some cases, how it saved a life.

Orlando Segarra, formerly of Havana, Cuba, was one of the outstanding cadets of the Class of 1959, the year Fidel Castro overthrew the Batista regime in Cuba.

Saturday, Orlando came for another Homecoming, and recounted again for us that his 22 years in a Cuban prison were made easier for him because of "the Castle Heights discipline. The discipline you folks taught me here on this Hilltop."

I was pleased to be included, but I knew the elements of discipline he and others learned were the composite of many efforts and of a system installed and instilled long before my arrival.

It was the rigorous, demanding no-nonsense -- even mystic -- philosophy and practice developed by this school, which demanded adherence from its pupils, that had convinced Orlando he was a survivor, and, to a major degree brought him home to The Hilltop.

Neither cloudy skies, threat of storms nor an amputation could keep **James J. "Jayboy" Sanders**, 1942-43 battalion commander and a loyal alumnus, from attending the Heights reunion.

Jayboy departed Heights for the US Army, fought in France, was wounded, but returned for a career in manufacturing and head of Sanders Manufacturing Co., in Nashville. This year, he appeared in a wheelchair and minus one leg, which was amputated because of circulatory problems. He, too, is a firm believer in Castle Heights disci-

James J. Sanders as '43 senior.

229

pline, a derivative of which is needed as he learns to walk with a man-made leg.

Jim Legg, Class of 1955, has another take on the disciplinary system cadets remember and practice. He disdains suggestions he is smart, but he prides another quality.

"I think," he says. "That is what Heights gave me – the willingness and desire to think. I went through Basic Training and I was trained. At CHMA, I was taught."

Pete Rademacher, Class of 1948 and gold medal winner in the 1956 Olympic Games, rarely misses a Heights Homecoming - and never fails to bring his gold medal, which he delights in showing.

The medal bears scars and nicks from falling on concrete, Pete says. When he appeared on a stage, as he did during a long promotional career, he would casually toss his medal into his audience. He always recovered it. You don't argue with a heavyweight boxing champion.

John and **Dick Means**, both Class of 1944, are twins and Lebanon natives. John is clean-shaven. Dick has a lush, white beard. I accused

Dick of wearing a beard to distinguish him from his twin.

"Not so," said Dick. "I simply wore out my razor."

And now a more somber note. We said goodbye to **Jay Cleveland**, Class of 1955 and former Heights Commandant, during a service at Wilson County Memorial Gardens. He died May 30, after back surgery. His wife, Susan, and his children deferred burying his ashes until Heights friends could attend services. [*Yearbook Dedication, page 312*]

Former CHMA Commandant Jay Cleveland.

• Jay after Heights earned a BS and MS in education, Middle Tennessee State University, after attending Sewanee, University of the South. Served on CHMA faculty 1973-1983, taught U.S. History and served as Commandant for eight years. Subsequently Director of Admissions at Virginia's Massanutten Military Academy. Jay's wife, Susan Wheeler Cleveland, was a Penn State University grad, and the couple had two sons who attended Heights -- James Albert and William Wheeler. Susan died in 2008, and both she and Jay are buried in Lebanon.

• In addition to Jay and his sons, other family CHMA students were brother, Robert '59, and father, Jay Sr. '29. Matriarch of the family was Alice Mae Philips Cleveland, born in Nashville 1883, married in 1902, and moved to Lebanon in the early 1920s. She died in 1978. Her homestead at 425 West Main [across the street from home of CHMA founder, I.W.P. Buchanan and now United Methodist Church parking lot] was a two-story landmark for Heights cadets on walks to and from town.

Mayor's status change: now an alumnus
• *October, 2007*

If alumni of Castle Heights could vote in Lebanon municipal elections, and if Mayor Don Fox ran for another term, his incumbency likely would be extended for an additional four years.

But most of them can't vote here and the mayor has announced he is not a candidate for re-election. But he's still alert to a favorable environment such as the one he found Saturday at Heights' alumni luncheon.

A loyal member of the "town boys" in yesteryear's "town vs. Hilltop [cadets]" engagements, **Don Fox** abruptly found his status changed when Academy graduates during their annual meeting inducted him into the CHMA Alumni Association.

Along with fond memories of vying with cadets when he and they were high school age, since Saturday Fox has a certificate that confirms he now is a Height alumnus, albeit an honorary one.

Alumni Association President **Rob Hosier** was fervent in his praise of the mayor.

Said he: "Everything we have asked of him, he has done if at all possible. He is the alumni association's true friend."

New CHMA alum Don Fox initiated restoration of Main as Lebanon City Hall.

Frequently, the Association has needed city assistance, especially since city hall formerly was Main Building on the Heights campus and a building [former home of Commandant Col. D. T. Ingram] immediately across the street from city hall is alumni headquarters

From the beginning of the city's tenure on The Hilltop, the mayor recognized and admired alumni activities and Academy heritage.

After the school closed its doors in 1986, Main rapidly deteriorated. Rather than see it steadily worsen, some of us secretly hoped it would just collapse since restoration appeared extremely unlikely.

Enter Don Fox, mayor of Lebanon, and in this matter, a visionary. He envisioned a restored building, standing tall on Lebanon's highest hill. Patiently and adroitly, he won support for plans to buy the property and move city headquarter into a restored Main. This may have been the mayor's signature political coup. It brought to Lebanon not only a city hall without parallel in any town, but also to Fox the eternal gratitude of Heights alumni.

"Town-gown" competition is history in this city, and the mayor in his new status will not have to choose a side.

o o o

Former cadets in large numbers returned to the old campus for Homecoming activities and for class reunions last weekend. We attended reunion of the Class of 1957, gathered for its 50th year anniversary.

The most famous member is actor **Roger Davis**. The most honored is **Bob Peel** of Paris, Tenn., once a pilot in the US Air Force and a prisoner of war during the Vietnam War. Bob received a sustained and an emotional standing ovation.

Generalissimo of the class gathering was **Ted Lavit**, maybe the most loyal alumnus in Academy history. Ted came to Castle Heights when he was seven, and graduated from both Junior and Senior schools.

Castle Heights literally was his home. The house mothers were his mothers, fellow cadets were his family, and teachers were his disciplinarians.

J. M. Ditmore was a post-graduate in the Class of 1957. During his senior year at Clarksville High School, he was a much publicized all-star football player.

Ted Lavit as '57 senior.

At Heights, he was just another private in a platoon taking orders from a younger, smaller cadet. In a regimented environment, his academic performance was honored as much as his athletic prowess. It was a different way of life for this football star.

Despite his new role in life then, he loves Castle Heights and stands as loyal as cadets who attended four or more years.

"My time at Heights was a turn-around year. My life came into focus. There were no frills, and we learned what was important. It was probably the best year of my life," he said.

Interestingly, many post-graduates and one-year cadets share these sentiments. **Earl Cato** and **Frank Clayton**, exciting running backs and members of the Heights Football Hall of Fame, and **Dr. Murphy Green**, star back on the 1955 team, rarely miss Homecoming.

Heights Homecomings may have special significance because the school no longer exists -- except in the minds of its graduates.

And its teachers.

11 years of Heights' love and still counting

As JB Leftwich noted, Theodore Howard Lavit '57, originally of Brooklyn, N.Y., is perhaps "the most loyal alumnus in Academy history." But then, consider: He came to Castle Heights when he was seven and made his unique mark on The Hilltop for 11 consecutive years.

And though his accomplishments were singular, he was likely -- at least during his Senior School years -- to be referred to as "LavitandWood" or "WoodandLavit" by fellow cadets. That due to his close friendship with another Heights "lifer," John Anthony Wood '57, originally of Oakland City, Ind. -- who was at the Academy 10 of Ted's 11. Each did move to his own drummer, but they seemed inseparable.

The Cavalier in 1957 featured an article on the 10-year friendship of Ted Lavit [right] and John Wood, who both started in the Junior School and were referred to by Senior School cadets as "woodandlavit" or "lavitandwood."

While a small number of other Heightsmen graduated after 10-12 years at the Academy, none did so with a fellow classmate as his shadow. Both were on *The Cavalier*, football and swim teams, class officers [Wood president, Lavit treasurer], and in Heights-Y and Heights Christian Fellowship. Lavit also played baseball and golf, and was on the debate team. Wood ran track, and was a member of the Round Table Council and Honor Council -- and was perhaps motivated by his brother, Russell, a 1951 Heights graduate and All-America swimmer and diver for the Tigers.

Lavit earned his BA at Centre College of Kentucky, his JD from Vanderbilt, and has practiced law in Lebanon, Ky., for more than 50 years -- litigating in state and federal courts. He and his wife, Wanda, have been married more than 20 years, and together have five children, seven grandchildren.

As for Wood, Lavit reports, "John began college at Vanderbilt, joined Sigma Chi, and initially played football. He subsequently returned to Oakland City, enrolled in Oakland City College, and married and had two children. He and his wife separated, and John went to Salinas, Calif., and worked for the U.S. Department of Health.

"Unfortunately he died in 1964, way too early, and I attended his funeral in Oakland City. He was buried with his Heights' ring," Lavit continued.

Lavit's relationship with The Hilltop did not end in 1957, however, and he served multiple terms as president of the Academy alumni association that existed while CHMA remained open. He also helped organize the Castle Heights Foundation, which bought the Academy from the Macfadden Foundation in 1974, and was on its board of directors.

"In August, 1986, the Foundation Board voted to close the school, for all of the reasons JB has written about, and the vote was 18 to 1," Lavit said. "I think often of my dissenting vote."

Lavit was instrumental in formation of the Castle Heights National Alumni Association in 1987, and has served on its board since its beginning. He was one of the originators of the HNAA's effort to buy and restore the Col. Dan Ingram house on the former campus to serve as alumni offices and historic records center, and was a key in the raising of funds for that purpose.

Attorney Ted Lavit, 1990s.

The latest and perhaps most exemplary example of Lavit's loyalty to the Academy and the concept that Castle Heights "will be forever," was his leadership of the successful 2012-13 campaign to raise $340,000 to buy the Rutherford Parks Library -- remodeled and used for more than 10 years by a Lebanon insurance agency -- to serve as the Castle Heights Military Academy Alumni Archives & Museum [*page 339*].

Ted Lavit '57, referred to by JB Leftwich [right] as "maybe the most loyal alumnus in Academy history," has worked more than 40 years to keep Castle Heights viable or -- since its 1986 closing -- "alive." He and JB worked together for 12 years on the Heights Foundation to oversee operation of the school.

"I had the honor and privilege of delivering the commencement address in May, 1986, not knowing it would be the last one ever given," Lavit said. "As I told that final group of seniors, I want you to know how I feel about Castle Heights. Now that I'm approaching the end of my career, I would trade all of my tomorrows for my Castle Heights' yesterdays." [A reception followed the speech at which, according to Lavit, "JB made special remarks and presented me with restoration of my stripes." Ted offered no details as to why the stripes were "missing."]

Extraordinary weekend
looms for CHMA alumni

• *October, 2009*

Alumni from far reaches of the country are gathering today and tomorrow on the Castle Heights campus for their annual Homecoming and to attempt to recapture memories of events that amused them, startled them and shaped their lives.

Paul Holsen, Class of 1959, recalls an event that happened not on the campus but at the Lebanon Municipal Airport where the late Arch Agee, a veteran pilot, taught Heights cadets to fly.

Following a flying lesson that didn't go according to plans, Arch tried to be realistic with Paul, advising him he "would never make it as a pilot." But Arch never gave up, and Paul did make it.

"I flew 54 years worldwide, many of those years with the CIA, Air America and the Secret Service for President Johnson," Paul said. "Just as Arch hoped, I proved him wrong. He was a great guy."

Paul brings with him '59 classmate **Orlando "Landy" Segarra**. Landy was among four or five cadets that year from Havana and the only one who did not view Fidel Castro as Cuba's messiah.

Orlando Segarra '59, JB Leftwich reminisce at 2009 Homecoming.

During the first two decades of my tenure at Castle Heights, Col. Harry L. Armstrong was president of the Academy. I served with three other presidents, but in my dreams – almost every night – Colonel Armstrong is at the helm.

Most teachers were in awe of the Colonel. He was a kind man, but he never lowered the barrier that separated him from faculty and staff.

When ball-point pens hit the market some time in the '40s, I saved $2 and bought my first one. Later, as I had a conversation with Colonel Armstrong, he asked to use my pen. Then, he absentmindedly put the pen in his pocket.

I didn't have the nerve to ask him to return it. I walked away and began saving my coins for a new one.

Times have changed and relations with bosses have changed. And

Col. H. L. Armstrong commanded the respect of cadets and faculty throughout his 33 years at the Heights' helm.

so have ball-point pens. There probably are more than two dozen in our household.

Seeing and reconnecting with graduates of the '40s when I was a young teacher remain pleasures with extra dimensions. Two out-of-town regulars from the Class of 1943 are **Bill Burnett** of Milan, Tenn., and **Charles Lacy Fields** of Clarksville. Both played on the undefeated 1943 Mid-South Conference football champion team. As did Heights loyalist **Bascom Cooksey Jr.** of Lebanon, who died three years ago. Both Lacy and his brother **Richard Fields** '48 of North Carolina are dentists. Dick Fields was one of the most gifted cartoonists in the history of the Castle Heights newspaper.

Earl Cato, one of the Academy's great running backs, became a loyal alumnus and rarely misses a Homecoming, albeit he travels quite a few miles en route from his home in California. Another star on the 1953 team, tailback **Frank Clayton**, usually attends. **Jack Caruthers**, Warwick, R.I., also travels far.

The spotlight this weekend will be on members of the Class of 1959, here for their 50th reunion. More than one-half of the surviving members of that year's 100 graduates are expected. Among them will be **Stan Huguenin**, originally from Sarasota, Fla., and **Bob Cleveland**, Bronxville, NY, a pair of student editors nonpareil. Stan and **Sandy McMath** of Little Rock, Ark., were state champion debaters.

Two of my former student editors died this year. They – **Stan Harvill** '51 and **Gordon Baskett** '47 – also were nonpareil. And so were **Edward McClellan** '57, a model for editors who followed, and my longtime friend, **Leonard Bradley Jr.** '58.

Among my pleasant memories are the formal dances, highlights of the Heights social season. I remember especially the beautiful girls in their full-length formal gowns and the cadets in their dress white uniforms.

Faculty members formed a receiving line for each formal dance. Cadets were expected to escort dates through the line and to introduce them to teachers and faculty wives in the receiving line.

I wonder if this happens anywhere in this age.

Memories, loyalties, love keeping CHMA alive

• *October, 2010*

There was a tinge of color in the trees, the day was warm but not unpleasant, and the campus of the old Castle Heights Military Academy swarmed with alumni seeking to recapture what was while sometimes coloring their memories with what never was.

Last weekend was Homecoming.

Heights no longer exists, but the City of Lebanon with headquarters in what was once old Main works to preserve the Academy atmosphere and spirit. Running contrary to the usual pattern of returning alumni, attendance appears to increase each year despite the realism of dwindling numbers since no new personnel were added after the 1986 closing.

I was the tie who crossed all classes. I began in 1941 and remained for 38 years.

Another feature of the Academy rested in its romantic aspect. Cadets, wearing their uniforms of gray and white marching each Sunday to church or in the formal Spring parades caught the eyes of many girls, rendering the Academy a birthplace of young love.

John Durant '41, recalled an important incident that occurred in the gymnasium, which was transformed into a ballroom for formal dances.

"I don't remember the occasion, but my girlfriend came from south Georgia for the dance. A little-known [at the time] singer named Fanny Rose Shore [later Dinah] entertained. I was so overwhelmed I got down on my knees and proposed at this dance in the gym. She accepted, and we enjoyed 62 years of marriage."

Rob Collins and **Garrett Kinley** were classmates for four years at Heights, graduating in 1955. Rob, attending the wedding of Garrett in 1959, met for the first time Garrett's bride-to-be, Jane Pritchett. Although their careers took them in different directions, Rob and Garrett maintained off-and-on contact.

After a number of years, Garrett and Jane divorced. Rob's marriage to Carole Leonard also ended in divorce.

You're ahead of me now, but Jane and Rob rediscovered each other and in 1999 they married, 40 years after first meeting.

"I think Jane has married more members of my class than anybody," Rob quipped.

There were a plethora of other stories.

John Bradley '63 remembered how he gained new respect for newspapers while he was editor of the Heights' paper.

Said he: "When I began work on *The Cavalier,* my opinion about the use of papers changed dramatically. After going to *The Lebanon Democrat* to publish the paper, I started viewing newspapers with reverence. So, I announced at home to my mother that we would no longer wipe muddy feet or shine shoes on newspapers."

Dick Meier '43 remembers his introduction to Heights.

"I have a freshman remembrance that even after 71 years vividly sticks in my mind. It has to do with Cadet Capt. **Jacob Priester** '40. I roomed on third floor of Halls Barracks where he was division officer. He chose me as his unofficial cadet orderly with such duties as sweeping the hall, carrying his laundry to Main and picking it up the next week after it was cleaned.

"Once he ordered me to shave, and I wondered what to shave since I was barely 14 years old. But shave I did.

"My great moment came during 1939 graduation. He came to me, and with a big smile, stuck out his hand and said: 'Good job, Meier. You will do o.k.' What a boost!"

Dick did do all right. A generation later, his son **Richard "Rick" Meier** '66 came to Castle Heights, and he, too, "did all right."

Highlight of the weekend came when the name of former cadet **Bobby Bradley** '60 was added to the War Memorial that fronts Main / Lebanon City Hall. A graduate of the United

Dick Meier
as '43 CHMA senior.

States Naval Academy, he was lost in an airplane mishap at sea.

His brothers Leonard Jr., John, Bill and Tom, and his sister Mary Elizabeth were present. All five brothers are Heights graduates, and all served in the U. S. military.

And this old teacher in some cases did right, justifying herewith a bit of boasting to express my pride in and love for Heights.

For the first time, the Alumni Association presented a plaque to a former faculty member, expressing the alums' gratitude for many years of service. It is the most treasured award I ever received, and I was completely unaware it was in the offing.

My response: "If I had my life to live over, I would do the same thing again."

War Memorial honors Bradley, 76 other Heightmen

Lt. Gen. John Bradley '63, one of five sons and a daughter of longtime Heights' Headmaster Lt. Col. Leonard and Mary Ann Bryan Bradley, knows well of "the very special young men and women who served a cause much bigger than themselves, the patriotic veterans who remain 'forever young,' those who are deeply missed by his or her family."

And at Homecoming 2010, General Bradley -- who flew more than 330 combat missions as a fighter pilot in Vietnam -- was asked to speak to those gathered at the Castle Heights War Memorial rededication and the inscription of yet another Heights cadet who was one of those "who served a cause much bigger than [himself]" during the Vietnam War -- Ensign Robert Bryan Bradley '60.

Bobby Bradley '60 was '64 U.S. Naval Academy grad.

"Everyone in our family always felt Bobby was a cut above the rest of us," General Bradley said. "He was smart, accomplished, athletic and so personable. His classmates and teammates regularly selected him as a leader. Hank Thorn wrote about Bobby in *The Cavalier* during their senior year, calling him 'The Fiftieth Boy,' a reference to the framed essay that hung for many years on the wall of Main. We all believed Bobby WAS the Fiftieth Boy.

"Bobby was the best of our family, with the possible exception of our mother, who taught him sweetness and loyalty. She taught him to treat everyone just the same.

"Our father, who could at times be demanding, taught him the importance of hard work and of being honest in every part of life.

"Our brother, Leonard Jr., was closer to him than any of the rest of us. No one misses him more than he. We still talk among ourselves in reverential terms when we speak of Bobby.

"Our brother, Bill, wrote one of the most enduring memorial essays 15 years ago about Bobby [delivered at a cemetery celebration in his honor]. It is a treasure, as is Bill.

"Our sister, Mary Elizabeth, always looked so much like Bobby -- we

Rededication of the Castle Heights War Memorial and the inscription of Ensign Robert Bryan Bradley '60 took place 2010 Homecoming weekend. On hand to honor their brother, Bobby, and 76 other listed Heightsmen were Lt. Gen. John Bradley '63, Leonard K. Bradley Jr. '58, Mary Elizabeth Bradley Ogren, Col. Thomas Bradley '69, and Billy Bradley '65.

can see, in her face, how he would appear if we were still blessed to have him.

"Our bother, Tom, and I followed Bobby into aviation. All of us wanted in some way to, 'Be like Bobby.'

"Bobby once was described by our father as, 'the Prince of the Family.' We all knew how he meant it. No parent could have asked for a better son, no sibling could have had a better brother.

"Bobby was serving our country in the way he most wanted. After a night takeoff, the aircraft was swallowed into the dark Saturday night sky, a seeming black overcast. The sky was undivided between the darkness of air and water, a sky without top or bottom. In fact there was no sky, only total blackness. Suddenly, he was, 'Lost at Sea.' After all these years, we still don't know how or why. There will be no answer.

"The especially beautiful National Cemetery of the Pacific, in Honolulu, has an inscription from Abraham Lincoln as a centerpiece that I think captures the feeling of any family which has experienced the most painful loss of a son or daughter, brother or sister, aunt or uncle:

"...the solemn pride that must be yours to have laid so costly a sacrifice upon the alter of freedom."

Bobby Bradley and three other Heightsmen killed in Vietnam -- A.G. Broumas '49, H.L. Brown '55, C.A. Ward '55 -- are honored on the Heights War Memorial along with three from the Korean War, 69 from World War II, and one from World War I -- 77 in all.

o o o

The Bradley family -- as with the Leftwiches, Hosiers, Lucases and Ingrams -- for almost 30 years was part of the Heights' campus 24/7. [Though the Leftwiches and Hosiers did not live on campus, their Academy positions and childrens' Heights attendance made them as integral as the other three.] Leonard Bradley Sr., a native of Nashville, Tenn., earned his BS and MA from Peabody College, and joined the Heights faculty in 1942. He served as Headmaster 1958-1973, when he accepted an offer to help organize and serve as headmaster of Lebanon's Friendship Christian School [about 600 students in 2014 in preschool, elementary, middle and high school facilities]. He retired from FCS in 1982. He married Mary Ann Bryan (sister of Lindsey Donnell's wife, Elizabeth) of Watertown, Tenn., in 1939, and they had a daughter and five sons [all of whom graduated from Heights):

^ **Leonard K. Bradley Jr.** '58 - University of Tennessee graduate, began 28-year career for Tennessee State Government in 1968; retired after professorships at Tusculum College and Vanderbilt University. Thinks of Bobby as "best friend I have had, and to this day I carry his second grade picture in my wallet." [*Complete background, page 177*]

^ **Robert Bryan Bradley** '60 - Graduated U.S. Naval Academy in 1964, and lost at sea in 1965.

^ **John Bradley** '63 – US Air Force Academy 1963-66, BS University of Tennessee '67. Served 1967-2008 as USAF commissioned officer, including one-year South Vietnam duty at Bien Hoa Air Base, flying 337 combat missions in "close air support" of soldiers, Marines. Commander, Air Force Reserve 2004-08, overseeing more than 70,000 reservists in 125 countries worldwide. Retired as Lieutenant General with more than 7,000 hours in fighter aircraft. Married Jan Underwood, Decatur, Ala., in 1975, and they have one daughter. After 2008 retirement, he (as President, CEO) and Jan started non-profit Lamia Afghan Foundation, to build schools for Afghanistan girls.

^ **William "Bill" D. Bradley** '65 - BA, University of Tennessee. TSgt. US Air Force, serving in Vietnam during four-year career. Retired Division of Budget Director, Tennessee Department of Finance + Administration. Married Nannette Peeler of Waverly, Tenn., in 1998; four children.

Following 40 years of US Air Force service, Lt. Gen. John Bradley [Heights '63] and his wife, Jan, formed in 2008 the Lamia Afghan Foundation to build schools for girls in Afghanistan. As of 2014, six schools were completed, serving 5,000 girls near mountains west of Kabul. The foundation also has shipped about three million pounds of clothing, blankets, medical equipment, school supplies and food.

^ **Charles Thomas "Tom" Bradley** '69 – BS, University of Tennessee; MPS, Auburn University-Montgomery. Attended Air War College, NSN Postgraduate School. USAF active duty 1974-2004, retiring as Colonel, Office of the Chief of Staff, Headquarters USAF, Pentagon. Executive Director, CEO of Air Force Historical Foundation 2006-2010. Member Heights NAA Board of Directors 15 years. Married Sandra Ann Gregory of Loyal, Wisc., in 1983. She retired from USAF in 2006 as Brigadier General, with more than 29 years of service. They have two sons.

^ **Mary Elizabeth Bradley** - Graduated Lebanon High School 1973, and was member of state champion girls basketball team 1970-71. BS, David Lipscomb College, 1977. Worked as auditor for State of Tennessee Comptroller, then with accounting firms in Colorado and South Dakota. Married to Jim Ogren, American Airlines captain and retired Naval Reserve officer. According to her brothers, "it's pretty well accepted without dispute she's the best athlete in our generation."

• John Bradley's interest in flying was influenced by his uncle, Lt. Col. Charles W. Bryan, CHMA '48, US Naval Academy '52, and brother of Headmaster Leonard Bradley's wife, Mary Ann. In June, 1971, Colonel Bryan (left) met with John -- already stationed in Vietnam as a captain -- at Udorn Royal Thai Air Base, Thailand, the evening before Bryan's final mission (his 100th) flying unarmed reconnaissance over Vietnam. Earlier, Colonel Bryan was Commander, T-38 Flying Training Squadron, Laughlin AFB, Texas, overseeing advanced jet pilot training for hundreds of airmen. Charles' wife Audrey Robertson Bryan, is sister of Tommy Robertson, Heights Class of 1949.

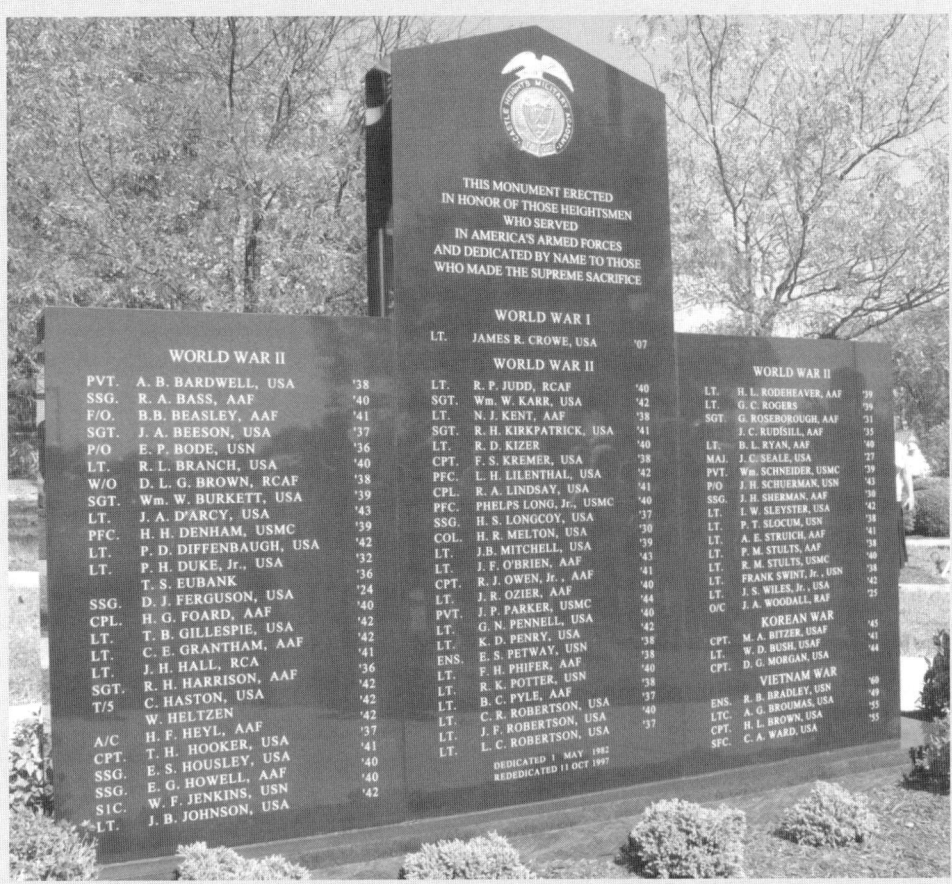

Funded by CHMA alumni and friends through the Heights National Alumni Association, this War Memorial -- located near Lebanon City Hall / Old Main building -- honors the 77 Heightsmen killed in World Wars I, II and Vietnam.

• Among remarks by Brig. Gen. Alonzo J. Walter Jr. '45 at May, 1982, dedication of the first CHMA War Memorial between Macfadden gym and auditorium:

"I am honored to be here 39 years after I first looked upon this Hilltop, and 37 years after graduation…I was as proud that day to be a "B" Company corporal as I am to stand before you as a US Air Force general…The Heightsmen we honor today would join me in praising our school if they were here. Many were cut down only months after leaving Heights…We are here to accord special recognition -- but I'd like to submit that while their names are inscribed because they made the supreme sacrifice, we honor them because they lived, because they served our country well in time of need, and because they came from the same mold we did -- Castle Heights. That makes us proud!…Perhaps if we had been stronger and more resolute in other times, wars which claimed the Heightsmen we honor today might have been avoided…. Thank God there are still schools such as Castle Heights which prepare well-rounded American citizens by stressing fundamentals -- duty, honor, country…"

Main Building, Castle Heights Military Academy, Lebanon, Tenn.

CASTLE HEIGHTS, LEBANON, TENN.

Main Entrance to Campus of Castle Heights Military Academy, Lebanon, Tennessee

CASTLE HEIGHTS, LEBANON, TENN.

Main Drive on Campus, Castle Heights Military Academy, Lebanon, Tenn.

Main Building, Castle Heights Military Academy, Lebanon, Tenn.

Buchanan Hall-Castle Heights Military School-Lebanon, Tenn.

E-90

MacFadden Auditorium, Castle Heights Military Academy

Chapter Seven
Addenda

"It is the writer who might catch the imagination of young people, and plant a seed that will flower and come to fruition."

-Isaac Asimov, Author

"If you have other things in your life—family, friends, good productive day work—these can interact with your writing and the sum will be all the richer."

-David Brin, Scientist

THE DRILL:
JB Leftwich wrote more than 2,500 columns during his 35 years as a newspaper journalist. Though hundreds were about Castle Heights Military Academy and his love for the institution, its students, faculty and staff, the majority were about life and people away from The Hilltop -- some serious, humorous, emotional, light-hearted. Selections in this chapter demonstrate his gift for writing regardless of the topic.

Overleaf Photo:
Histric postcards featuring Castle Heights used by cadets, faculty, Lebanon residents and visitors to communicate timely "news of the day."

A Lesson in the rhymed, nonsense poem
• *January, 1985*

We are approaching the city of Limerick and the conclusion of a week's tour of Ireland with three busloads of Middle Tennesseans, largely first-time visitors to the Emerald Isle.

Our driver, who spent a few years in the United States and kidded us constantly about our Southern accents, invited us to try our hands at writing limericks - an invitation lacking appeal to most of our group.

It appealed to me.

My affection for the limerick began in 1937 in a journalism class taught by the late Dixon Merritt, once editor of *The Democrat* and former syndicated columnist. Mr. Merritt was author of the famed pelican limerick lauding the bird whose "beak can hold more than its belly can."

Our driver, the ultimate story teller and an Irish historian, throughout the trip indoctrinated us with the history of the island, with special emphasis on the Irish patron saint, St. Patrick. Thus my initial effort:

> *Said Patrick with a tug of his shawl,*
> *I've been practicing my Southern drawl,*
> *With a few more lessons*
> *And the good Lord's blessings*
> *I'll be able to talk like y'all.*

Writers of limericks have explored a wide range of subjects - history, the Bible, current events, mythology, fables. Often limericks are social commentaries dealing with life styles, mores and foibles. In the following, I used a fable to comment on a couple of modern topics:

> *The old woman who lived in the shoe*
> *At last figured out what she must do.*
> *She applied for food stamps*
> *And kicked the man out*
> *Who lived in the shoe with her, too.*

The common thread of all limericks is humor. The limericist looks at life with wry humor. Furthermore, the limericist does not take himself seriously - he knows he is writing doggerel.

Inspiration (I use the word guardedly) to the addicted writer of limericks can surface at strange times - while mowing the lawn, looking at TV, or even in church. This one came during a sermon:

247

Said Jonah to answer the whale's questions,
I'm the cause of your belly's congestions.
You're really not well, sir.
You need Alka-Seltzer
A half-ton for your stomach's digestion.

Although the minister was discussing Jonah, my mind wandered to young David and his monumental upset of the Philistine giant:

Young David he said to Goliath:
Common sense to this battle appliath
Just leave us alone
And I'll drop this old stone
And we'll spend a few weeks with our wiveath.

Politics is a good breeding ground for limericks. This one written early in the presidential campaign turned out to be less than prophetic:

Said Ronnie, as he sat there with Nancy,
I view this campaign as quite chancy.
George Bush must bow out
He hasn't the clout
Geraldine is more to my fancy.

Limericks can be pure fancy. They don't have to comment or observe. They can invent impossible situations unrelated to reality. Like this one:

There once was a mouse (a wee mammal)
Who placed a big bet on a camel
A lofty ambition
But a bad proposition
For a mammal on a camel to gamble.

And this one:

A spaceship with an alien invader
Flying north of this planet's equator
Sat down in a field
And met there Brooke Shield
And said, take me to your leader -- later.

I looked in the dictionary for a definition of a limerick and found, "a rhymed, nonsense poem of five anapestic lines."
Then I looked up the definition of anapestic.

Everybody needs to own a 'Hell Box'

• *December, 2010*

In the lobby of the building housing the *Lebanon Democrat* stands a Merganthaler Linotype machine, mutely testifying to an age when it and others of the same genre revolutionized the printing industry.

The Linotype also bears testimony to the ruthless stampede of technology, beneath its steamroller.

If it had a voice, as some future obsolete machine will have, the linotype would say: "Here I stand, useless in a world of computers and advanced photography and engraving. But there was an era when I was the most important implement in moving the written word to the presses and finally the printed page."

I suppose that as cold type replaced hot metal, "printer's devils" and "Hell Boxes" gave way to young ladies with scissors and drawers full of logos and column titles.

The Hell Box was a container for bits and pieces of machinery, metal type that nobody could classify [pieces of leading], items that just showed up, and any other scrap without a designated place.

At this point, I digress to recall Robert Spears, the most remarkable printer's devil I ever knew. He also was the neatest person I ever knew in a printing operation. Robert could clean the big press, battle pounds of printers' ink, and emerge spotless. When I walked through the shop and touched nothing, I emerged smudged.

Printer's devils were apprentice printers, the rank beginners in the trade. Theirs were the duties of cleaning the presses, sweeping the

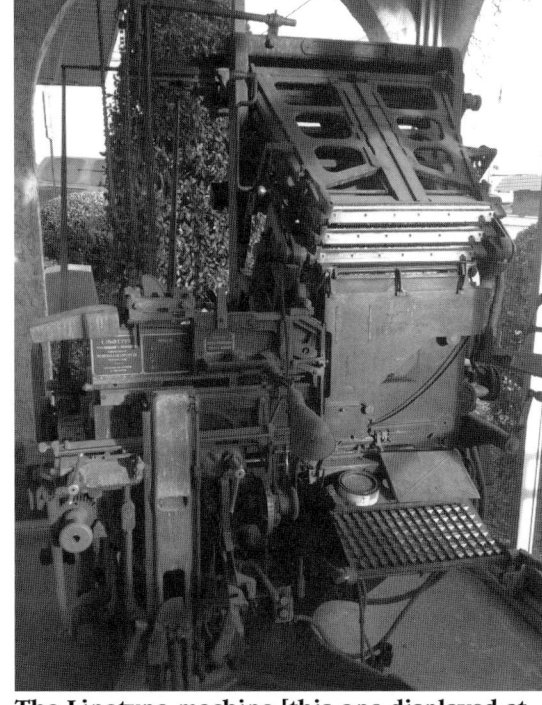

The Linotype machine [this one displayed at *Lebanon Democrat*] revolutionized the printing industry. A single operator used the typewriter-type keyboard to turn out in minutes hundreds of lines of metal type ["slugs"] then arranged by skilled craftsmen to form entire newspaper pages ready for printing.

floors, and, as they advanced, distributing the handset type.

Occasionally, we would go through the Hell Box and find important missing or useful items. In a print shop, you seldom threw anything away; you threw it into the Hell Box.

Although, we didn't call it a Hell Box – Mama would never have allowed such terminology – we had on our farm its equivalent in which we saved things for some unanticipated future use. It was sort of a miniature attic for small wheels, bolts and screws.

I have a Hell Box in the top drawer of a dresser, and about once a year I dig through it to retrieve screws, shoe laces, buttons and golf tees. Stowed away are bits and pieces of what I used to be.

One of my buddies of years past has a Hell Box in which he stored bottles with tiny bits of booze therein. That was his way of never exhausting one of his life necessities. He never owned an auto, never learned to drive one, and did not want one. Booze was a different matter until late in life he decided to become a teetotaler.

I wonder if today's newspapers have Hell Boxes, and I wonder what one would find in one. I also wonder if other organizations have Hell Boxes. In today's world of technology, bits and pieces are probably stored in computers.

Everybody needs a Hell Box. It lets us delay decisions to trash things, and prevents loss of items of later value. It eliminates clutter on desktops, tables and shelves. Just pitch it into the Hell Box and out of sight. Dig through it later to retrieve valuables and to discard useless ones.

Everybody also needs a Hell Box for discarded ideas, customs and prejudices. A mental Hell Box to clear your mind, so you can focus your thoughts on other matters.

How much sadness and heartbreak could we avoid if we tossed our hatreds, ill-conceived ideas, prejudices and bitterness into a Hell Box for later examination? How many marriages would be salvaged if we owned and used an emotional Hell Box? How many wars would never have been if every nation used a Hell Box?

But mental Hell Boxes should not be depositories only for bitterness. You should toss into them a few fun ideas, a few happy thoughts, an occasional joke and an item or two you value. So when you dig into their contents in the future, you will find things to enliven your day.

And as for the revolutionary Merganthaler Linotype machine? It should stand not only as a monument to discarded technology, but as a warning to advanced technology.

Who knows? Some future visitor may find in the outer lobby of this newspaper an obsolete computer or an obsolete press.

Or even an obsolete writer.

Indignity of losing to small rodent
• *January, 2001*

If I had a hit list, this guy would head it. Indeed, his would be the only name on it. I would rejoice if a small meteor took him out.

To say I dislike him would be putting it mildly. I despise him, just as I did his father and his grandfather, who also tormented me. My antipathy stems from one fact: He continues to outsmart me. After doing battle with three generations of this character, I admit the current version is smarter than I. As were the previous two generations.

This assaults my self esteem. How can I, with some degree of human intelligence, continue to be outwitted by this miserable creature?

0 0 0

"The squirrel," she said as I came in the door, "is in the bird-feeder."

I felt the color drain from my face, my pulse quicken. I looked out the window. There perched on the squirrel-proof feeder was my public enemy number one, placidly eating the birdseed.

I'll fix him, I said. She said nothing, but a slight grin conveyed much.

I went outside. Unalarmed, the squirrel eyed me. Did I detect a slight smile? I do know the corners of his mouth were upturned.

"You blanketyblank," I yelled as I rushed him. The squirrel took flight, landing gracefully on the ground some distance from the feeder, then scampering up the nearby tree where he eyed me in amusement. He knew my rage would simmer, I would go inside, and he would resume.

I went to the garage, found a plastic gallon bucket, slit it vertically along the side and half way on the bottom, and fitted it upturned around the iron rod that supports the feeder. I think I have him this time, I said, trying to suppress my glee. Next day, I came home and she greeted me.

"The squirrel is on the birdfeeder."

After exercising my routine of "scaring" the squirrel, we sat by the window to watch. In due course, the squirrel returned, ran up the iron support, tried unsuccessfully to tilt the bucket, gave up, returned to the ground and surveyed the feeder. Then he leapt onto the birdbath, took a four-foot leap to the feeder and resumed his meal.

I'll fix that, I told her. I'll elevate the bucket. Fast forward to the next day. I arrive home; she greets me with her familiar refrain.

"The squirrel is on the birdfeeder."

I went outside. The squirrel scampered up the tree and watched me go back inside. This time he made a leap from the birdbath to the top of the upturned bucket around the iron rod. Now the birdfeeder was close enough for him to reach with a slight jump.

"He's outsmarted you again," she said.

I'm not through, I said. I'll get him yet. I tied the bucket higher and farther away from the birdbath. I knew the squirrel could not get enough leverage to make a leap this distance.

I arrived home next day, and decided to bypass her and her message. I went around the corner to view the feeder. The squirrel was not there, but the feeder was swaying in still air. I eyed the tree. There, perched high on a limb, sat the squirrel, still chewing on birdseed.

I felt like Elmer Fudd in the Bugs Bunny cartoon. I fumed. How could this dumb squirrel continue to outwit me? I went inside. She looked at me and said nothing.

I am going to move the feeder farther from the birdbath. I'm going to outsmart that (expletive deleted) squirrel yet. I watched. The squirrel returned, raced up the iron rod, bypassed the bucket and landed on the birdfeeder. I saw him accomplish this feat three times, never figured how he was bypassing the bucket. His agility is amazing. Michael Jordan would be envious.

Maybe if I placed the feeder on the opposite side of the street he would become roadkill. Another idea. I took the lid from a metal popcorn container and placed it above the bucket, but the squirrel has called it a day and disappeared. At last, maybe I have outsmarted him.

0 0 0

"The squirrel is back on the feeder," she said as I walked in the door.

I'll get him, I said. I have another idea.

I got the three-gallon metal popcorn can, bored a hole in the bottom, pushed it up the bird-feeder support rod, locked it into a rigid position, then placed the original plastic bucket on top.

That's really clever, she said. When she thought she was beyond my hearing range, she added:

"But my money is on the squirrel."

Of ex, re, former ample and prosequences
• *Winter, 1995*

'Tis time now for a few more words on words.

For example, let us consider "Cease and Desist." This phrase has an undertone of legalese and means simply: Stop what you're doing and do not resume. Hence, the opposite of the phrase should be "Decease and Sist," which by rules of logic should mean continue action.

Therefore, the next time you want to tell somebody to start and go, simply tell him (or her, of course) to decease and sist.

Now let us examine prefixes, "de" and "ex." De is a negative prefix and ex means former. So, if you offer an example, you are, in effect, offering a former ample. Since ample means plenty or enough, example must mean formerly there was plenty or enough.

Now, as for "descend," which means the opposite of ascend. But isn't the prefix as in ascend superfluous? We don't need the word ascend. All anybody needs is cend. Former ample: Cend the steps. Then, descend the steps.

If you "deplore" the condition of the world, you must have plored it before it got the way it is. Former amples: Defuse, delay, deject. If you are sad, you are dejected. If you are happy, are you jected? And defame, deform, defer. If you don't put something off, do you fer it. It's perfectly obvious that de as a prefix is negative.

But, how about the word "dependable?" This word poses a problem. To negate it, one must prefix it with the negative un. Undependable. This adds up to a double negative and everybody knows how teachers of English grammar deplore double negatives. A solution is pendable. Former ample: He is worthless -- absolutely pendable.

Thence to the word "repeat." Everyone knows re means to do the same thing again. Such as in do. "Redo your homework, Wilbur. This is a poor former ample of preparation."

Since repeat means to state the again, peat must mean to state it the first time.

Former ample: "Honey, would you please take out the garbage?" she peated.

"What did you say?"

"I said get off your fat duff and take out the garbage," she repeated.

Let me pause here to say the above is not a personal reference. I always take out the garbage -- or suffer the consequences.

Which brings us to prosequences. Since con is the negative of pro, one assumes prosequences are things one enjoys.

Back to re. A former ample: Remove. When you remove something, you're moving it again. Such as: "Move that chair over here," and later "Remove the chair."

Therefore, if the surgeon tells his [or her] patient, "Your appendix is inflamed and I must remove it," he means, of course, "I moved your appendix to where it is now, but I must remove it and place it elsewhere."

Consider "regurgitate." The positive of this is gurgitate. Former ample: "Hey, Elmer, quit playing with your food and gurgitate your oatmeal."

And in conclusion: un which everybody knows is a negative prefix. Undo is the opposite of do. Uncouth is the opposite of couth. Former ample: "His manners are perfect. He is truly a couth person."

All of this brings us to the word "ravel." And unravel. Is ravel the negative of unravel?

And if all of these words don't send you into a tailspin (is headspin the opposite of tailspin?), consider this sentence from *The Tennessean* in a report of a tragedy:

"Lebanon police also say they have investigated numerous complaints of domestic violence by Deborah Jones against her husband over the past year"

Insert the word "filed" before the word "by" and the meaning is clear.

Whatever happened to editors?

At last: human logic triumphs
• *March, 2005*

Our squirrel is back, ready for another season of Black Oil Sunflower Seeds and another exercise in outwitting the master of the house where the little rodent's favorite birdfeeder is concerned.

It's a running battle between a little four-legged mammal and an aged humanoid, with the creature formerly from the wild but now a domesticated animal boasting a series of undefeated seasons. With his brilliant record, if he were coaching football, he would be in the class of legends with Bud Wilkinson and Bear Bryant.

With his athletic skills, if he were two-legged and stood 6-11, he would command more than enough salary as a basketball player to corner the market in sunflower seed.

And if he were of the proper dimensions, he would have won in Athens enough gold medals to build his own version of Ft. Knox. But he is none of the above. He is simply a thief of Dicksonian dimensions, an innovative thinker of Edisonic depths, and blessed with athletic skills of Jordanian proportions.

To put it plainly, I am not equipped, mentally or physically, to compete with this bushy-tailed rodent. But I try.

I hung the birdfeeder in mid-autumn. Suspending it from a shepherd's crook. I then filled it with sunflower seed, and awaited results. There was little delay. When I looked outside, there he was, sating his appetite. I shooed him, went into the garage, found a quart of motor oil, and squirted a generous amount on the iron rod support. It was a successful plan.

The squirrel came around the corner of the house, hit the rod at full speed, and for a moment, looked like a cartoon character clawing thin air before plunging to the bottom of a canyon.

"Ha, I've outwitted the squirrel," I bragged to my wife.

Next day, when I returned from an errand, she greeted me.

"The squirrel's back on the feeder," she announced.

The oil had dried, and traction was good. I had to try a new tactic. I moved the feeder from the shepherd's crook and suspended it from the roof overhang. He had a counter move. He mounted a shrub, jumped to a window screen and thence to the bird feeder.

Undaunted, I removed the window screen.

Undaunted, he mounted a shrub, jumped to the screen frame and thence to the feeder.

I elevated the feeder about six inches. He climbed a tree, ran the length of an overhanging limb, jumped to the roof, climbed down the suspension chain, and gorged on sunflower seed.

I removed the feeder, suspended it with a thin but strong string, hung it once more and awaited results.

The squirrel ascended to the roof via the tree limb, raced to the bird-feeder suspension and eyed it suspiciously before testing his skills. He made the leap to the string, found it had enough substance for his grip and descended to the feeder.

I lowered the feeder, removed the string, threaded it through a stainless steel tube and placed the feeder in position. The steel tube did not challenge him. He descended the tube with the skill of an acrobat.

The plot thickened. His friend joined him, using the same route. One squirrel was inside the feeder, the other hanging down to the seed by his hind legs gripping the top of the feeder.

I tapped the window from inside -- the outside squirrel made a flying leap, sending the feeder into a spin as the other squirrel, trapped inside, through glazed eyes viewed a spinning world.

I lowered the suspension tube and greased it with Vaseline. The squirrel hit the tube and panicked. I had won.

"I have outwitted the squirrel," I announced.

Later, my wife called my cell phone.

"The squirrel's back on the feeder," she said.

Back at home, I hung the feeder from a shepherd's crook, placed a cone-shaped baffle around the supporting rod and awaited results. The baffle, with a hole larger than the rod, was secure but not snug.

Later, the squirrel climbed the rod, poked his head through the hole between it and the baffle, and found he could neither advance or withdraw. He was trapped, and I had him.

"What are you going to do about him?" she asked.

"Let him go, of course," I said

A great-grandfather's report: A 'miracle child'
• *JB Leftwich, August, 1999*

We were on the plateau of our lives with a large and caring family, all apparently in good health, all frequent visitors and with all adults gainfully employed. A granddaughter's wedding was one week away, and our annual family vacation soon would follow. Our 60th wedding anniversary [JB and Jo Doris] was soon to come. Abruptly, our lives changed.

Preface: August, 1998. Our granddaughter, Peri, and her husband, Brian Wright, were on the phone, calling to announce she was pregnant with her first child. On April 12, 1999, Hannah Page Wright was born, apparently a healthy baby girl.

Day 1: Thursday June 24, 1999, 6:00 am: Our son, Jim Leftwich, was calling. His granddaughter, Hannah, was in Vanderbilt University Children's Hospital in critical condition.

Day 2: Dr. Cecilia Meagher, a cardiologist, found the problem: An extremely rare anomaly of the coronary artery which occurs in about three in one million babies. Hannah's heart was damaged.

Day 5: June 28. The family gathered in the waiting room while Dr. Davis C. Drinkwater Jr. performed the delicate surgery necessary to give Hannah a chance to live. We paced, we talked, we prayed. We even laughed some. Humor relieves tensions. There were intermittent reports on the surgery and finally the announcement that Hannah had survived her operation. We hugged everybody in sight.

But there was discomforting news. Hannah's heart had arrested during surgery and had to be massaged back into action. She was on a machine which assisted heart function, but she could not remain attached indefinitely because of the danger of blood clots.

Day 7: At high risk, Hannah was separated from the heart machine, and all did not go well. Again, her heart arrested, and again, medical personnel carefully and doggedly massaged it back into operation. Hannah was suffering strokes, and an all-night vigil was underway.

Day 8: Our family was on a roller-coaster. There were encouraging snippets only to be dashed by the reality of her precarious journey. The medical team was fighting seizures. She was responding to treatment.

Day 9: Friday, July 2: Except for Hannah's parents, Peri and Brian, and grandparents, Jim and Carolgene, the extended Leftwich family left for

Knoxville for the wedding rehearsal dinner for granddaughter, Anna.

Day 10: A wonderful wedding. Never before had Anna looked so beautiful. In his wedding prayer, the Rev. Stewart Jackson, Birmingham-Southern University chaplain, prayed for little Hannah during an emotion-choked moment. At that very instant, Hannah was undergoing a trauma which threatened to take her.

Day 21: During the previous week, Hannah survived minor crises, but showed signs of stability as her life was sustained by a respirator. But another decision had to be made – should we cancel the annual family vacation? We decided to not cancel. Except for Hannah's segment of the family, most of the others assembled at Gulf Shores, Ala. Our ally was our grandson-in-law, Lynn, a physician who was able to talk to Hannah's doctors and keep us informed.

Day 23: An excruciating decision had arrived for Peri and Brian. Obviously, Hannah could not remain on life support indefinitely. They said, yes, remove the support and make Hannah as comfortable as possible.

Day 24: The life support system was taken off. Whether her heart could sustain her remained to be seen. In the waiting room, her parents were discussing the worst case scenario.

Day 25: Vacation ended. We drove from Gulf Shores to Vanderbilt to find a happy grandmother, Carolgene, calmly rocking her granddaughter. Hannah had survived. For the first time in days, parents and grandparents could hold their baby.

Other major elements in this story:

The Minister: The one who stepped forward was the Rev. Sandy Hodge, pastor of Inglewood United Methodist Church. Sandy understood the family's needs and how to meet those needs. "An angel," said Hannah's grandmother.

Hospital and Staff: Doctors, nurses, cardiologists, surgeons and case workers of the pediatric intensive care unit were skilled professionals and compassionate human beings. The hospital got an A+.

Ronald McDonald House: A Godsend for this distressed family.

Epilogue: Hannah went home where her little heart functions at 15% capacity. Her journey to good health is hazardous, and her constant care is demanding. But she has already surprised some experts. Maybe she will surprise some more.

A grandfather's tribute: A 'remarkable life'

• *By Jim Leftwich, June 2012*

In 1999, my father, JB Leftwich, wrote a column about my granddaughter Hannah's birth and first 25 days. My daughter, Peri Wright, kept Dad's column in Hannah's scrapbook, and has requested a final chapter.

It was not really unexpected, but it was startling when the remarkable life of my 13-year-old granddaughter came to an end. Hannah lived her life with severe complications; the result of high-risk surgery to mend a rare congenital heart defect. She could not walk or speak. She was fed through a tube. She never ran or sang or danced. But she smiled. Oh! How she smiled!

Her smile was a miracle in itself. Thirteen years ago our daughter, Peri, and her husband, Brian Wright, made the painful decision to remove life support after surgery. They said goodbye to Hannah, and put her in God's hands. The neurosurgeon had said if she lived she would never smile or recognize anyone, and would live in an almost comatose state. But Hannah and God had other

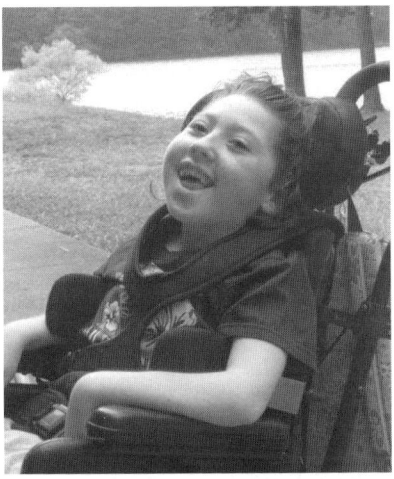

Hannah Page Wright -- featured in columns by two Leftwiches 156 months apart -- was a "miracle baby" for 13 years, bringing love and joy to all who knew her.

ideas, and she went on to live gregariously and mostly happy. Along the way she taught so many of us some of life's most important lessons.

Lesson 1 - A smile is worth a lot.

After Hannah came home from the hospital, Peri and Brian settled in as caregivers, learning more about medicine than an accountant and human resources manager ever intended. Over the years we all prayed for Hannah. As a father, I wanted to fix my little girl Peri's difficult situation, and as a grandfather, I wanted Hannah well and normal. My prayers were somewhat conflicted, and I never quite understood what to ask. As I watched their lives unfold, I began to realize the exact right people were showing up at just the right time.

For example, in the hospital, my mother-in-law asked her preacher to come by. It turned out that the Rev. Sandy Hodge had spent much of her ministerial career as a hospital chaplain and was able to give extraordinarily helpful counsel. The good-looking young dentist that Hannah fell for turned her appointments from terror to pleasure. There is a long line of the right people showing up at just the right time.

Lesson 2 - Answers to prayer are all around us.

Many showed up for Hannah's funeral. I walked over to a child in a wheelchair and asked how she knew Hannah. She said, "I ride to school with Hannah everyday. We have been next to each other on the bus for several years. Hannah was my friend." Wow! Hold the bus! Hannah had friends? That was a new thought for me.

Later a special boy named John from Hannah's class came over and dragged me to a monitor showing Hannah's video, produced by my older grandson, Hannah's brother, Josh. John was very animated and wanted me to see Hannah on the screen. I later learned Hannah always giggled at John's movements and John loved Hannah, frequently saying, "Kiss Hannah, kiss Hannah!"

Then I began to notice Hannah's friends were all around; from the neighborhood, day camp, school. Hannah's teacher provided colored chalk for the class to write something to Hannah on the playground sidewalk, which they did. But it didn't stop with her class. The next day the playground was covered with spontaneous chalk-messages to Hannah. Hannah's world was much larger than I had imagined.

Lesson 3 - Never underestimate the value of a life.

Hannah loved attention and contact with people, especially kids. She loved it when her little sister, Maddie, got tired of walking and sat on Hannah's knees while her mom pushed the wheelchair. She was content and happy watching baseball in her dad's lap, or cuddling with her mom at bedtime. For the most part she was easily entertained with a Blue's Clues DVD, enjoying it even more if someone was with her.

For 13 years I watched Hannah live her life; a life which begged consideration of questions about happiness and quality of life. It was hard to ponder her life and what might be going on in her mind. But ponder I did, agonizing over her situation and that of my daughter. As I brooded, Hannah smiled. Somewhere along the line I realized Hannah loved us, and after all, what is more important to happiness than love?

**Lesson 4 - The only true measure of the quality
of life is loving and being loved.**

HANNAH PAGE WRIGHT
April 12, 1999 - May 13, 2012

Letter to a Heightsman ...

- *October 15, 1993*
- *JBL corresponded with many CHMA grads through the years.*
  This is an example.

Now, let me see if I can reconstruct the letter I had almost finished before the computer failed and wiped out everything I had written. It seems impossible I have allowed so much time to elapse since last I heard from you. I could not believe the date on your last letter -- June 25.

So what happened to summer? Already, we have had light frost, and some of the late blooming flowers have peaked and started deteriorating. And soon -- late next month -- birthday number 74 will come and pass, and time will move even faster in search of birthday number 75.

We remain moderately healthy. Jo Doris has arthritis...My heart has been out of rhythm...This has not affected my activities to a major degree. I am still walking, painting, repairing and grumbling, albeit the pace is slower...

Last weekend was Homecoming at Castle Heights with special emphasis on the Class of 1943, many of whom were and are good friends. These are the boys -- now 68 years old -- who still call me Captain Leftwich. The '50s call me Major, the '60s Colonel, and the '70s call me JB. I never have become accustomed to the informality of the young.

Chuck Ward '42, my first *Cavalier* editor [*page 166*], returned for Homecoming. Jo Doris and I took him and a female friend out for dinner and recalled times that were and some that probably were not. Just as with you, I have remained in contact with Chuck throughout the decades. He, too, never quite drained the printer's ink from his system. Chuck thinks the calendar year should begin on September 1, arguing that September marks the beginning of the academic year and, perhaps just as important to him, the beginning of the football season.

My two grandsons attending the University of Tennessee went [to an away game], stopping over in Atlanta to see the Braves play. They were planning to spend the night in the Fiji house with their fraternity brothers, but changed their minds and headed back to Knoxville after UT got a lesson in fundamentals. I thought it was interesting that the college kids, despite all the press coverage on misbehavior by fans of both schools, just went on about their business and shared their hospitality with their brothers from the visiting school.

It seems impossible that your children are now adults...My son, Jim, shares your feelings about a daughter's wedding. All of our clan, three generations totaling 21, were present. This may never happen again as the grandchildren move from school into their careers. Two grandsons will graduate from college this scholastic year.

October 16...

My computer is in my home so there are interruptions. Nothing brings to her mind more things for me to do than my sitting down to write. It appears that my facing a keyboard is an inspiration to her.

October 17...

Twenty-four hours after the above graph, I am back to my keyboard. I was not aware at the time, but she was standing behind me as I wrote. Said she: "We need to go see about buying a new clothes dryer." She could have added, "as you promised." I stopped in mid-sentence, closed the computer and went with her on a mission that led far beyond the appliance store. I shall not list details.

I am amused, not angry. I am so thankful she is here and I am here with her. We have been together 55 years. (She just interrupted my train of thought to ask a question about a crossword puzzle clue. Now she is discussing the characteristic of her puzzle.)

I dug out old negatives [of old Tennessee barns] and had two prints made. One at Kroger's, the other custom made by a photo studio here. I have been out of photography so long now that I was testing the waters with these two. I'll have a couple of others reprinted to give you a choice. It is flattering to have you want them. One year ago, a local bank did a showing of my prints and presented me with a plaque for "many years of public service." The Chamber of Commerce gave me a plaque and made me a lifetime member, and *The Tennessean* gave me a plaque for "promoting values embodied in the Bill of Rights." To be candid, I've done little, probably nothing, in promoting the Bill of Rights, but *The Tennessean* wanted to give me a plaque during its annual banquet for letter writers and guest columnists. Somebody probably said: "Hey, give him this one." All the above distinguishes me for longevity. (She just announced that on her own she had thought of the word in her puzzle.)

I, too, treasure our enduring friendship. Indeed, "friendship" is too generic. I treasure our close and loving relationship.

Coach

Lessons from a 70-year marriage

- Published July, 2009, by Sam Hatcher, *Wilson County Trend*
- Written by Lynda Leftwich Newton, Jim Leftwich '69,
  Barbara Leftwich Froula, Jack Leftwich '70

It was not an auspicious beginning and would hardly have foreshadowed a 70-year marriage. JB Leftwich and Jo Doris Prichard drove across the Tennessee state line into Kentucky in 1939 to be married. They planned to keep this union a secret, but Jo Doris' Mother was not fooled -- and so they began their life together living with the bride's parents, Jim and Alta Prichard.

Both were students at Cumberland University. JB had completed two years at CU and Jo Doris one. He continued as a student while Jo Doris interrupted her college education to work as secretary to Wilson County

JB and JoDoris Leftwich attend mid-'50s Heights Christmas dance.

Extension Agent Jim Ward. JB worked part-time at the *Democrat*.

After his Cumberland graduation, JB began his long career with Castle Heights Military Academy. In those years Heights was not just a place where he reported to work, but also a place where the families were involved. The [Lt. Col. Ralph and Rebecca] Lucas, [Maj. Lindsey and Elizabeth] Donnell, [Maj. Leonard and Mary Ann] Bradley, [Maj. C.V. and Elsie Mae] Baker families as well as many others were an important part of Leftwich life. Every spring there was an Easter egg hunt for the young children followed by the parade of cadets. At Thanksgiving the families were invited for lunch.

As young Leftwiches began arriving, the couple began building a house at 136 Castle Heights Avenue – only a block and a half from The Hilltop. This was important, as families in those days were fortunate to have one car. [In 2010, that location is a part of the parking lot for Immanuel Baptist Church.]

Having four children -- Lynda, Jim, Barbara, Jack -- to educate was a driving force for JB and Jo Doris. In addition to his teaching career, JB was county correspondent for the *Nashville Tennessean* and he developed a photography business. He took pictures at Heights functions,

The Leftwich's son, Jimmy [left, second row], was a member of the 1956-57 Junior School Glee Club directed by Jeanette H. Kremer [far right]. Considering Mrs. Kremer's classical musical background, one might consider it unlikely the very roots of "southern rock" would be taking form under her guidance. But among the vocalists is Duane Allman [left, first row], who with his brother Gregg -- also a CHMA student at this time -- formed the Allman Brothers Band in 1969. Gregg was a fourth grade student of Mrs. JB Leftwich.

Also in the chorus: Alan McClellan [fifth, first row], third of the McClellan brothers from West Virginia to graduate from Heights: Edward '57, Myron '58, Alan '62.

including graduation. He often would stay up all night before the final Sunday Circle "dismissed" developing pre-graduation event photos.

Jo Doris began her teaching career when a vacancy occurred mid-year in the fourth grade at Heights. One of her students was Greg Allman who grew up with his brothers to form the Allman Brothers rock/blues band. [She still has a necklace given to her one Christmas by Greg. And he always signed his homework with, "I love you, Mrs. Leftwich."] So began a time of teaching, going to school, being active in the First United Methodist Church Women's group, and, of course, raising a family. She spent most of her career at Lebanon Junior High School teaching science, and later as Sam Houston Elementary librarian.

So what accounts for this marriage longevity? They endured the highs and lows of anyone who lives more than 80 years. They supported each other in "sickness and in health." (She nursed him 20 years ago,

• Jeannette "Ma" Kremer [as she was affectionately called by cadets] was a graduate of Chicago's Cosmopolitan School of Music and the University School of Music, Ann Arbor. She studied in New York and Paris, and had extensive teaching experience. Her son, F. S. Kremer, was Heights' "A" Company commander 1937-38, and his sword was "willed" to each succeeding "A" commander by Mrs. Kremer after he was killed in World War II. As a cadet, Kremer complained the Academy had no fight song, so his mother wrote, "Hail, Castle Heights!"

when he had a heart attack resulting in by-pass surgery. He nursed her through back surgery and a ruptured appendix. As a result of the heart surgery, he was advised to walk two miles a day -- which he has continued, probably contributing to his longevity and alertness at 89.)

By the way, a story told by Dad about his hospital stay: "Leonard Bradley Jr., longtime family friend and one of my former math and journalism students, was visiting my family in the hospital waiting room while I was in surgery. The surgeon emerged and told my children the operation was successful, but they probably would never see me looking worse than I now looked. Leonard without missing a beat told the doctor, 'They never saw him during an 8 a.m. algebra class.'"

They continue to be interested in life. They read daily. They keep up with children/grandchildren/great grandchildren through e-mail. JB continues contact with many of Heights grads. The family continues to have two get-togethers a year – Thanksgivings and summers.

So, what are the lessons for those of us following in Gen II, Gen III and Gen IV:

• **Never forget who you are.** Years ago Dad was on a plane delayed in landing. He began a conversation with the lady seated beside. It ended with sentiments similar to these: She - "What do you do anyway?" He - "I manage rental property." (This after his CHMA retirement.) She - "I was sure you were a teacher." He was and still is a teacher for all of us.

• **You can do whatever it takes.** Multi-tasking, though a current term, was practiced. Mother taught school, attended college classes, reared four children and looked after her Mother. She prepared all our meals – eating out was rare. We frequently had biscuits for breakfast. Cereal was a Sunday night meal.

• **Two strong people can stay married** [enough said about that].

• **You can change with the times.** Dad developed computer skills and is now on e-mail, also Facebook. Mother, while an excellent traditional cook, was never afraid to try new recipes. One night Mother ("Momommy" to the grandchildren) declined to reveal the main dish [rabbit] until after they tried it.

• **Continue to improve your mental capabilities.** Both played Bridge (though Mother at one time said, "You don't think I taught him everything I know, do you?") and they continue to work challenging crossword puzzles. They read newspapers daily.

• **You don't have to live in the past.** While we all enjoy hearing stories of Mother and Dad's early years, they maintain their interest in others. Not just family and friends, but people at church and in the community. Mother's apple cake is still requested for church events.

• **Be true to your values.** We all know what they represent.

JB's secrets for young husbands
• *October, 2009*

Two events, each of note in an otherwise usual year, occurred in 2009 and transformed it into a year for me to remember.

One, I reached an age plateau of four score and ten. Two, our marriage reached an anniversary of three score and ten. Neither number falls into the category of the unique in the wide view of happenings. Whatever one achieves, he or she soon discovers others with records of a higher dimension.

Two close friends celebrated their 70th wedding anniversary last year, and a local minister preached a sermon at age 101. Years ago, Dr. L. L. Rice, a legend in the histories of Castle Heights Military Academy and Cumberland University, delivered an hour-long speech on his 100th birthday. Without notes. As a newspaper reporter, I covered the speech. I thought he might never shut up.

Our anniversary -- Jo Doris and me -- though not a longevity record, prompted demonstrations of friendship and heart-warming tributes, likely typical of any durable marriage, nonetheless observations and tributes we cherish. And my birthday promoted Generation IV members of the family to fashion their own tributes to this aged patriarch.

Great-grandson 10-year-old Jon Stewart created a birthday card bearing the message: "When life gives you birds, you fly away!"

I've given thought to this message, surmising there is profound thought therein that I am missing. I even Googled these words, and turned up nothing. These are his thoughts, and I hesitate to inquire further. Perhaps, he is advising me to use whatever abilities I have and not to lament talents I don't have. It could be he is observant. Thinking back and leveling with myself, I acknowledge having envied persons with talents beyond my humble ones.

But in my defense, I have had defining moments when my senses told me I had done well in some tasks, however simple.

Another written message came from grandson-in-law Sean, who, after receiving a pocket knife as a gift, wrote a poem in our honor, concluding with these words: "Thus we got a lil' blade as engagement plunder . . . Now have paired butcher & sharp'ner none can cleave asunder."

Could it be that the language of this young century has morphed into profundity that we who existed in the early years of the last century find beyond our grasp?

Perhaps, the most touching thoughts came from Molly, teen-age great-granddaughter, who wrote a poem citing her special relationship

Attending the 70th anniversary celebration for JB and Jo Doris Leftwich were children from two prominent Castle Heights families -- the Leftwiches and the Bradleys [Leonard and Mary Ann Bradley] -- who grew up together on The Hilltop: Barbara Leftwich Froula, Lynda Leftwich Newton, Jack Leftwich '70, John Bradley '63, Tommy Bradley '69, Bill Bradley '65, L. K. Bradley Jr. '58, and Jim Leftwich '63.

with me and memories we created together. Her reflections brought a special glow, assuring me family affection can extend through generations.

Mattiebeth, 3, had no pertinent words, but she supervised as I picked items off the floor. When I failed to recover an item, she gave me a "gotcha" look and gleefully called my attention to it.

The following are thoughts of this ancient senior citizen who realizes advanced years do not necessarily bring wisdom but, more to the point, bring time to contemplate. Hence, these words from this imperfect husband to younger husbands:

- Kiss your wife often. Kisses are renewable.
- Hold her at least a few seconds every day.
- Don't worry about your spats. Fusses relieve tensions. Just keep them in bounds. Make up before the day ends.
- If possible, have separate checking accounts.
- Learn to say, "That's all right," even when it isn't.
- Help with the dishes, and take out the garbage. Even make the bed.
- Be sensitive to her moods. She's not always the same. Neither are you.
- Chances are she's pretty. Tell her so.
- Tell her occasionally when one of the children does something commendable, he must have her genes.

267

- If she looks nice in a new garment, tell her. If she doesn't, fib.
- If she's a fair cook, compliment her cooking. If she's an artist in the kitchen, compliment her frequently.
- Open the door for her. Seat her.
- Remember her birthday. If not with a gift, with a hug.
- Engage her in conversations.
- Remember your wedding anniversary and tell her how fortunate you are to have her.
- Say "Thank you," frequently. Learn to say, "I'm sorry."
- She never gets too old to enjoy hearing, "I love you."

Just as in so many instances, I wish I had thought of these admonitions earlier in life.

- Though child-raising tips were not among JB's "secrets," he -- with direction from wife, Jo Doris, and with their four children as evidence – had as much to offer in regard to parenting as in husbandly advice:

^ **Lynda Leftwich Newton** attended Castle Heights summer schools 1959-61, and graduated from Lebanon High having served as *Blue Flame* editor. Journalism degree from University of Tennessee, organizing and editing school's first daily newspaper [*Daily Beacon*], and named a Torchbearer -- highest award for grads who exemplified academic excellence and community / university service. Worked for *Knoxville News-Sentinel* before professional management training career with Dale Carnegie with her husband, the late Glyn Ed Newton. They have two children, four grandchildren.

^ **James L. "Jim" Leftwich** is 1963 Cum Honore graduate of Heights, member of National Honor Society, Heights "Y," football squad, wrestling team co-captain. Attended University of Tennessee, earning BA from Memphis State University. Retired after 40 years in financial services. He and wife Carolgene Page, retired teacher of hearing impaired, have been married 48 years and have two children, five grandchildren.

^ **Barbara Leftwich Froula** attended Heights summer schools 1961-62, and graduated from Lebanon High where she played basketball and was sports editor of *Blue Flame*. Earned BS from University of Tennessee, worked in Knoxville area as Fire Protection Specialist for Rural/Metro Fire Department and Knox County Fire Prevention Bureau. Mother of two children, with three grandchildren.

^ **Jack H. Leftwich** is 1970 Cum Honore graduate of Heights, and was member of National Honor Society, Heights "Y," football and track teams, and swimming team captain [holding several CHMA event records]. Spent more than 40 years with various technology companies, and remains active in that field. He and wife Debbie Hobbs, career realtor, have seven children, 10 grandchildren.

Changing face of a public square
• *April, 1996*

JBL Note: The verses were written by my son, Jim Leftwich, who recalls more than three decades ago stepping on asphalt bubbles as his mother led him across traffic lanes on the Square to an island of parking meters. Says he about the tar bubbles: "I liked to hear them pop."

A recently refurbished -- but still stone-faced -- General Hatton gazes from his elevated vantage point upon a town square far different from the one he surveyed when he first was placed in the center of Lebanon's business district.

Indeed, the encircling businesses have evolved almost 100 percent from the establishments staring back at the statue in 1937, my first year in this city -- albeit as a student, until two years later.

The Westside Hotel, a lawyer's placard,
Penny parking meters, whittler's discard,
Tobacco juice, popcorn seasoned air
No longer embellish my hometown square.

Quick, now, which is the only current business on the Square that was in operation 60 years ago? McClain and Smith is gone. And Askew's and Eskew's. So are Baird and Safley, Draper and Darwin, the court-house, the jail and Rose's.

Cat's Paw and Oertell's in the corner pocket,
Produce and goods at the farmers' market,
Bartering, dealing, on the court house step,
No record or ledger was ever kept.

If you answered Seat's Studio, you are correct. Ah, Waldo Seat! Frugal with himself, generous with his friends. Tenaciously hanging onto 8x10 cameras long after 35mm's had swept the country. Arguing until the last that no little camera could equal the large format cameras he used. He was right, you know. At the time.

Waldo Seat, in latter years partners with Lillard Barrett, his son-in-law. The business is still in the same family with Sonny Barrett now at the helm. Same location.

Gum on the walk, the screech of a car,
Blistering pavement, bubbles of tar,
A passing nod, a warm "hello,"
And mamas with children in tow.

And those anchors of the old Square: Shannon's and Bradshaw's drug stores. Who could forget Homer and Harry Shannon? Homer standing in the door welcoming customers. Harry, with his belt well below a generous belly, behind the counter. And the merchandise, spilling from the shelves onto the floor. And the 35-cent plate lunch. None was ever better.

Cook's Hardware and the City Cafe,
McAdoos' store and a Princess matinee,
A cherry coke from Shannon's fountain,
All the domain of Robert Hatton.

Nothing was more invigorating than seeing a musical comedy on a hot July day in the Princess Theater with its air conditioning. Were there other air conditioned establishments here in those days? (Some wag once said the "No Smoking" sign got a bit scrambled. Said he thought Nosmo King was a movie star.)

Once bustling, the center of commerce
Is a memory now -- time in reverse.
The General, his post antiques and art,
Recalls local trade -- minus Walmart.

How many remember parking around the Square on Saturday night just to "people watch" on the sidewalks? 'Twas a different era.

Cadet days began at sunrise,
never really ended....

• *From 1950's Castle Heights promotional catalogue*

As Academy Public Relations Director (in addition to his classroom, publications advisor and photography responsibilities), JB Leftwich coordi-
nated production of the Heights catalogue sent to those inquiring about
the school. Excerpts from "**A Day at Castle Heights**:"

■ The cadet day begins at 6:30 a.m. with the sound of reveille. [Chances
are the room alarm clock was set for 6:00]....At 6:45 on the Hilltop,
the cadet corps is formed into four companies around The Circle, and
first sergeants are calling roll.

■ Long lines march to the mess hall, cadets stand at attention behind
their chairs, the Adjutant barks "Seats," there is the sound and move-
ment of chairs, and then the command, "Rest." Eight cadets at each
table, with ranking men at both ends. Cadets serving as waiters bring
trays of food, and by 7 a.m. breakfast begins. Faculty tables include
officers, some with families. Sick call sounds at 7:30, and those in
need head to the infirmary (either being granted medication or confinement to the facility). Cadets have 20 minutes until first class at
7:50, making sure they adhere to the "uniform of the day" announcement made at breakfast, and that their rooms are left clean with beds
made -- since some time during the next four hours they will be inspected by a faculty or cadet officer.

■ Classes end at 1:00 p.m. with "dinner" (lunch) at 1:10. At 2 p.m., cadets either attend study hall (if assigned) or remain in their rooms
for study. On Monday, Tuesday and Friday, cadets begin one hour of
military training at 2:40 p.m. On Thursday, military training begins at
2:10. On those four days, extra-curricular and athletic sessions begins
at 4 p.m., for seasonal varsity and junior varsity teams, intramurals.

■ Wednesday afternoons are one of four "town leave" periods, enabling
cadets to walk into Lebanon (or join with peers for cab service) for a
movie or other activity. Saturday and Sunday afternoons and Friday
nights are the other three "free" periods.

The Dug Out, located in basement of Ingram Hall, was center of cadets leisure on-campus time for decades. Heights' chapter of DeMolay, along with other student organizations, operated the facility's concessions with profits directed to campus improvements.

- Saturday mornings, at 10:30 a.m., is the most rigid inspection of the week [known as SMI], with military and cadet officers checking each room -- with room occupants standing at attention -- for dust, trash, locker orderliness, items out of place or disallowed, bunk beds sheets and blankets tightness, desk and drawer organization, sink and soap dish cleanliness, and individual personal appearance. Cadets hoped to avoid assignment of demerits for what to the inspecting officers was perceived as lack of perfection.

- Saturday nights, cadets remained on campus and could play recreational games in the Dug Out (game room with pool tables, TV, refreshment counter), attend a movie in Macfadden Auditorium, swim in the pool, or read, listen to records or write letters. That night as well as each evening, during unallocated times, cadets lined up outside two pay phone booths in Main to call home to family or girl friends. Formal or informal dances are scheduled some weekends

- Sundays after breakfast, cadets formed on The Circle by religious affiliation and marched into town for services at Lebanon churches.

Thought of as a "simple brass instrument," a bugle's sounds -- including those made by a trumpet -- on the Hilltop throughout each day and night signaled multiple complex routines, activities, formations, procedures.

During spring months, it was announced at Sunday "dinner" whether there would be a formal military parade at 4 p.m. that day. Advance notification was made to alert "day boys" (cadets living in Lebanon), area residents and visitors that a parade was scheduled.

■ On a daily basis, "supper" was served at 6 p.m., with cadets having marched into the mess hall. Most tense time of each weekday, dreaded by certain cadets but never feared by many, was the post-meal call to "Attention" by the cadet Adjutant, and his following announcement: "The following cadets will report to the Office of the Commandant...". Names of cadets "on report" for failing to follow rules/procedures -- such as sleeping in for BRC (Breakfast Roll Call), classroom misconduct, uniform mistake or other infractions reported by faculty, cadet and military staff officers -- were read aloud. After meal dismissal, the named cadets lined up outside the Commandant's office in Main and individually were called in for determination as to whether and how many demerits would be assigned. Cadets were "allowed" to walk off demerits during "town leave" periods. Cadets also could be demoted from any military rank they had achieved during their time at Heights in the event of "earning" a designated quantity.

■ "First call to quarters" by bugle was sounded at 6:50 p.m., with final

Informal weekend dances and sock hops, held in Macfadden Gym, were routine on the Hilltop. This one in the late '50s featured an appearance by Miss Tennessee 1958, Patricia Eaves, as part of a March of Dimes fund-raising campaign. [Obviously hair length was never a cadet issue.]

CQ coming at 7 p.m. In-room study was until 9:40, with taps at 10 o'clock. During this more than two uninterrupted hours, when there supposedly was no visiting room-to-room or playing of radios, the faculty "officer in charge" [OC] made his rounds to observe -- through formal peep holes in each door -- cadets at study. [Consequently, each barracks had a subtle signaling system -- usually involving radiator pipes -- dependent on cadets on first floor of each dormitory making it known the OC had entered the building. The sound of cadets hurriedly returning to their rooms and the click of radios/record players being turned off was noticeable. And toward the end of each semester with final tests nearing, the glow of lamps from beneath room doors -- with peep holes covered temporarily -- could be seen by anyone walking the halls each night after Taps.]

Major/Captain/Colonel/JB says 'Farewell'

- Published *Lebanon Democrat, October, 2010*
- Written by Lynda Leftwich Newton, Jim Leftwich '63, Barbara Leftwich Froula, Jack Leftwich '70

Few of our Dad's readers were around in 1938 when he began his career at *The Lebanon Democrat*. His association began while he was a student at Cumberland University – he says he was paid $5.00 a week, and he considered that overpayment.

We suspect, though we have no proof, that Dad may be the longest continuously writing newspaper person in the state. Throughout his tenure he has attempted to teach and inform by sharing his own experiences and those of others with life in Middle Tennessee -- and at the former Castle Heights Military Academy. He also has kept himself informed in current events and has done some political commentary.

In recent weeks Dad's health has declined and he has decided to discontinue his weekly column. Occasionally he may submit one, but not on a regular basis. After all these years of writing, it is too difficult for him to say good-bye personally -- plus doing that might suggest he is "giving up" -- so we, his children, are doing it for him

He was reminiscing recently about his political opinions. Most of his readers are aware he has become conservative in his views. He hasn't always felt that way, and was remembering he once worked for President Lyndon Johnson's re-election. His changing viewpoint has often led to interesting discussions with those who did not make the same political evolution.

One of our family's favorite stories about Dad's early years at *The Democrat* involved our Mother, Jo Doris, who was working for the late Jim Ward, Wilson County Agent. In that position, her pic-

JB's last Homecoming was 2010, where he was presented with the initial Castle Heights National Alumni Association plaque honoring former faculty for service to the Academy -- in his case more than 45 years, plus continued love and dedication to the school for almost 25 years since its closing -- or 70 of his 91 years. Subsequent honorees announced at Homecoming: Gene Hale [2011], Cordell and Oleta Winfree [2012], and Sgt. Major Rodney Arthur [2013].

ture was made with some sheep. Dad, and others at the *Democrat*, made up a dummy front page using the photo and a headline referring to her as "Little Bo Peep." At the time, Mother thought it was authentic, and she was not amused. As time passed, it has become more amusing to her.

For many years, Dad was advisor to Castle Heights' award winning newspaper, *The Cavalier*. One of his proudest achievements was teaching these young men, and watching as many went on to successful careers, some in journalism.

The weeks that *The Cavalier* was published, Dad often had to spend time Saturdays at *The Democrat*, where it was printed. While Dad read copy, we spent more time than would have liked in the old newspaper shop on East Gay Street. Tagging along on Saturday morning, we amused ourselves watching and listening to the metallic clink of the Linotype as it miraculously transformed lead into lines of backward letters. When the press was running, it produced a rhythmic beat as papers were printed, emerging folded at the end of the machine. He was at home in the newsroom with news people.

Dad was very fond of his manual typewriter and never transitioned to an electric one. Once computers were introduced, he became proficient with its usage, and his grandchildren often bragged about that. He continues to communicate with family, friends and former students by e-mail.

Dad never lost his zest for the written word, especially for words well written. He continues to look at newspapers with a critical eye. When we wrote letters home as college students, he never hesitated to edit our letters and give us suggestions for improvement..

As with most writers, Dad always appreciated his readers. He did sometimes question the number of people who actually read his columns. At least once, however, readership was proven to him. At Christmastime he wrote a column which included a recipe for his Mother's jam cake. Inadvertently an ingredient was omitted. He heard from many who wished to try the recipe and wanted the correct amount. (He subsequently issued a correction, and has included the recipe in many Christmas columns since.)

He feels privileged to have worked with many outstanding newspaper professionals. In addition to his association with *The Democrat*, he was for many years county correspondent for *The Nashville Tennessean*.

Dad has great loyalty to you, his readers, and hopefully, he may occasionally write a column. But if he doesn't, be assured you will always be close to his heart.

- 30 -

JB Leftwich took many dramatic and memorable photographs of Castle Heights Military Academy cadets, faculty and facilities during his Hilltop tenure, but perhaps the most iconic -- certainly one of the most popular -- is this late '50s shot.

Chapter Eight

Yearbook Dedications

"It requires a real sense of dedication to persevere through the heartaches and drudgery incident to the teacher's profession... A teacher lives on in the lives and characters of those he [she] has touched and inspired. He is an instrument of divinity in the shaping of human destinies. In large measure we feel our faculty has a generous share of those who 'gladly teach!' Great is the school so blessed."

— **Col. H. L. Armstrong, 1956**

THE DRILL:
1942 marked the first year JB Leftwich served as advisor to the Castle Heights yearbook, then called *The Hill Top*. [At the suggestion of Commandant D. T. Ingram, the annual subsequently was named *The Adjutant*.] Traditionally the book each year was dedicated to a CHMA faculty or staff member based on decisions of the publication's editor and editorial staff. Following are copies of yearbook dedications from 1941 through 1986 [the year the Academy closed], with exceptions of 1943, 1944, 1978 and 1981 when dedications were not designated.

Overleaf Photo:
A collection of CHMA yearbooks maintained by the Heights National Alumni Association

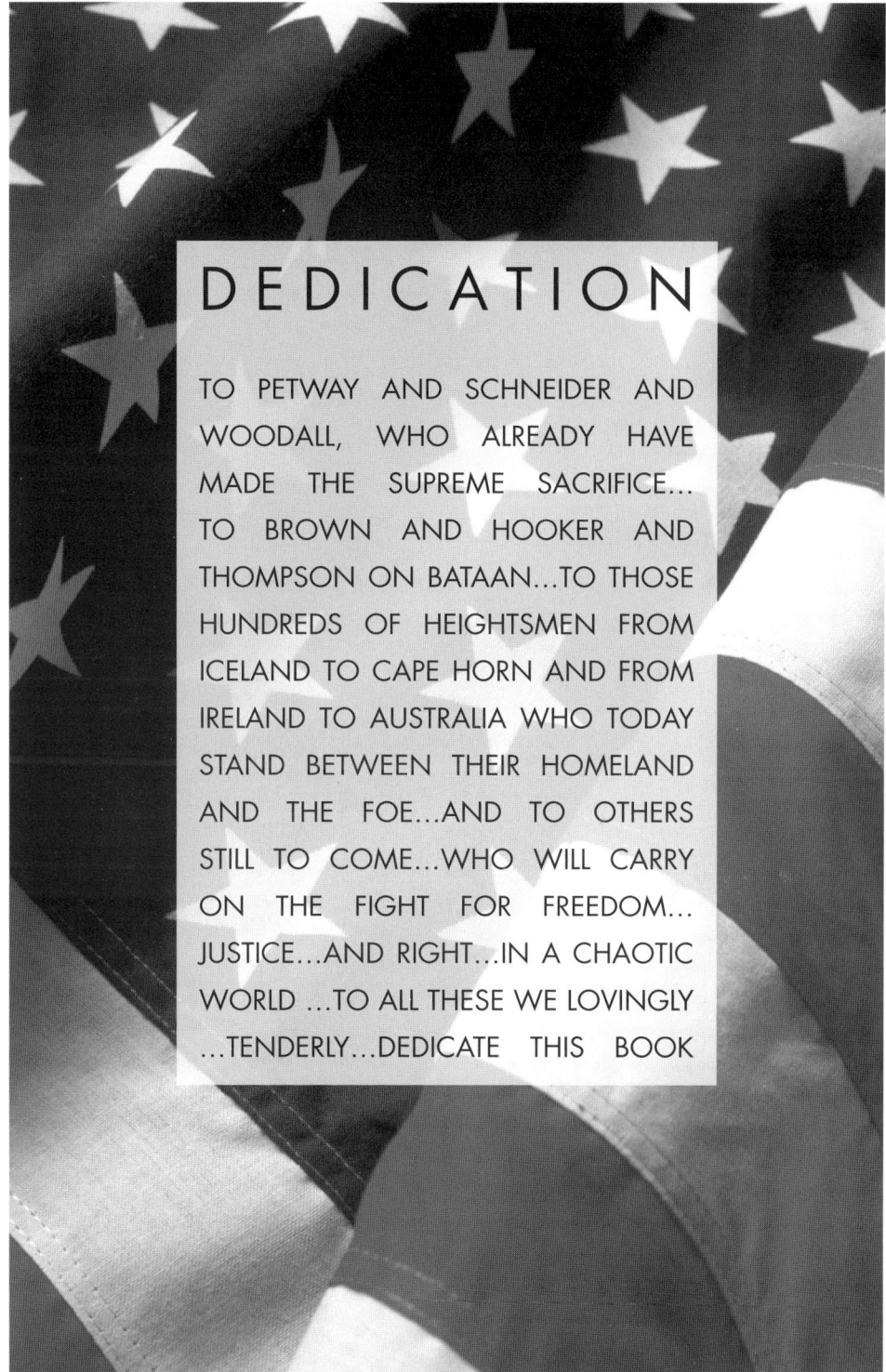

DEDICATION

TO PETWAY AND SCHNEIDER AND WOODALL, WHO ALREADY HAVE MADE THE SUPREME SACRIFICE... TO BROWN AND HOOKER AND THOMPSON ON BATAAN...TO THOSE HUNDREDS OF HEIGHTSMEN FROM ICELAND TO CAPE HORN AND FROM IRELAND TO AUSTRALIA WHO TODAY STAND BETWEEN THEIR HOMELAND AND THE FOE...AND TO OTHERS STILL TO COME...WHO WILL CARRY ON THE FIGHT FOR FREEDOM... JUSTICE...AND RIGHT...IN A CHAOTIC WORLD ...TO ALL THESE WE LOVINGLY ...TENDERLY...DEDICATE THIS BOOK

FOR FREEDOM'S CAUSE

To the boys who have gone before,

To our predecessors—

To those who have trod the path before us—

To those alumni who lay down the cap and gown

For the rifle and bayonet,

We dedicate this book.

They looked at things in the same way we do.

They got their demerits, made their low grades,

Looked over the world in general over a coke in the commissary,

In the same way that you and I do.

After December 7,

One by one they left,

To go and fight and die.

They were no different than we.

Life was sweet.

They had their wives, mothers, sweethearts, children.

When the bugle sounded, they were ready.

They gave their youth, freedom, lives.

It is to these—

Our honored dead—

That we dedicate this memorial,

Our 1945 yearbook.

IN MEMORIAM

KILLED IN ACTION

BASS, RALPH T.
BEASLEY, BUDDY B.
BEESON, JOHN A.
BODE, EDWARD P.
BRANCH, ROBERT L.
BROWN, DAVID L.
BURKETT, WILLIAM W.
D'ARCY, JAMES A.
DENHAM, HARRY H.
DIFFENBAUGH, PETER D.
EUBANK, THOMAS
FERGUSON, DAVID J.
HALL, JAMES H.
HARRISON, ROBERT H.
HELTZEN, WALTER
HOWELL, ELMER G.
JENKINS, WILLIAM F.
KARR, WILLIAM W.
KENT, NORRIS J.
KREMER, FREDRICK S.
LILIENTHAL, LESLIE H.
LINDSAY, ROBERT A.
LONG, PHELPS, JR.
LONGCOY, HARRY S.
MITCHELL, JERE B.
PETWAY, EDWIN S.
PHIFER, FOREST H.
PYLE, BEN C.
ROBERTSON, CECIL R.
ROBERTSON, JOHN F.
ROBERTSON, LEROY C., III
RODEHEAVER, HOMER
SCHNEIDER, WILLIAM
SEALE, CLYDE
SHERMAN, JOHN H.
SLEYSTER, IRVIN W.
SLOCUM, PHILLIPS T.
STULTS, PAUL M.
STRUICK, ALEXANDER E.
WILES, JOE S.
WOODALL, JOHN A.

MISSING IN ACTION

HOOKER, THANE
KIZER, RICHARD D.
MELTON, HARRY R.
OWEN, ROBERT J.
OZIER, JOHN
PENNELL, GEORGE N.
RANDOLPH, CLIFFORD J.
RUDISILL, JOHN C.
RYAN, BERTRAM L.
SCHUERMAN, JAMES H.
STULTZ, RICHARD

Dedication

The position of Castle Heights as one of the leading military schools in the nation is due to the determination and ability of a few loyal men who have devoted their lives to that end. Heights' history is rich with such names as Col. I. W. P. Buchanan, Dr. D. E. Mitchell and Prof. O. N. Smith—all leaders in the field of education and all dedicated to the principles of Castle Heights.

To this select group must be added the name of Col. Harry L. Armstrong.

Beginning in 1909 when the school was in its infancy, Col. Armstrong has devoted his life to helping create a military academy recognized as one of the best in America. He serves as president of Castle Heights, but more than that, he represents the finest quality found in schools of this type.

In this man cadets who have attended Castle Heights have found a friend— a man who believes in boys and who has practiced that belief for nearly forty years.

It is with the profoundest respect that the Senior class of 1946 sincerely dedicates the Adjutant to our friend, Col. H. L. Armstrong.

1947

MAJOR DAN KENDALL

How often have we marched with quaking heart and trembling knee into a neat little office in the Main and faced a huge bear of a man seated behind piles of records—our records? How often have we looked into snapping black eyes glaring out at us from under heavy dark eyebrows? How often have we gulped and tried to conjure up a reasonable facsimile of an excuse for an academic failure?

And still, how often have we realized that the huge man underlaid his demands for "work and still more work" with a tone of sympathy and friendliness? How often have we since come to the conclusion that this man has exacted a more determined effort from us and through his suggestions and demands made us realize that he had our best efforts at heart?

In this man we cadets have found not only a task master but a friend—a man who believes in boys and who has practiced that belief for nearly twenty-five years.

It is with the profoundest respect that the Senior Class of 1947 sincerely dedicates the ADJUTANT to our teacher and friend—Major Dan Kendall.

Our Appreciation...

1948

A few short months ago they walked among us; worked, studied, played—shared our hopes, joys and sorrows.

Why they were taken from us, we know not. We try not to ask these questions—lest it hurt us more. We try not to mourn for they would not have wanted it so.

We dedicate this yearbook to Charles and Joe not in a spirit of tearful bereavement but with pleasant remembrance.

They died too young to achieve "greatness" or "success" in the recognized material sense of the words. They did not die for some noble cause or high ideal, but for reasons unknown to us. Perhaps it was because He wanted two devoted friends, loyal comrades that He took them from us. These Creighton and Walters were.

"When God picks blossoms for His own garden it is fitting that He pick the finest flowers."

These two were not earthly saints. They were boys through and through and would appreciate no undue sentimental flattery. These qualities were what made us love them and why saying "good-bye" was so hard.

To Charles Walters and Joe Creighton we respectively and lovingly dedicate this book.

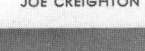

JOE CREIGHTON

CHARLES WALTERS

COL. DANIEL TAYLOR INGRAM

The Old Dominion, the mother of statesmen and military leaders, has given Castle Heights one of her truly great sons. We honor and respect him for his fierce loyalty to Virginia and his love for everything typical of the gentleman of the old South. Fresh from Virginia Military Institute in 1921 Captain Daniel Taylor Ingram came to Castle Heights as military tactical officer, coach of baseball and track, and instructor in history. Holding that position until 1928 he became commandant, with the rank of Major and it is in that capacity that he has been known and loved by thousands of cadets. .Two years ago he was promoted to the much deserved rank of Lt. Colonel.

Throughout the years he has not lost his slow Virginia drawl, which we sometimes love to copy behind his back and which has made us forget that laboriously planned technical alibi when we faced him to answer those military reports that have had a way of appearing opposite our names on the bulletin board. If he has been severe and exacting, all his demands have been tempered by just impartiality, fairness, and a deep personal interest in every cadet.

To a greater extent, perhaps, than anyone else who has ever lived on "The Hill" he represents the true spirit of Castle Heights. It is, then, with sincerest appreciation that we dedicate this issue of "The Adjutant" to a truly fine southern gentleman, Lt. Col. Daniel Taylor Ingram.

DEDICATION

Dedication . . .

Miss Mary Fahey

Perhaps no other person has given so liberally of time, efforts and means to the cadets of Castle Heights Military Academy.

For more years than she likes to remember, she has been the adopted "mother" of hundreds of boys away from home and confused by the complexity of a new environment.

She has sewed on stripes, cooked waffles, mended shirts, heard tales of woe, shared happiness and sorrow, played Dorothy Dix, arranged dates, and understood the hundreds of problems that confront "her boys," the cadets of Castle Heights.

She has lived and died with the football teams, kept her fingers crossed for the basketball teams, and mentally run the races with the track teams.

In sincere gratitude we pay tribute to the loyalty and love of Heights' Number One Fan and dedicate this edition of THE ADJUTANT to Miss Mary Fahey.

Dedication

If the Heights cadets were to get together a list of virtues and characteristics most desired in their instructors there would be many.

Every cadet dreams of the day he will return to his Alma Mater and be greeted by old friends among the cadets and faculty. There is always some member of the faculty you seek out first—the one with a serious expression on his face which changes to a cordial smile when he greets you. He's the man who makes you feel at home—the one who remembers you.

Then as you view the old meeting places your mind switches to a member of the faculty always willing to give you help. . . . Maybe you were homesick or maybe you did badly on a test. He had a way of making you realize how to conquer your upset emotions. He gave his students a square deal, gave aid where it was needed, showed you he wanted you to pass.

In the trophy case are the symbols of Heights victories. Here are "The Cavalier" prizes, won by time given in extra-curricular pursuits.

To the man who combined these virtues, the members of the ADJUTANT staff dedicate this book

MAJOR J. B. LEFTWICH

Major Tom Harris

In an age of grim forebodings and pessimistic views of the future, a man who can impress his associates with humor and fun is indeed a rarity. The man who made the deepest impression on the seniors of 1952 was capable of sugar-coating the seriousness of knowledge imparted in English classes with spontaneous and often unexpected humor.

But this man was not given solely to the lighter side of life. His sincerity and friendliness were much valued by the seniors and underclassmen who came to know him. His willingness to go a little further in behalf of some delinquent student was well known by members of his classes.

And so, it is with deep appreciation for these moments of laughter combined with an underlying sincerity that we dedicate the 1951 edition of The Adjutant to Major Tom Harris.

Dedication

DEDICATION

LT. COL. RALPH A. LUCAS

The cadet corps of Castle Heights can never forget the deep, booming yet kindly voice that has meant so much to so many, over the years. His constant desire to help; his tireless efforts on our behalf; most of all the kind understanding we loved so well are all features we shall never forget about the man who is fondly known as the cadet's friend, Lt. Col. Ralph A. Lucas.

Ever since he joined the staff of the academy in 1938, the boys have felt that here was a man to whom they could take their troubles, and know that they would be solved the way a real man would solve them. Because of his hard work to help the school maintain the name it has today, he was promoted to the rank of major in 1948, and then, in 1951, to Lieutenant Colonel, the rank he holds today.

As headmaster, his problems are many, yet there is always time to smile a cheery greeting, or say something that makes you feel better inside than you felt before. So, it is with humble gratitude that we, the Adjutant staff of 1953, do lovingly dedicate this yearbook to one of our best and most loyal friends on the Hilltop, Lt. Col. Ralph A. Lucas.

D E D I C A T I O N

This year the dedication is to a man who not only did a good job with his scheduled duties but in his spare time formed new organizations which aided the school in many ways. His friendly and helpful advice aided many cadets to continue through times which seemed the darkest. Because of his friendliness, his helpfulness, and his endless work to improve both the school and cadets, we, the 1954 Corps proudly dedicate this annual to Maj. Arthur H. Mann.

During his first year on the Hilltop, he started the Roundtable Council, an organization which brought the corps and the faculty closer together. The Debate Team, under his guidance, had an outstanding record both of his years here.

At the beginning of this year he was promoted to the rank of major and upped to the position of associate headmaster. The DeMolay boys know how much he has done for them in straightening the records.

These are some of the highlights of Maj. Mann's achievements during his three years here, because if we listed every little thing it would take many more pages. The Adjutant staff of 1954 is honored to be able to dedicate this book to such a helpful and friendly person as Maj. Arthur H. Mann.

MAJOR A. H. MANN

MAJ. PAUL WOOTEN

D E D I C A T I O N

He came to us just three years ago and yet he was not a stranger. Having served in the business office and the Junior School for many years before, he was more a part of Heights than we realized.

To say that he immediately became well thought of or popular with the corps would be an understatement.

In the capacity of assistant commandant he has disciplined us in a manner that causes us to respect and admire him. In the classroom, the "man with the silver dollar" has added the personal touch that makes education a thing to be sought. His life is in harmony with those about him. In times that can often be trying, to find someone with such friendly wit and a zest for living is indeed a rarity. Through such actions he has become a source of inspiration to many of us. It is with this in mind, that we, the Adjutant staff of 1955, affectionately dedicate this edition to Maj. Paul Wooten.

1956

DEDICATION

MAJ. LEONARD K. BRADLEY

As freshmen and sophomores we had little contact with the quiet man whom the juniors and seniors had affectionately nicknamed "The Wizard." We little realized during those first two years the influence he would have on us.

Then, we became juniors in his chemistry class. For a while we thought he was trying to crowd four years of college chemistry into a one year high school course, and if by chance we passed, we became "Little Wizards"; finally, though, we realized that his purpose was to prepare us for college. This he did, and for life too, because chemistry never became so important that there wasn't time for him to help us with our personal problems.

Because he took time to help us, because he understood us, and because he was fair, we, the ADJUTANT staff of 1956, take great pride in affectionately dedicating this edition to MAJ. LEONARD K. BRADLEY.

MR. E. L. MARTIN

DEDICATION

Frequently overlooked when honors are attributed to an educational institution is the man who guides its business affairs.

No private school can be successful without a sound business system through which its fees are collected and its expenditures are wisely made.

Seldom are affection and gratitude showered upon business people . . . but these expressions are often misdirected. Those who are concerned with the welfare of Castle Heights know Mr. E. L. Martin, our business manager, is due our esteem and admiration.

In an age where material values often overshadow moral vitrues, Mr. Martin stands out, not only for kindness, firmness, and devotion to duty, but for the time-proven principles of honesty and integrity.

It is with a sense of deep appreciation for the many, many hours that he has devoted to this institution that we dedicate this issue of The ADJUTANT to Mr. E. L. Martin.

Mr. Earl Price and Mr. Martin

MAJ. C. H. HURD

DEDICATION

Remember when as a freshman, you first went to the library and timidly asked the librarian for a book? You were probably rather scared at first by the "shiny-headed" man's gruff-sounding reply, but if you looked closely you saw a smile creep over his face as he assisted you.

Then the years passed; and you were a senior. You came to know "Uncle Peter" as one of the best friends you could ever have at Heights. You joked and talked "pal to pal" with him and by this time you weren't the least bit shy around him.

Sometimes you tried to turn the library into a social club, or when you became too "excited" over a magazine article, he had to exert discipline. You didn't care though, for he was always right. He commanded unwavering respect by always being fair, tolerant, and "one of the boys" at heart.

Therefore because of his genuine, Christian friendship; and because of his unwavering duty to Heights since 1942; we of the 1958 senior class and this staff of the ADJUTANT take great pride in devoting this yearbook to Maj. C. H. Hurd.

MAJ. LINDSEY DONNELL

DEDICATION

Versatility is a quality sought by many men, but found only by few. Even rarer is the man who will continuously give his time and efforts to others. Combine the two and an outstanding Christian character is formed.

During the past 22 years, such a man has been on the Heights faculty.

Among the many positions he has held are: headmaster of the junior school; football, track, soccer, and tennis coach; athetic director; and head of the mathematics department. Regardless of what he does, however, the welfare of the boys has always been his chief concern.

Many will recall his originality both in and out of class, or his encouragement during soccer games. But all will remember the guidance, friendship and high principles that exemplify the life he lives.

For these reasons, we of the 1959 ADJUTANT staff dedicate this book to Major Lindsey Donnell.

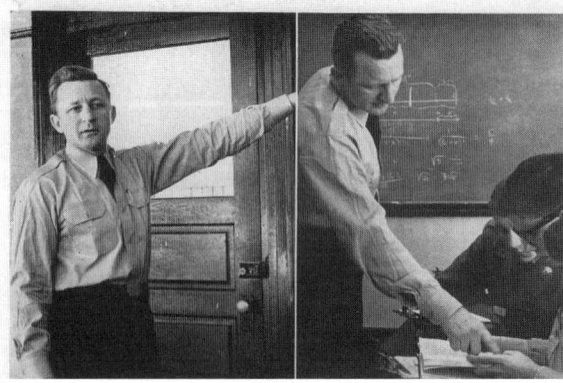

1960

Dedication

Wrestling fans

Mrs. Ed Loyd and Mrs. Wallace Foremon

The prospect of satisfying the appetites of 550 hungry boys three times each day would frighten any mere male, but a pair of efficient ladies have taken the task in stride.

For many years these two have set an ambitious goal for themselves: the preparation and serving of nourishing and appetizing meals to Heights cadets and employees. To say that they have attained their goal would understate their noteworthy success.

It would be false to state that each meal is met with unanimous approval by each member of the corps. Such is not the case, but neither it is true that

the meals mother prepares are always heartily endorsed. As a matter of fact, a dietician's job is more often than not an unappreciated task.

But it would be just as false to state that Heights dieticians are not unappreciated. Hardly anyone would deny that Heights food is superior to that of any other institution and that special meals at Heights are classics.

So, well filled and happily anticipating tonight's meal, the staff of the 1960 ADJUTANT affectionately dedicates this book to Mrs. Wallace Foreman and Mrs. Edward Loyd, the academy's unsurpassed dieticians.

12

297

1961

In Tribute to . . .

No one can deny the value of the improvements at Heights during the last two years by the installation of the public address-bugle system and the closed circuit telephone system.

These two projects, each requiring a great deal of work and planning, are the products of one Heights faculty officer, one who received no extra compensation for the work but who performed the task because he is devoted to the betterment of the school and is endowed with enthusiasm for any task he undertakes.

This enthusiasm can be clearly seen in other areas, too. Fine marching bands have become a tradition at Castle Heights. These bands are another product of the hard work and devotion of this man.

Heights now has an amateur radio club, providing an additional extra-curricular outlet for many cadets. This organization owes its start and subsequent progress to him.

And the wealth of surplus equipment in evidence over the campus—new chairs for the dining hall, new beds for many of the barracks rooms, additional equipment for various departments and classrooms—has increased the efficiency of the physical plant.

In grateful acknowledgment of his valuable services to this institution and in appreciation for his devotion to the improvement of Heights' physical facilities, the staff of the 1961 ADJUTANT dedictes this book to Maj. Laurence Dillon.

Maj. Laurence Dillon and friend, Mary Elizabeth Bradley, as they cruise on Old Hickory Lake in the school cruiser, The Sweetheart of Castle Heights.

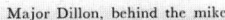

Major Dillon, behind the mike.

MAJOR ROBERT HOSIER

Maj. Robert Hosier . . . Maybe he's not the happiest-looking, but few men on the campus have done more for Heights while he's been here. As a matter of fact, not many members of the faculty have been here longer than the irreplaceable swimming coach.

Although humor prevails in abundance during his classes, Coach Hosier seldom cracks a smile with the exception of a very light and barely audible chuckle. He is known as the most adept dry wit on the Hilltop.

But affording laughter to the cadets in his classes is not the only contribution Maj. Hosier has provided the school. He has produced nine Mid-South champion swimming teams for the academy and has never had a team to finish lower than third in a Mid-South tournament. In one streak, his teams won six straight Mid-South championships. But again, this is not the most important function of Coach Hosier.

Maj. Hosier puts first what is first at Heights: academics. Everyone who has ever been in any of his classes knows this to be true. He follows academy regulations with an almost fanatical fervor. His major concern is helping the individual cadet, and many times he has been heard to state that a swimming meet should not interfere with a help session, be it afternoon CQ or Saturday morning school.

The gauge used to measure cadets is composed of the accomplishments in four fields: academics, sports, military and religion. If the faculty were measured by the same guage, Maj. Hosier, a staunch Episcopalian, would rate high on the list.

Dedication

Coach Hoiser conferring with '62 swim captains, Joe Gribble and Jan Faltin.

DEDICATION

Proverbs tells us that "a fear of the Lord is the beginning of wisdom; with wisdom comes understanding; with understanding, knowledge." This biblical excerpt is the essence of the philosophy of one of our faculty members.

We, the cadets of Castle Heights, are greatly indebted to this man—not for any single aspect of physical or mental ability, but for his life and his presence at the academy.

To understand him and his dedication to learning one must know something of his life.

He was born in Gallatin, Tenn., and, according to his own statement, was one of the "rottenest kids" around, being the bully of the neighborhood. He never made exceptional grades in high school, in one year at Vanderbilt University, and in another year at the University of the South.

Then came an event that was to change the course and outlook of his life—he became a cadet at the United States Military Academy at West Point where he was to spend four of the roughest years of his life. Here he was to develop into a fine athlete on the track, gain an appreciation for learn-

ing, and find understanding.

After West Point came a rapid rise to the rank of colonel in the Army, overseas duty where he was wounded, director of logistics for the initial invasion of the Italian peninsula, and eventually a responsible assignment in the Pentagon.

Retirement from the service came as a result of the wounds he suffered in the European theater.

Then there were graduate work at George Washington University, assignments in private and public high schools, and in 1953, Castle Heights. Later, he left Heights to study at Vanderbilt University and Peabody College, then back to his job as head of the mathematics department here.

Castle Heights is an institution of learning for those who sincerely want to learn. No man, in his efforts to explain and demonstrate the importance of understanding and human thought, could better represent the purpose of this academy.

With grateful appreciation to this symbol of intellectual liberty, human and academic understanding, the editors dedicate this book to Col. Harvey Loyd Brown.

1964

MAJOR STROUD GWYNN
Head Football Coach

His lifetime record as a head football coach is 146-68-21 and he is justly proud of it. His Castle Heights teams won the Mid-South championship in 1948, 1953, 1957, and 1962. Since becoming head football coach in 1947, Major Gwynn has had winning seasons in all except four years.

But Major Gwynn is much more than a successful football coach. He is a Christian gentleman, dedicated not only to athletics but to every phase of school life and devoted to honesty, fairness, and high moral principles.

In recognition of these qualities and for his long years of faithful service to Castle Heights, the staff dedicates the 1964 ADJUTANT to Major Robert Stroud Gwynn.

DEDICATION

Col. Morgan (right) with his son, Capt. Bobby Morgan.

During a chapel talk.

During faculty meeting.

"Our seal is light and truth" is the official motto of Castle Heights Military Academy. Possibly none of the instructors on The Hilltop abide more by the slogan than Lt. Col. R. Kenneth Morgan, and it is to him that the 1965 **ADJUTANT** is dedicated.

Head of the language department, Col. Morgan has dedicated himself to teaching and dealing with boys for more than 40 years. From the time he became head of Morgan School in Petersburg, Tenn., he has been recognized as one of Tennessee's leading educators.

He was head of the school, founded in 1885 by his father, from 1935 until 1950 when its doors were closed. He then served as superintendent of the Tennessee State Training and Agriculture school, before joining the Heights faculty in 1955.

As Director of Religious Activities here, Col. Morgan has displayed a lasting and influential concern for a life of "Light and Truth" for cadets. Widely known as a church leader, he has been a delegate to many national religious conferences.

It is for these accomplishments, characteristics, and devotion that we dedicate the 1965 **ADJUTANT** to Lt. Col. Kenneth Morgan.

Dedication

The language of success is described in one's natural character. The universal language is religion. The language of America is English. The 1966 ADJUTANT is dedicated to a man who is dedicated to language—Lt. Col. Paul Wooten.

Loyalty to his profession and Castle Heights and a sincere interest in the cadets of this institution are two aspects of his character that blend to produce his success as a teacher. Nevertheless, character alone does not qualify a man for teaching. Training in that field is essential and this instructor, born and reared in Lebanon, accomplished this at Cumberland University. He then furthered his preparation at Middle Tennessee State College, where he obtained his Master's.

An interest in young people does not assure effective communication with them. Patience and understanding are "musts," and the ideas of this instructor have forded the barrier.

He was first associated with Castle Heights in 1932 when he became a member of the staff, serving in the business office. He remained in this department until 1942 when he rendered his services to his country in World War II. After serving as an officer in the United States Army for four years, he returned to The Hilltop in 1949.

He resumed his work at Heights as the commandant of the junior school. Three years later, he moved to The Hilltop as a senior school instructor. With time and experience, additional responsibilities accumulated as he took the job of assistant commandant and finally acting commandant. Feeling that successful teaching and "commandanting" were incompatible, he resigned his job as commandant and devoted his entire time and efforts to teaching English. This undivided devotion to a particular field allowed him to excel, and he progressed to the position of Head of the English Department, where he has remained.

His extracurricular activities include directing the Castle Heights Civil Air Patrol and score-keeping for the basketball games. But academics rate highest with Col. Wooten as they do with Castle Heights, and he can usually be found in his classroom during help sessions and Saturday morning school.

For these distinctive qualities, the 1966 ADJUTANT is dedicated to Lt. Col. Paul Tomlinson Wooten.

A DEDICATION TO

CAPT. MERLIN SANDERS

To his wife and five children, he is a devoted husband and father. To his athletic teams, he is a concerned coach who does more than is expected. To the Reserve Army, he is a captain. To everyone, he is a pleasant person whose sharp and ready wit is never really cutting. He is a lot of things to a lot of people, but most important he is a teacher—not just an instructor among thousands, but a real teacher among a few. For these qualities which make him a respected and effective teacher, the 1967 ADJUTANT is dedicated to Capt. Merlin Sanders.

DEDICATION

Dedicating a yearbook is never an easy job for a staff, but this year one fact stood out when the editors were making the decision. Looking back through the years, we discovered that one distinguished faculty member was completing his twenty-fifth year of teaching service to Castle Heights and to its cadets.

He came to Heights in 1943, making 1968 his silver anniversary as an academy instructor. Years of dedication and service—this sums up this man's attitude toward teaching and his value to Castle Heights. Those who have been through his classes will testify to the sacrifice and extra effort he puts into his work, to the enthusiasm he has for his teaching, and to the interest he shows for the individual student.

He is known and liked for his pleasant disposition, his sincere manner, and most of all, for his dedication to the teaching job he does so well. It is with a great deal of pleasure that we in turn dedicate the 1968 ADJUTANT to a most respected member of the Heights faculty, Maj. John L. Sweat.

DEDICATION

When cadets reach their senior year at Heights, they are forced to make some important decisions at a very prominent stage in their life. In order to make these decisions, they look for help — not only from their parents but also from the school faculty.

Since it is often difficult to receive assistance from parents at a boarding school, the seniors, along with the other cadets, seek aid from dependable and trusted members of the faculty.

When the staff of the annual got together to decide what faculty member deserved the honor of having a yearbook dedicated to him, they remembered well the favor one man gave to them — his advice.

Over his eleven years at Heights, many cadets have come to him with their problems, and he has risen to a post which is entirely devoted to directing the lives of cadets.

A pleasant disposition, a good sense of humor, and a sincere approach to teaching combine with his special talent of helping cadets as the reasons that the 1969 ADJUTANT is dedicated to Maj. Gene E. Hale.

16

1970

Dedication

Because of your ability to instill in students a desire to learn . . .

Because of your ceaseless devotion to Castle Heights and your great concern for its betterment . . .

Because of your wit and loyal service which inspire us . . .

Because you have given so completely and unselfishly of yourself and your time without the least hesitation . . .

And most of all because we respect you . . .

To you, Lt. Col. C. V. "Ace" Baker, on your silver anniversary of service to the academy, we dedicate this, the 1970 ADJUTANT.

DEDICATION

The 1971 ADJUTANT staff is proud to dedicate this yearbook to a teacher who is close to most of the staff. As the physics teacher, and instructor of two Senior mathematics courses, he has been faced with many of us for two classes every day.

Although this alone probably warrants some award, there are other qualities for which he deserves recognition. Among these are an interest in the students' work combined with an ability to encourage the students to learn for themselves, and a thorough knowledge of the subject matter coupled with a readiness to admit mistakes.

For these reasons the 1971 ADJUTANT staff dedicates their annual to Lt. Col. R. Thomas Wiley.

DEDICATION

His day at Heights begins while most cadets are still in bed sound asleep.

Twenty years of distinguished service to his country in the military has earned him the respect of cadets, administration and faculty alike.

In the triple capacity of assistant commandant, military supervisor and instructor he has consistantly proven his unchanging dedication to the Hilltop and the principles it strives to teach. Because of that steadfast dedication, we, the yearbook staff, dedicate this, the 1972 Adjutant, to **SGM John S. Richards.**

1973

The 1973 ADJUTANT is dedicated to a man whose commitment to Castle Heights has earned him the respect and admiration of everyone associated with the academy.

After a long career in the service of his country, he came to Heights six years ago and established himself as both a teacher and a friend. His success as "coach" of both the Honor Guard and the Color Guard is unparalleled.

For his loyalty, his sincerity, and above all for his dedication to the cadet corps of Castle Heights, we are proud to dedicate the 1973 ADJUTANT to M/Sgt. Marvin C. Pelfrey.

DEDICATION

DEDICATION

In his twenty-two years at Heights he has been an important influence in the lives of numerous students. In his positions of English instructor and assistant headmaster, he is in contact with several students daily and his advice has been a source of help to many in academic as well as extra-curricular catagories.

After spending four years in the Junior School, he came to the Senior School and quickly established himself as one who gave straight answers. In his past years as weightlifting instructor he helped young men develop their physical potential. He also shows a genuine concern in his students in particular and in all Castle Heights students in general. For these attributes, as well as his sincere dedication, the yearbook staff dedicates the 1974 ADJUTANT to Major Bobby E. Todd.

dedication

The 1975 Adjutant is dedicated to a teacher, a coach, a man, and a friend.

This man has earned the respect, admiration, and friendship of every person on the Hilltop. His impact on Castle Heights has been profound. He has drawn us closer as a cadet corps, and has molded us into adults.

He has instilled in each of us a feeling that can only be described as "spirit". He has given us things that shall remain with us forever, among these things are memories, and our memories of Castle Heights would not be complete without him.

He continually proves his dedication to Heights, so it is only fitting that we dedicate the 1975 edition of the Adjutant to Col. Jay P. Cleveland.

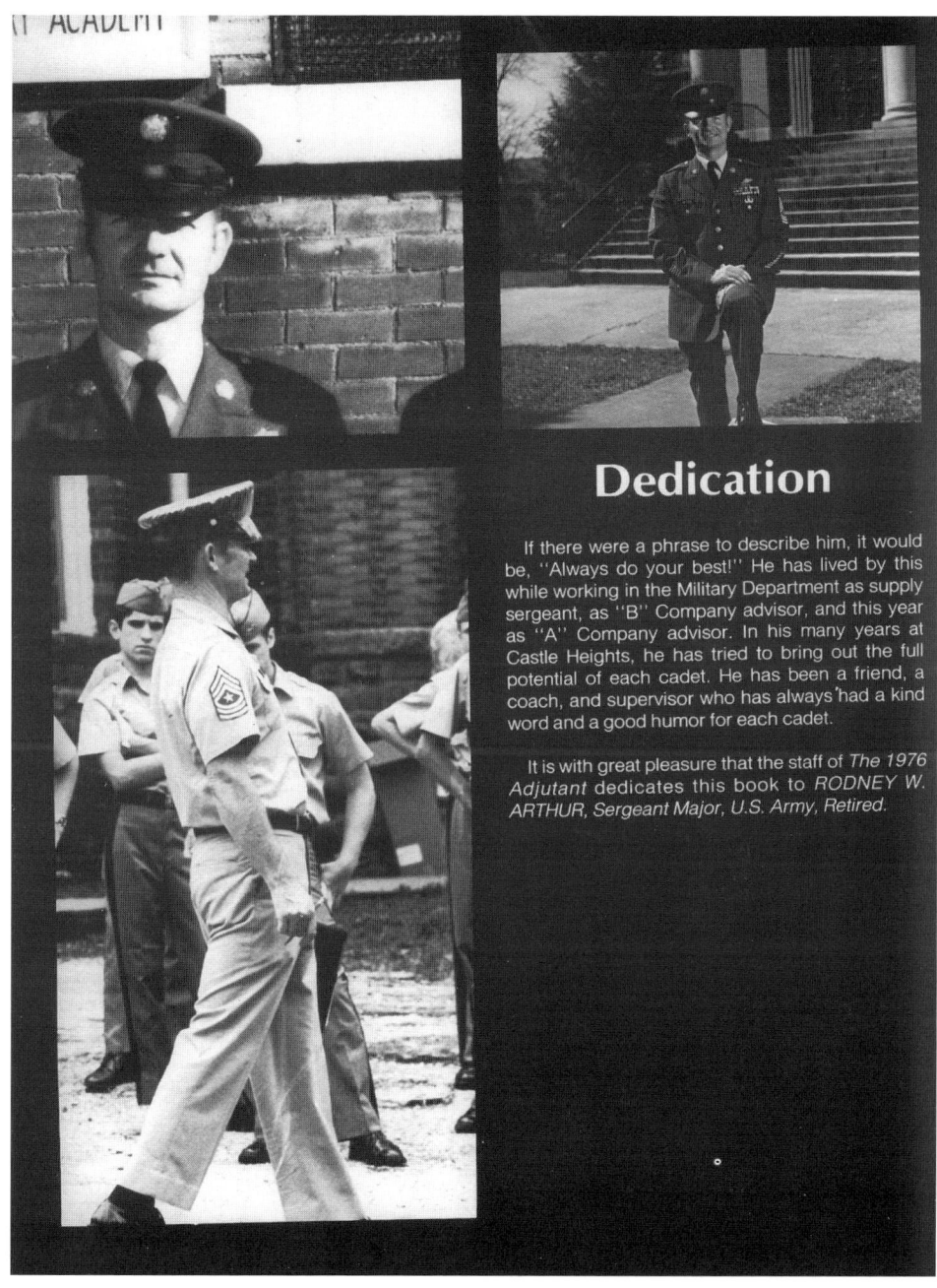

Dedication

If there were a phrase to describe him, it would be, "Always do your best!" He has lived by this while working in the Military Department as supply sergeant, as "B" Company advisor, and this year as "A" Company advisor. In his many years at Castle Heights, he has tried to bring out the full potential of each cadet. He has been a friend, a coach, and supervisor who has always had a kind word and a good humor for each cadet.

It is with great pleasure that the staff of *The 1976 Adjutant* dedicates this book to *RODNEY W. ARTHUR, Sergeant Major, U.S. Army, Retired.*

Dedication

Teacher!

One of the most respected words — and sometimes a misused word — is the word "teacher."

College degrees do not a teacher make.

Showing us "how" is not always teaching. Even prompting us to ask "why?" is not always teaching. Filling our minds with knowledge and techniques is not always teaching.

A teacher makes us reach for the sky instead of the horizon, strive for the peaks instead of the plateaus, depend on effort rather than potential, respect attitude as much as altitude.

Teacher!

Major John Graves.

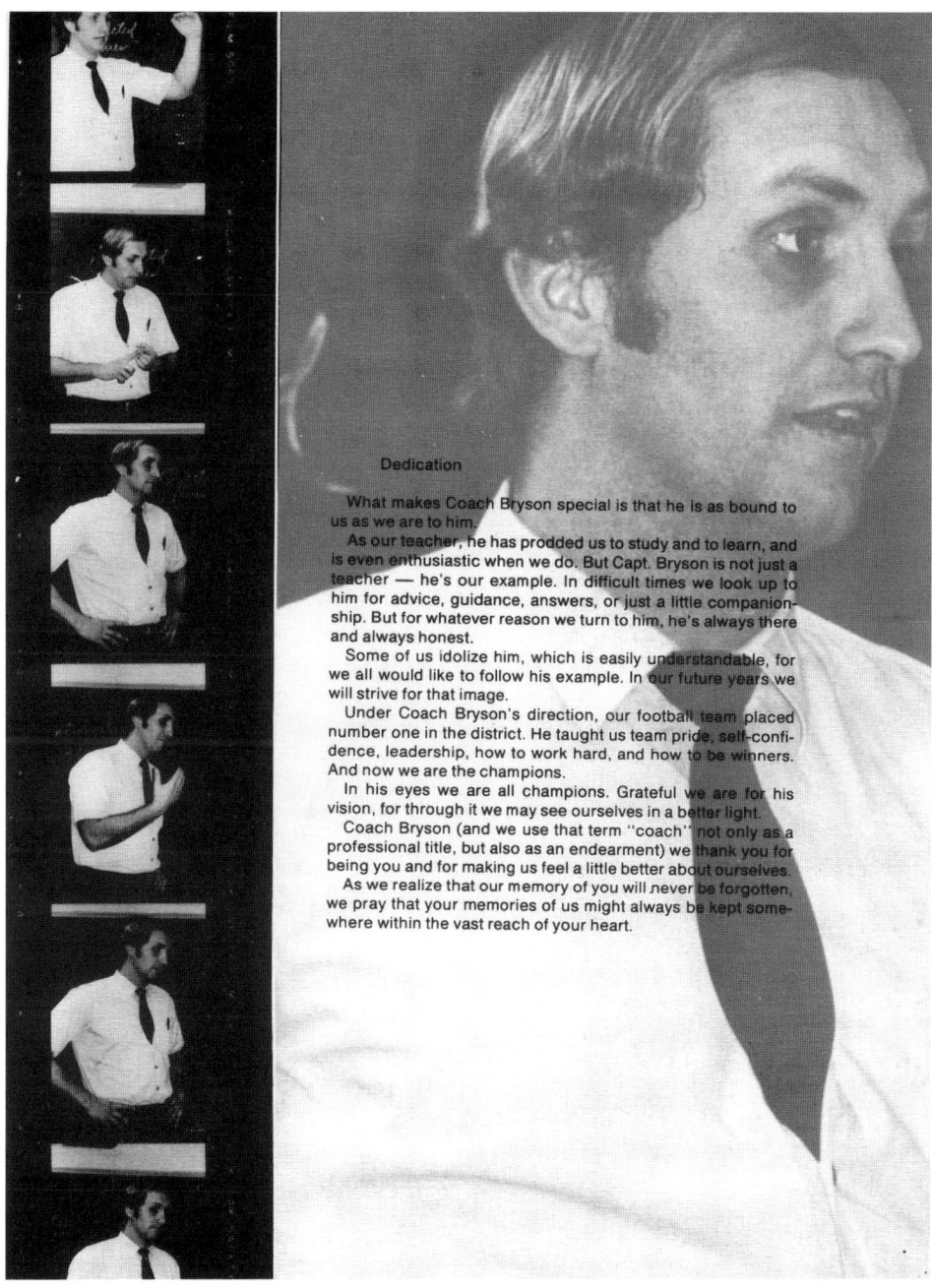

Dedication

What makes Coach Bryson special is that he is as bound to us as we are to him.

As our teacher, he has prodded us to study and to learn, and is even enthusiastic when we do. But Capt. Bryson is not just a teacher — he's our example. In difficult times we look up to him for advice, guidance, answers, or just a little companionship. But for whatever reason we turn to him, he's always there and always honest.

Some of us idolize him, which is easily understandable, for we all would like to follow his example. In our future years we will strive for that image.

Under Coach Bryson's direction, our football team placed number one in the district. He taught us team pride, self-confidence, leadership, how to work hard, and how to be winners. And now we are the champions.

In his eyes we are all champions. Grateful we are for his vision, for through it we may see ourselves in a better light.

Coach Bryson (and we use that term "coach" not only as a professional title, but also as an endearment) we thank you for being you and for making us feel a little better about ourselves.

As we realize that our memory of you will never be forgotten, we pray that your memories of us might always be kept somewhere within the vast reach of your heart.

1980

DEDICATION

This year the Adjutant staff is dedicating our book to memories of Col. Don Franklin. Don Franklin first came to Castle Heights in 1959. He stayed two years and then left to go to Ross Gear as a personnel manager. However, the attraction of academic life together with his love of sports proved too strong to resist and Don Franklin returned to Castle Heights in 1970 as line coach.

Col. Franklin, as you might expect, has been quite a football player. Graduating from Lebanon High School, he was chosen as an All North Central Tennessee football conference league standout, and was named to the Nashville-Tennessean All-Mid State football team. At M.T.S.U. he became a member of the All-Ohio Valley conference football team.

Quite honestly, we can say Col. Don Franklin is a gentleman and Christian, liked and respected by all of those who make up the Castle Heights organization.

The 1980 Adjutant staff is proud to recognize this man.

1982 *[No 1981 Dedication]*

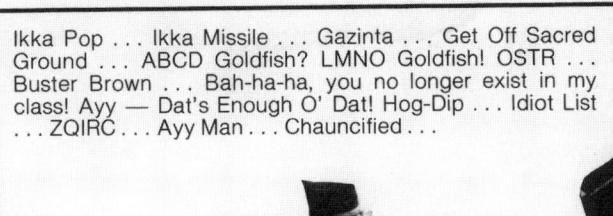

Ikka Pop . . . Ikka Missile . . . Gazinta . . . Get Off Sacred Ground . . . ABCD Goldfish? LMNO Goldfish! OSTR . . . Buster Brown . . . Bah-ha-ha, you no longer exist in my class! Ayy — Dat's Enough O' Dat! Hog-Dip . . . Idiot List . . . ZQIRC . . . Ayy Man . . . Chauncified . . .

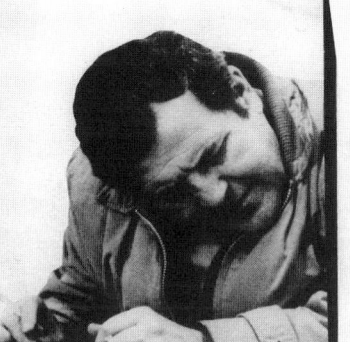

DEDICATION

This Yearbook Dedication is a token thank-you to a man who has devoted so much effort and time to his school and to his "people." Educated at Fishburne Military Academy, Massachusetts Institute of Technology, and The University of North Carolina, he came to us in the fall of 1973 after serving on the teaching staff of Staunton Military Academy for nine years. He is a very special, very private man.

We learned of his qualities in many ways: answering reports to him when he was Assistant Commandant, serving confinement under his direction, visiting with him when he was the Officer-In-Charge, and attending his classes in Algebra, Integrated, Physics and Calculus. He must hold the Castle Heights record for Help-Sessions. He was always in the classroom on Saturday morning, patiently waiting for us to arrive. We knew him as "The Major" until he was promoted to Lieutenant Colonel last year. His peers call him "Prep School Man."

For his selfless dedication, professionalism, and unyielding will to lead us to achieve, the staff of the 1982 ADJUTANT dedicates this edition to LTC Dixon H. Ward, TEACHER!

Dedication

Maj. Lancaster came to Castle Heights in 1961 after a successful career in the music department of public schools in Hamilton and Davidson Counties. He soon established himself as a man upon whom the students, Administration, and fellow faculty could depend for a consistently good performance. Directing a high school band is comparable to balancing an eel on your nose, and Maj. Lancaster seems to have found a system that works. His bands have participated in Christmas and other parades with dignity and have brought honors to the school. Besides public presentations, they have played for parades, pep rallies, retreat formations, and other significant school events. In the classroom, Maj. Lancaster is known by his students as a teacher who knows his subject, can express himself well, and demands a degree of perfection for successful completion of his course. Few are the students who leave Maj. Lancaster's Algebra I class and find themselves unprepared for Algebra II. A true professional, Maj. Lancaster projects the best image which a teacher can attain: He cares.

Dedication

Mrs. Toplovich came to Castle Heights in June, 1968 after having been recognized as an outstanding teacher in the public schools of Wilson County. At the time she departed from her previous post as Senior English instructor, her principal verbally regretted "losing our best teacher." Mrs. Toplovich entered the language and English departments at Castle Heights with the same attitude which had made her successful in other situations. She worked hard, and expected as much of her students. The results of Mrs. Toplovich's labors are most apparent — her students remember her as a demanding, fair, intelligent, and inspiring instructor whose efforts have helped them greatly at the college level. Mrs. Toplovich also involves herself in other activities which she pursues with equal vigor. Her value as a cheerleader sponsor and drama coach is considerable. Her sponsorship of European cruises is especially noteworthy because of her erudite and cosmopolitan personality. A real, genuine lady — a true professional teacher in the strictest sense of the word — Mrs. Peggie Toplovich.

DEDICATIONS

Rodney W. Arthur, Sergeant Major, U.S. Army, Retired

There is no one word to describe him. Everyone stood a little taller and did a little better whenever he was around. Always trying to bring out the best in us, he had a friendly smile and an encouraging word to greet us. His leaving was certainly our loss. We lost a friend and a father, who listened and gave us advice. We will remember him as Assistant Commandant, "B" company advisor, and a fair man.

It is with great honor, indeed, that the Adjutant staff of 1984 dedicates this book to Sergeant Major Rodney W. Arthur.

Major General Ned D. McDonald, Jr.

Major General D. McDonald came to Castle Heights in 1979 to attain the position of Superintendent. For five years he devoted his time and effort to the improvement of the Academy. His leadership has guided us and his personality has befriended us. His dignified manner and pride of the Cadet Corps projected through his work. He gave so completely of himself without the least hesitation. Keeping us informed and commending us for our performance as a unit will be a trait we will miss.

For these reasons, it is our privilege to dedicate the 1984 Adjutant to Major General Ned D. McDonald.

Dedication

Maj. Doris Inman came to Castle Heights senior school in 1979. Over the last six years, Mrs. Inman has been involved in the Senior School English Department and several extraciricular activities. She was the Dean of Women for many years and sponser of the Heights Christian Fellowship in the past.

Her family was also involved at Castle Heights. Ltc. Robert Inman, her husband, was Headmaster in the Junior School while one of her children is an alumnus and the other graduated this year.

Cadets over the years have grown to love and respect Mrs. Inman. In class she was a demanding teacher but gave her students all of her attention. When she was Dean of Women, the boarding girls that she lived with thought of her as a second mother. There is a very close bond between Mrs. Inman and this year's senior class because the majority of us started our long trek through the Senior School with her for Freshman English and this year we are ending our journey with Mrs. Inman as our Senior English teacher. We all have a very special relationship with her and a great fondness for the women who has seen us grow and mature from teenagers to young adults.

We, the Senior class, dedicate the *1985 Adjutant* to Mrs. Doris Inman for her years of outstanding service and devotion to the Corps of Cadets and the Academy.

DEDICATION

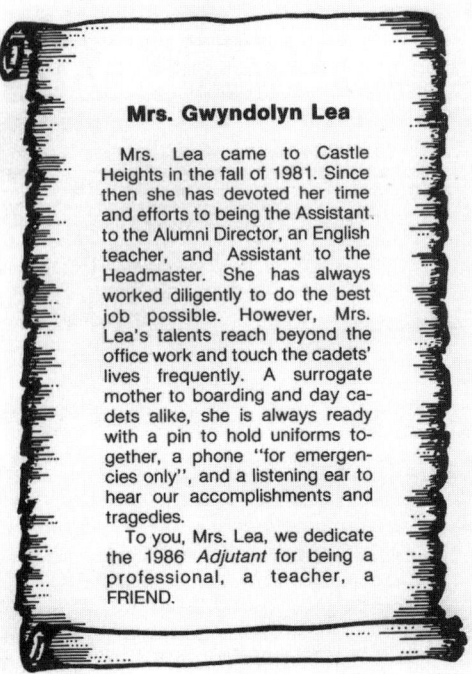

Mrs. Gwyndolyn Lea

Mrs. Lea came to Castle Heights in the fall of 1981. Since then she has devoted her time and efforts to being the Assistant to the Alumni Director, an English teacher, and Assistant to the Headmaster. She has always worked diligently to do the best job possible. However, Mrs. Lea's talents reach beyond the office work and touch the cadets' lives frequently. A surrogate mother to boarding and day cadets alike, she is always ready with a pin to hold uniforms together, a phone "for emergencies only", and a listening ear to hear our accomplishments and tragedies.

To you, Mrs. Lea, we dedicate the 1986 *Adjutant* for being a professional, a teacher, a FRIEND.

At time of publication, *Adjutant* staff did not know the 1986 year-book would be the Academy's last. This salute to that year's 33 seniors is fitting tribute to the more than 8,000 Castle Heights Military Academy graduates of The Hilltop over more than 80 years.

Seniors

June 1, 1986 . . . What a day to remember! The senior class, lined up waiting to receive diplomas, looked stunning in all of its glory. All of our accomplishments, all of our work, was brought together to this point in time. The feelings were so overwhelming; the comradey was stronger than it had ever been before. And within an hour — it was over.

So now we look back to that fateful day when we were together for, perhaps, the last time, and we smile. Only a few months have passed, now, and our lives have taken a fresh turn. We gaze upon this page and laugh, remembering the days we laughed together. Yet, the impact has not yet reached its full potential. For, in fourteen years — at the turn of a new century — when we are rummaging through our attics and stumble across this book, we will find this page and gaze upon it once again. However, mixed in with the laughter will be wishes for yesteryear . . . and it is then that the true meaning of this book will come to life.

> *May the Lord bless thee, and keep thee; the Lord makes his face shine upon thee, and be gracious unto thee.*

And before you close this book — this prayer goes out to you:

> *Foristan Et Haec Olim Meminesse Juvabit.*

(Perhaps some day it will please you to remember these things.)

Vergil, The Aeneid, Book I

The Cavalier

Chosen by Chapter   1st Inspection

the westerner world

Sophs Go To Polls
— Leaders
The Line O'

'Pink' Carpet Unrolls For John Kenne

Eleven Opens Season
Vs. Loyola Today

The COLLEGIAN

Wilson County's
GOOD NEWS

Vol. 4   Lebanon, Tennessee   No. 27   August

A Salute To J.B. Leftwic
By Jack Hendrickson   Pages 2 & 3

Quill and Scroll

International Honorary Society for High School Journalists

The Staffs of

"The Cavalier" and "The Adjutant"

Lebanon, Tennessee

bestow upon

"Coach" J. B. Leftwich

Publications Adviser

this Scroll in recognition of his devoted interests in the creative work of young people in journalism and the writing arts.

In Testimony Whereof we have affixed our signatures
this 20th day of May, 1959

_____   _____
Cavalier Editor   Adjutant Editor

This is to certify that

J. B. Leftwich

is a member of

Sigma Delta Chi

Professional Journalistic Society

having been initiated by the   University of Tennessee   Chapter

on the

Quill and Scroll

s free
to read,

EFFERSON

DISTINGUISHED ADVISER AWARD
for exemplary service to scholastic journalism.

J. B. Leftwich

TENNESSEE HIGH SCHOOL PRESS ASSOCIATION
The University of Tennessee / School of Journalism

Chapter Nine
Roll Call

"I need to achieve, and satisfy myself of the worth of that accomplishment. I have to be close to the main stream of things, although I'm usually an observer and a reporter rather than a doer. I'd like most to be remembered as a teacher."

-JB Leftwich, 1979

THE DRILL:
In the fall of 2010, former editors of *The Cavalier* and *Adjutant* began a campaign to raise a minimum of $25,000 to fund a JB Leftwich CHMA Editors' Scholarship at Cumberland University. In just over six months, more than $30,000 was donated, and $1,000 scholarships have been awarded thus far to four CU students for 2011, 2012, 2013 and 2014.

Perhaps as meaningful were the words of praise, respect, admiration, gratitude and love offered by the men he mentored for more than 35 years as "Coach" -- and those that flowed again when the news of his death in July 2011 was announced.

Overleaf Photo:
Awards, commendations and professional recognition for JBL were commonplace.

Working closely with his editors as equals was a JB Leftwich desire and objective.

We knew him as 'Coach'

• *Philip S. "Stan" Huguenin '59 / July, 2011*

Written at request of Sam Hatcher, then-publisher of
WILSON POST, at time of JB Leftwich passing

My first nine teachers -- all in Sarasota, Fla. -- were Miss/Mrs. Read, Wright, Hill, Miller, McQueen, Rushing, Tatum (homeroom and English), Mr. Davis (homeroom, history), and Mrs. Antrim (homeroom, Latin).

They all were above-average or excellent educators, helping me over nine years to learn the basics of multiple subjects ... reading and loving it, writing in legible cursive, chemistry, mathematics, English, history, social studies, science, geography, biology, art and other specialties. (Latin not so much.)

One educator over three years, however, changed and shaped my life.

By ninth grade, my behavior and grades were not up to "expected standards," so my parents' solution (primarily Mother's): Castle Heights Military Academy for my sophomore, junior and senior years. Basically the entire Heights faculty was superb. This was in the late '50s when many observers believe Heights, its corps of cadets, its educators and administration were at their zenith.

The extraordinary educator who literally impacted my future -- and those of hundreds of other cadets -- was Maj. (military school ranking) JB Leftwich. Those of us mentored by him in his role of advisor to *The Cavalier* and *The Adjutant* came to appreciate, admire and respect him as much more than just a "teacher" or "educator." (He also taught mathematics and algebra, but square roots, fractions and hypotenuse triangles were not my thing.)

Major Leftwich was a vital and important person in many lives on The Hilltop, in our personal growth and maturity, and in ways that helped many of us select and excel in professional careers. He also was a counselor, friend, advisor, perfectionist and outstanding journalist. The editors and editorial staffs working for him were driven to meet his standards of excellence, his desire for perfection. If in our story assignments, writing of articles and laying out of the publications graphically we did not meet these standards, he pointed out the weaknesses and challenged us to fix them. He expected, too, that each week, each month, each semester, our knowledge -- and willingness to think "outside the box" -- would expand and improve.

He loved sports and took pride in accomplishments of Academy teams and players, especially those lead by coaches Stroud Gwynn (football), Ralph Lucas (basketball), Lindsey Donnell (soccer and tennis), and Robert Hosier (swimming). Major Leftwich encouraged detailed sports coverage in the publications, using it as a means -- for his staffs and the entire corps -- to recognize individual accomplishment, the importance of organization and training, the importance of individuals joining as a team, a single unit, to help secure victory.

By his example, we learned the power and beauty of the written word, and we understood the difference and importance between an objective "news" story -- written to tell the reader "who, what, why, when and where" -- and a bylined column (whether in sports or the editorial section) written to offer a personal opinion or point of view. And because JB loved photography and knew how to tell a story through a lens, we saw that creatively linking words, headlines and photos enhanced the reader's understanding and clarity of what we reported.

We learned to treasure accuracy, spell correctly (using a dictionary was mandatory), and how essential it was to make certain that sources were quoted correctly. A major benefit, too, was that the planning and organizational skills used to put out a newspaper every three weeks --

or a yearbook in eight months -- and the teamwork required by the entire publications staffs benefitted us while at Heights and as we moved on to the rest of our lives. Multi-tasking, staying focused and striving for perfection were essential

Off campus, his accomplishments and initiatives as a husband, father, grandfather and selfless community activist have been documented by awards, citations, plaques and trophies over many years -- again demonstrating to us that while our work was important, and to be done as close to perfection as possible, we had other more important obligations away from the "office." While his love of teaching, his students, and his chosen career -- and of Heights -- is extreme, it is throughout his extended family we find the real evidence of this primary Major Leftwich emphasis. The ultimate, of course, being his devotion, caring, concern and love for his Jo Doris -- his better half for more than 70 years and the partner giving him the freedom, encouragement and praise that helped him change hundreds of young men and women's lives.

Around 1900, Henry Brooks Adams, grandson of John Quincy Adams and great-grandson of John Adams, said, **"A teacher affects eternity; he can never tell where his influence stops."**

JB and Jo Doris Leftwich married in 1939, and devoted more than 70 years to their children, grandchildren, Castle Heights, First United Methodist Church, Lebanon and Wilson County.

And during coaching careers at Miami University, Northwestern and Notre Dame, the legendary Ara Parseghian said, **"A good Coach makes players see what they can become rather than what they are."**

Two perfect descriptions of Major Leftwich by prominent professionals made in two different centuries. The Major has been classified as a "teacher" -- a creative, innovative, successful, effective, patient and understanding "educator" -- his entire career. Those of us fortunate enough, however, to be in his classrooms and on the staffs of one or both of his publications pay our tribute and respect by calling him "Coach."

It seems a broader, more specific, more loving description for a man who, indeed, will never know just how far his influence has reached or whether it will really ever stop.

329

B. Edward McClellan '58

Professor Emeritus, History of Education and American Studies/ Indiana University

Major Leftwich recruited me to write for the *Cavalier* when I was in 7th grade, and it turned out to be the break of a lifetime. He taught me how to write, how to copyedit, even how to set type for headlines. More important, he taught me the importance of precision, the beauty of a well-crafted sentence, and the satisfaction that comes from striving for excellence. A man of strong character, he also was the best moral educator I ever encountered. Because JB made me a careful writer, my first publication came back from the reviewers without a single editing mark. I had learned at the feet of the master.

Tom Bradley '69

Retired USAF Colonel/Pentagon

Colonel Leftwich was a huge figure in Tennessee high school journalism by the time I started writing for him my freshman year. [My first byline resulted in a trip to the Superintendent's office. I had written exactly what I believed I had been told by a school authority; Colonel Leftwich stood by me, and no bad consequence resulted.] I was associate editor of *The Cavalier* and *Adjutant* co-editor as a senior, a highly productive year of growth and maturation thanks to coach. During the four decades after graduation, he was my most trusted counselor outside family, and soon my best friend -- which he remained until he died. The last time I saw him [March 2011], we both knew it was likely our last talk, and we thanked each other for a lifetime of friendship.

Richard Reeves '48

Retired Attorney [including U.S. Army, Fort Benning], Tampa FL

Captain Leftwich asked me to be editor of the '48 *Adjutant*. I had never been involved in journalism at Heights, but he said he knew a busy, organized person would do a good job. I had tremendous respect for JB, and learned a lot working on the yearbook. He wanted everything done exactly right. It was a privilege to work for him. He was a good man.

Marshall Cox ' 50

Retired Attorney, New York

What JB taught me during my two years editing *The Cavalier* -- how to write succinctly and to deadline, how to put together information, how to manage time and work with others -- I could not have gotten elsewhere. They proved to be invaluable when I went on to Vanderbilt University, and while there worked three years at *The Nashville Tennessean*.

Being able to write succinctly and to the point was just as useful at Ohio State University law school, and then during my 39 years practicing law in New York City and Washington, D.C. I will never forget those wonderful Friday nights at the *Lebanon Democrat* when we put the paper together . . . It was truly hands-on newspapering, and I loved it.

Rodger Tarr ' 59
Distinguished Professor, Emeritus / Illinois State University
I had JB for plane geometry my first year at CHMA [11th grade]. "Major" wrote my parents to tell them he advised me to drop PG, and take it my senior year after I "adjusted." He was correct; as a senior I had a 98 average, helping me graduate third in our class. His true legacy is loyalty. To be sure, he was honest, nurturing, even stern, but we all knew, in the end, he was loyal to us and thus to the principles of CHMA. JB Leftwich was Heights, and a very important person in my life.

Jerry Anderson '56
CEO, Anderson Construction Company
I attended Heights my junior and senior years. Before I enrolled, I had a bad attitude towards school and authority in general. Major Leftwich was my plane geometry instructor. After about two weeks, he sat me down after class and -- among other things -- said, "You could be the smartest boy in this class if you would apply yourself." He encouraged me into journalism, appointed me Assistant Sports Editor of *The Cavalier*, and got a few of my game stories published in the Nashville paper. In 1956, Pete Rademacher came to Heights to speak at Chapel on his way to becoming Olympic Heavyweight Champion. I did an interview with him that later won a statewide award for "Best High School Sports Story of the Year." From a boy with all D's on his 10th grade report card, I graduated from CHMA third in a class of 92. Without question, JB Leftwich was one of the most influential men in my life.

Joseph Lipscomb '66
Professor, Institute Director / Emory University
Reporter, writer, editor, math teacher, photographer, entrepreneur with a knack for doing well by doing good… Charming conversationalist, raconteur, humorist and master marketer of the things that mattered, including Castle Heights… Husband, father, colleague, advisor, counselor, disciplinarian and cheerleader.

JB Leftwich was all of these things.

Perhaps using "mathematical induction," JB Leftwich found it easier in 1968 to know which identical twin -- Tom Bailey [left] or Bob Bailey -- went with which publication. Tom was *Adjutant* editor [and class salutatorian] with Bob as Activities Editor. Bob was *Cavalier* editor [and valedictorian] with Tom as Associate Editor. Dr. Robert Bailey earned his Ph.D. at the University of California - Berkley, and worked for Rockwell Scientific Co.; Dr. Tom Bailey earned his Ph.D. at University of Texas, and worked for TRW Aerospace

For three unforgettable years [Joe Lipscomb was the only three-year editor of the CHMA newspaper], I had the privilege of sitting in the *Cavalier* office, a few feet away from the overloaded but ever-organized desk where "Colonel Leftwich" planned, plotted and adroitly managed a diverse portfolio of professional and personal commitments.

I had never seen anyone do so many things so well at once. But I had come to Heights from a small nearby town, so I remember thinking maybe my comparison pool wasn't very large. Now, after five decades of working alongside touted folks in academia, government and industry, my views from long ago hold firm. JB Leftwich was a genuine Renaissance Man. He was a polymath of sorts, with the intuition and analytical talent to create so much. And it was all done with elegance and grace – a sense of balance, perspective and integrity.

In the summer after Heights graduation, I had the opportunity several others from the *Cavalier / Adjutant* staffs had enjoyed previously: joining, thanks to a Colonel Leftwich recommendation, the reportorial staff of the *Nashville Tennessean*. During my first week, various editors around the paper's City Room were trying to figure out exactly who I was, and my instinctive response was to say I had been working under JB Leftwich at Castle Heights. One state editor remarked, "Well, if you worked with Leftwich, you worked with the best." He was exactly right.

James T. Snoddy '70
Printing Industry Executive / Georgia, Illinois, Tennessee
I was editor of the 1970 yearbook, and also had Colonel Leftwich for advanced math my sophomore year. He truly was a father figure, and treated all with dignity and respect. Furthermore, he was an excellent teacher who always got the best out of his students. Under his direction, I finished in the top 10 in a couple of regional math contests. I recall so many, many good things about Colonel Leftwich and am proud to have been one of his students.

Doug Brinkman '59
Engineer [projects in Texas, Mexico, Guam [Naval facilities]]
Secondary career: Trauma Center Paramedic
It is difficult to put into words how thankful I am to have crossed paths with Major Leftwich at a time when I was at a cross road. I knew the high school I was attending would never prep me for university engineering courses. For my family to afford sending me to CHMA was a sacrifice. When I started in his classes, I knew this was the person who was going to help -- and extra sessions only enforced my feelings. After three college degrees and at our Heights class 50th reunion, I was able to give him a big hug and say "thank you."

David Hall '61
Retired Newspapers Editor / Executive
Chief recollections of being tutored in journalism by Coach are two: 1] He taught young men the best principles of the craft, and expected us to apply them at the professional level; 2] He expected *The Cavalier* staffs to plan and execute each issue on their own. He was wise with counsel, exacting in expectations . . . JB Leftwich's tutelage enabled me to find my career early. The inspiration of those years at Heights enabled me to forge a 40-year career on daily newspapers, forming the skills and values necessary to edit four publications in St. Paul, Denver, Northern New Jersey, and Cleveland. .... I remember the time from fall 1957 to spring 1961 as among the finest, most inspirational years of my life.

Harry Leggett '52

Owner President / Life Insurance Company,
Funeral Homes, Cemeteries

I can never think of Heights without thinking of "Captain" Leftwich --
to this day, my favorite teacher. He was at every track meet, wrestling
match and football game (I was three-year letterman in each) -- always
there with his camera. He knew all of us cadets and remembered us. In
the 1970's, I had a serious blood clot and while in the hospital in Little
Rock, my wife came in and said, "Harry, look who's here." I looked up,
and it was JB Leftwich. I can truly say my life has been richer for having
known him.

Jim Gamble '62

Senior Intelligence Officer / Department of Defense,
Redstone Arsenal Alabama

My years at Heights were especially rewarding due to the life and character of our mentor and friend, Maj. JB Leftwich. My life is richer and my
professional career successful in part due to the life's model he demonstrated daily. Major Leftwich, my Dad, and others set me on the right
path, and what I was taught I am now passing on to my kids.

Tom Bailey '68

Engineer Manager, Northrup Grumman Corporation

Colonel Leftwich persuaded me to join *The Cavalier* after a math class
my sophomore year. Near-term benefit was being excused from afternoon military drills; long-term was learning writing and organizational
skills used in college and throughout my professional career. Colonel
Leftwich taught me to write quickly, concisely and with precision. My
journalism background helped me excel as a defense contractor because
I did not need help (as many engineers do) in translating my work into
English.....I grew up quickly at Heights, thanks to Colonel Leftwich. I
got my first chance to manage others [*Cavalier* editor 1966, *Adjutant*
editor 1967]; I made my first overnight trips [to school newspaper con-
ventions]; and I gave my first speech to strangers [lady writers in Nash-
ville]. I met and wrote about honest and corrupt politicians, murderers,
Vietnam War widows, civil rights activists and beauty pageant winners.
I have a lifetime of memories from my five summers as a reporter

LeRoy Dowdy '62

Retired University Professor

I join with all those profoundly touched by JB Leftwich in pointing out he has been a "coach" to me in life as well as in journalism. His roles as father, citizen, philosopher and all-round admirable human being have been an extraordinarily worthy example for all of us. Late in life, Coach was a role model of how to deal with physical challenges with grit and determination.

Leonard K. Bradley Jr. '58

Tennessee State Government 1968-95

Faculties / Tusculum College, Vanderbilt University

As I expect is true for many of JB's students and editors, my experience with him still is one of the greatest seminal events of my life. I took all five of his math courses -- and that made math simple in college, as well as in helping my kids with homework. We Bradleys lived across the street from the Leftwich family and grew up with their kids. Jo Doris was like a second mother to us.... My continuing dependence on JB is writing, at which he was better than almost everyone I have read. He particularly liked sports writing for its liberty, imagination and flexibility, and I did that for three years for *The Cavalier* and the *Adjutant*. I spent most of my life writing for newspapers, then writing Tennessee laws and speeches for governors. ....I cannot write anything important without thinking of Coach. And as I think of Coach, writing and family are constant in my mind, almost every week. Though he is not with us now, I cannot get him out of my mind. In fact, as I wrote this tribute, I must have reviewed the wording two dozen times in fear he would correct me for my mistakes. I corrected quite a few in case he was watching, but I expect he would want simpler sentences. And I'm afraid I misspelled "simpler," but I could not find it in the dictionary. Maybe I should have said "more simple." But then he would tell me to use the simpler word.

Chapter Ten
Looking Ahead

"History is who we are and why we are the way we are."
        -**David McCullough, America Historian**

"One faces the future with one's past.."
        -**Pearl S. Buck, Writer / Novelist**

THE DRILL:
Thanks to ongoing efforts of the Castle Heights National Alumni Association, its Board of Directors, its president, and many of the more than 8,000 alumni, the Academy and its spirit JB Leftwich so lovingly and proudly wrote about will continue to "exist." Four of the original structures are guaranteed survival into the future, and two of those will continue to house CHMA memorabilia and artifacts. There is reason to believe that even 400 years -- possibly longer -- after its 1902 founding, there will be a Castle Heights.

Overleaf Photo:
The Rutherford Parks Library, built in 1912, soon will serve as the "Castle Heights Military Academy Alumni Archives & Museum."

Photo Credit: Gary Moor '59

Initial volunteer "Library Work Day," organized by Ken Hall '71 to assist with Rutherford Parks Library refurbishing and landscaping, was in September, 2013. Members of classes from the '50s, '60s, '70s and '80s participated. Subsequent sessions have been held / are planned.

Alumni initiative ensures new CHMA museum

"To keep Heights alive, to keep what we had, to be able to reflect on our history through displaying our memorabilia and artifacts...and to continue a beacon on The Hilltop."

Thus Theodore "Ted" Lavit '57 reported to Castle Heights alumni and friends in May, 2014, about the successful purchase of the 100 year-old Rutherford Parks Library to serve as the "Castle Heights Military Academy Alumni Archives & Museum."

Impetus for the campaign to purchase the unique building -- occupied since 2003 by THW Insurance Services of Lebanon -- came at the October, 2012, meeting of the Board of Directors of the Castle Heights National Alumni Association. In less than nine months, the Association raised approximately $230,000 from Heights grads and supporters, borrowed $100,000 from the HNAA $200,000 CD, and closed June 3, 2013, for the reduced price of $330,000.

"The building was perfect for us, the location great, and we enjoyed our time there," said Rick Thorne, one of three founding THW partners. "We just outgrew the space, and were delighted the alumni were able to acquire it. We will always feel a part of Heights because of that building."

The library had been vacant for about 17 years when THW bought it in 2003. Interior remodeling and renovations were made at that time, though the HNAA expects to replace the roof, make repairs to windows, and improve exterior landscaping. Its Castilian architecture, Gothic entry and multi-colored glass centerpiece make the facility unique.

Don Ash '73 [left], host Fred Noe '75 and Mitch Damsky '74 were among those attending the "Beam at The Club" reception / silent auction in August, 2013, raising more than $20,000 for the Archives & Museum.

"We are hoping to open as the Museum/Archives by 2016 Homecoming," reported Association President Rob Hosier.

"We were working on this purchase for a year because we wanted a place suitable for a CHMA museum and archives," he continued. "We also wanted to make sure the beautiful old building was preserved. After getting all of the structural tests completed and proposing the idea to the Alumni Association Board of Directors, we signed the deal."

Lavit noted he is "proud of our alumni for perpetuating the memory of the school that developed young boys into manhood and who took on leadership positions throughout the world in so many fields."

"The fund raising drive to recapture ownership of the Library was an outstanding success," Lavit said. "The Heights spirit of old was revitalized, and what's so amazing to me and all of our Board members is that since the closing of Heights in 1986, we have seen nothing but increased interest, devotion, support and growth in our Association and in the idea of keeping Heights 'alive,'" Lavit continued. "And the fact that as an IRS charitable corporation we continue to grant scholarships annually to worthy and aspiring students entering or attending college."

Also assisting in the fund-raising efforts was the inaugural "Beam at The Club," organized by members of the Class of 1975 and attended by more than 300 in August, 2013. Main organizers were Fred Noe Sr., seventh generation Beam Family Distiller Don Ash, Tom Clemmons and Frank Bryant. More than $20,000 was raised, and the event -- including a silent auction -- is tentatively planned on an every-other-year basis.

According to Hosier, displays in three separate library rooms will include pictures, military and sports memorabilia, and other items focusing on faculty, staff and cadets -- most of which are now stored in the Ingram House. He said there are seven decades of composite class photos [each year's seniors] that probably will be rotated in the museum as well.

"We anticipate eventually being open to the public for perhaps three

This stained glass work of art is the centerpiece of the Rutherford Parks Library, and -- like the facility itself -- is more than 100 years old. It is in the center of the ceiling over the main library, and the glass is protected by a shingle roof with several skylights to allow filtered sunlight.

days a week at selected hours," Hosier continued, "and we want to utilize the central part of the building, charging a small fee, for area civic groups wanting to have meetings."

Hosier said the Ingram House will continue to serve as the main offices of the HNAA, and also continue as a display area for memorabilia and artifacts.

"Now we have the Rutherford Parks Library on the west wing of Old Main, the Ingram House on the east, and Main -- as Lebanon's City Hall -- still as the crown jewel at the top of Castle Heights Avenue," Lavit said. "Plus The Circle, where we met in formation at least four times daily, and the granite memorial with the names of those who fell in World War I, WWII, Korea and Vietnam all adding to the glory and prominence of

This *Dallas Morning News* article of July 21, 1912, reports a donation by student B. Rutherford Parks Jr. (1914 grad of Castle Heights School) made possible the new library on campus. Parks, president of Midcity Realty Co. in Dallas for more than 35 years, died at 77 in 1971. A lifelong resident of Dallas, Parks was in the real estate business most of his life, owner of Parks Investment Co., board member of Fair Park Bank, and active in multiple community organizations. He and his wife, Julia, had two daughters, five grandchildren. As for O. N. Smith: According to *Hail, Castle Heights!*, he joined the faculty in 1903 as assistant headmaster. He had done

DALLAS BOY'S GIFT TO COLLEGE.

Rutherford Parks Donates Library Building to Castle Heights School.

Containing among other illustrations a picture of the new school library, the gift of a Dallas boy now attending the school, the 1912-13 catalogue of the Castle Heights School at Lebanon, Tenn., has been received by The News.

Rutherford Parks of Dallas, a son of B. R. Parks and a junior student at the school, last year donated the money for the Rutherford Parks Library, which is now being completed and will be one of the finest buildings of the school.

The catalogue is handsomely gotten up and really serves as a record of the school year. It contains pictures of the faculty, the buildings and the athletic teams of the last year. Oscar N. Smith, a member of the faculty, is now in Dallas and said that he has secured about forty Texas students for the next session of the school.

grad work at Princeton, was a member of its summer school faculty, and brought with him to Heights the motto Sigillum Lux Et Veritas ["Our seal is light and truth"], the tiger symbol as mascot, and the maroon and gold school colors.

what was the great school we knew as Castle Heights."

Hosier and Lavit emphasized that new, continuing and expanded donations to the Rutherford Parks Library/CHMA Archives & Museum fund will be needed to help project success and perpetuity.

"Now, more than 100 years later, we are back on The Hilltop, in the midst of where a great Academy stood to develop bodies and minds of thousands of cadets through its dedicated faculty," Lavit said.

• The historic CHMA sign [*page 339*], originally at the main entrance starting in the mid-'60s, for many years was a feature at Lebanon's Legacy Farms owned by Jerry Bryson. Don Ash '73 asked Bryson to donate the signage back to Heights, and he and brother Dirk Ash '75 oversaw restoration, painting and installation on the Rutherford Parks Library grounds [within sight of Lebanon City Hall (old Main)] near Castle Heights Avenue. The Ash family dedicated the sign with a plaque to stepfather and mother Burke and Joy Ash Herron, both former Heights instructors.

Built in 1939 for Col. D. T. and Mildred Bowen Ingram and their three children -- Alice, Dan Jr. and John -- what became known as the Ingram House was first leased then purchased in the mid-'90s by CHMA alumni to serve as headquarters of the Castle Heights National Alumni Association.

Ingram House continues
as HNAA headquarters

Thanks to efforts of Lt. Col. Stroud Gwynn soon after 1986 closing of Castle Heights, much of the Academy's meaningful memorabilia was saved, preserved and protected for benefit of friends and alumni who would continue to return to the former campus.

Also through Gwynn's efforts, the Heights Alumni Association was reorganized from a social group that met at annual Homecoming events to a body responsible for its own business and financial affairs. He negotiated for the lease of the Ingram House on Hill Street for use as the Alumni House and offices, and in 1996 the facility became the permanent property of the Castle Heights National Alumni Association.

For more than 25 years, the Alumni House has served as headquarters for the HNAA Board of Directors and President Rob Hosier, as primary location for display of Heights exhibits, and for storage of hundreds of items related to the Academy's 84-year history. Though the new "Castle Heights Military Academy Alumni Association Archives & Museum" will become the major facility for memorabilia displays and exhibits, the Ingram House will continue to serve as offices and display area.

Since 1986, alumni generously have contributed to the Association to provide for the upkeep of the Ingram House. Foundation officials publish twice-yearly newsletters with information on HNAA and faculty / alumni, including activities and deaths; and organize, promote and conduct Homecoming celebrations the second weekend of every October. In addition, the Association in 2014 was in its 14th year of awarding 10 scholarships of $1,000 each to children, grandchildren and other relatives of those who attended and/or graduated from CHMA. The recipients have enrolled in colleges throughout the country. In 2015, the HNAA will change to five scholarships of $1,500.

"It is not surprising that Heights graduates continue to support and help 'keep alive' a truly wonderful institution that ceased to exist more than a quarter century ago," noted Hosier.

Working with Hosier in 2014, and most of them since 2000, are directors representing a cross-section of classes from 1945-1987: Dan Andrews '45, Don Ash '73, Tom Bradley '69, James Branum '70, Harry E. Bryan Jr. '57, Rondol Cartwright '57, Allen Chamberlain '84, Dan Coleman '69, Tom Elliott '47, Amy Beth Hale '87, Ken Hall '71, Frank Hartley '64, Richard Hosier '66, Ted Lavit '57, Larry McCown '71, John Means '44,

Photographs, trophies, uniforms, athletic awards and Cum Honore plaques (listing each year's most outstanding cadets as voted by faculty and administration) are among memorabilia on display at the Ingram House. Space for similar items stored away for more than 25 years now will be available in the new Alumni Archives & Museum scheduled to open in 2016.

Gary Moor '59, Philip Phillips '87, Peter Rademacher '48, Jerry Ream '59, Gordon Simpson '55, Tony Taylor '63 and Carleton Thackston '67.

Past directors are Leonard Bradley '58, Bro D'Arcy '47, Comer L. Donnell '58, Jack Goodner '72, John Flanagan '70, Scot Hendricks '76, Emily Kinnard Bell '83, Lisa Agee Reaney '85, and Clay Woods '59. Previous directors now deceased are Bill Barry '43, Sam Belote '38, Bill Burch '38, James Chamberlain '48, Bascom Cooksey '44, Mark Donnell '64, Ernest Pellegrin '48, Brian Rummell '40, Ron Wardlow '56, Horace Whitten '59.

The 100-year-old Mitchell House, integral to Castle Heights Military Academy history, became executive offices for the international Sigma Pi Fraternity in 2013.

Mitchell House legacy expanded
by international fraternity

"This will not just be Sigma Pi Fraternity's international executive offices, because the Mitchell House belongs to the community, the City of Lebanon and thousands of alumni and friends of Castle Heights Military Academy. We are excited to be here, and want people to come, make new memories and see a part of history."

That was part of remarks by SPF Executive Director Michael Ayalon in November, 2013, announcing official acquisition of the former CHMA Junior School headquarters from CBRL Group, Inc., holding company for Cracker Barrel and Logan's Roadhouse restaurants. The fraternity -- headquartered in Brentwood, Tenn., since 2003 -- has 125 chapters on North America campuses with more than 99,000 members.

"In 2010, our organization began a search for facilities that would feel more like a fraternity's headquarters, and the Mitchell House just made sense," Ayalon continued. "We were founded in 1897 (at Vincennes University in Indiana) by four cadets, so in some ways the fraternity and the House have similar histories."

According to Ayalon, Sigma Pi is the only Greek letter organization with an international philanthropic program -- the Altruistic Campus Experience project.

Construction on the house started in 1906 by Dr. David Mitchell -- one of the CHMA founders -- who made a fortune in the Pennsylvania min-

Once the setting for Castle Heights Military Academy formal dances, the restored Mitchell House remains available for special events, such as this June, 2014, wedding of Brittany Joiner [Mt. Juliet] and Matthew Taylor [Murfreesboro].

ing industry before moving to Lebanon in 1900 at age 24 with his wife, Elizabeth. [He enrolled at Cumberland University as a junior, graduated in 1902, and within days was elected CU president -- where he served until 1909.] The house is of stone and built in the classical revival architecture with wide porches, nine fireplaces and four white front columns. He spared no expense in creating the nearly 11,000-square-foot home, bringing stone masons, woodworkers and craftsmen from Pennsylvania.

Mitchell's wife died of typhoid fever in 1919, at age 42, and he in a distressed state moved to California, leaving the house for his two children and their maternal grandparents. It served as a residence until the early '20s, and was left vacant for 16 years until it became the Heights Junior School in 1936.

The house sat vacant for another 11 years after Heights closed until bought by Danny Evins '53 and his Cracker Barrel Old Country Store organization to serve as corporate offices. Through restoration efforts costing millions of dollars, the Mitchell House qualified for listing as an historic landmark on both the State of Tennessee registry and the National Register of Historic Places.

The Sigma Pi museum is on the first floor featuring badges, pins, trophies and original minutes from the first meetings. A robe and gavel from SPF brother Judge Curtis Shake, who served during the Nuremberg trials, also is on display. An expansion is planned to include more recent items from alumni brothers such as a football signed by Dallas Cowboys quarterback Tony Romo, a guitar from country star Tracy Lawrence, and reference to Jack Daniels Master Distiller Jeff Arnett. Two boardrooms provide meeting space, business offices are on the second floor, areas have been

346

A fountain featuring the Academy's tiger mascot, and the outdoor courtyard with CHMA seal and bricks naming every graduate are now featured at the restored Mitchell House, which served as executive offices for more than a decade for Cracker Barrel Country Store, Inc. -- founded by Danny Evins '53.

set aside for brotherhood initiations, and an attic and basement will be used for storage.

Historically, the Mitchell House was opened for weddings, reunions, photography sessions and events, and this is being continued (*http://www.mitchellhouse.org*). The grounds include the courtyard added by Evins that features bricks inscribed with the names of all CHMA graduates and the Academy's seal.

"As we look to the future, Sigma Pi will continue to go above and beyond to maintain the foundation that our founders built for the fraternity," Ayalon said. "The move to the Mitchell House is a new chapter in our history, and it is the perfect location for continuing to build on the legacy we have created over the past 117 years."

Cumberland University's Vise Library features the Castle Heights Reading Room, with pictures, plaques and athletic trophies of the Academy, a painting of Bernarr Macfadden, and photographs of Col. Harry Armstrong (33-year CHMA president) and co-founder L.L. Rice.

Heights, Cumberland maintain historic link

More than 110 years after the first primary linkage between Cumberland University and what would become Castle Heights Military Academy, the two institutions remain connected in a strong, historic relationship.

With the opening in 1902 of the Castle Heights School, the plans of CU graduate and mathematics professor I. W. P. Buchanan and CU graduate and president David Mitchell "designed to take youths from 12 to 25 and fit them for the best colleges, South or North, or for the business world" were realized.

Laban Lacy Rice, who like Buchanan had earned his doctorate from CU and was an English professor at the university, began his Heights tenure as instructor for Greek and Latin, became headmaster, and by 1913 was sole owner of the school. Rice served as CU president 1941-46.

After Heights was closed in 1986, portions of the revenue from a two-week auction of Academy materials and artifacts was delegated to Cumberland in a 1989 agreement involving the Heights Foundation and alumni association. As a result, Cumberland awards a Castle Heights scholarship each year, maintains CHMA's academic records for permanent reference, and pays tribute to the school by way of a Castle Heights Military Academy Reading Room at CU's Vise Library.

Among Heights related items displayed in the reading room are athletic trophies, selected photographs and paintings, and a number of plaques citing honored alumni.

Individuals with CU/Heights ties include book author JB Leftwich [editor of the *Cumberland Collegian* newspaper his senior year); 1957-58 CHMA headmaster and vice president and 1958-83 CU President Ernest L. Stockton Jr. [his father was CU president 1926-41].; Lindsey Donnell, CU All-America athlete, and other Heights faculty who were CU grads including Paul Wooten, Norm Cleveland, Thomas Fishburne and Charles Osborn. Harry Armstrong, who first joined the Heights staff in 1909, returned to CHMA in 1929 as president after a seven-year absence during which he served as superintendent of Lebanon's public schools and CU Dean.

Lebanon History Center includes Heights

Along with restoration of CHMA's old Main to serve as Lebanon's City Hall, officials in 1997 opened the City of Lebanon Museum and History Center in the basement of the facility.

Among exhibits and displays are four related to Castle Heights:

1) Survey marker formerly located on a large stone that still exists in front of the former Heights administration building and barracks;

2) Embossing device used on diplomas from Castle Heights School;

3) Dress uniform of JB Leftwich, loaned by the Leftwich family;

4) Plaque donated by the Daughters of the American Revolution honoring Lt. James R. Crowe, Castle Heights School class of 1907, who was killed in World War I.

James Miller as '57 senior.

Key organizer of the overall Center was James Miller '57, a graduate of David Lipscomb University, Nashville. He retired after teaching history for 30 years at Lebanon High School, and was an authority on local history, Middle Tennessee Indian culture and Civil War battles. He was a member of the Friends of the Nashville Symphony, Middle Cumberland Archaeological Society, Wilson County Historical Society and Sons of Confederate Veterans. He died at 68 in 2008.

The Center is open Monday-Friday, 8 a.m. – 4 p.m., with the main entrance from the parking area behind City Hall -- which also includes displays and prints of Heights.

Final element of final Castle Heights dress parade on Saturday afternoon of commencement weekend was stepping forward of all seniors from corps ranks to assemble for "pass and review" as remainder of battalion marched in their honor.

ACKNOWLEDGMENTS

Our thanks and gratitude to the following for their valuable assistance in the publication of this book:

Susan and Rob Hosier '63
Their loyalty, love, devotion and hard work are responsible for the very existence of the Castle Heights National Alumni Association, and their efforts on behalf of the publishing of this book were tireless, essential and generous.

Lt. Gen. John Bradley '63
William D. "Bill" Bradley '65
Col. C. Thomas "Tom" Bradley '69
L. K. Bradley Jr. '58
R. W. "Bob" Cleveland '59
William D. "Bill" Goodner '64
Paul J. Holsen II '59
Theodore "Ted" Lavit '57
Barbara Leftwich Froula / Lynda Leftwich Newton
B. Edward "Ed" McClellan '58
Gary C. Moor '59
Charles W. "Chuck" Ward '42
*
B. B. Branton, McCallie '69
Michael B. "Mike" Huguenin

PHOTO CREDITS

Gary Moor '59
(Above, Pages 336, 341)

Stan Dunlap
SD Photography,
Hendersonville, Tenn
(Page 346)

MR. AMERICA
by Mark Adams
HarperCollins Publishers
(Pages 196, 197)

Chris Carter
Sigma Pi Fraternity
(Pages 122, 345, 347)

JB Leftwich
(Pages 13, 88, 111, 128, 142,
157, 165, 170, 179, 182, 208,
236, 264, 274, 277)
Additional JBL pictures
throughout book from
Cavalier, Adjutant and
Academy catalogues

Seats Studio
Cadet senior photos

Jared Felkins
Lebanon Democrat
(Page 249)

Cumberland University
Vice President
William R. Richardson
(Page 348)

Hail, Castle Heights!
James A. Crutchfield/
Castle Heights Alumni
Association
(Pages 5, 24, 85, 97, 132,
144, 150, 153, 158, 179)

***GUARDIAN OF
THE LEGACY:***
The Mitchell House Story
H. Rogers Thomson/
CBRL Group, Inc.
(Pages 36, 121, 122, 345)

***Remembering
Wilson County***
Wilson Bank & Trust
(Pages 13, 123, 139, 272, 273)

Overleaf Photos: JB Leftwich captures 1959 seniors at attention [left] during final lowering of colors, and flinging hats [right] as "Dismissed!"

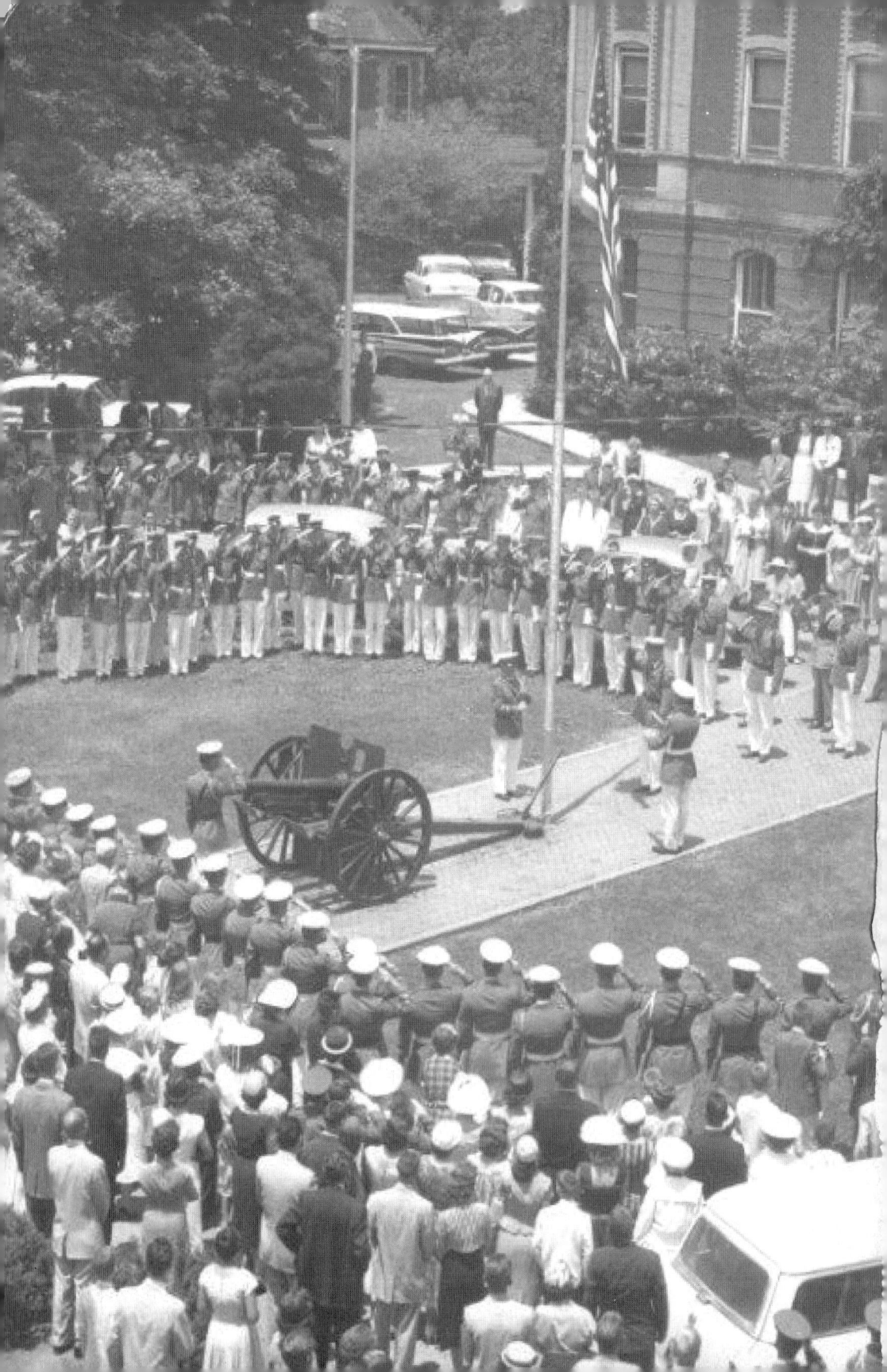